NEW SERIES NO. 202   MAY 1, 1931

UNIVERSITY OF IOWA STUDIES

HUMANISTIC STUDIES

VOLUME IV   NUMBER 5

A BIBLIOGRAPHICAL GUIDE TO OLD ENGLISH

A Selective Bibliography of the Language, Literature, and History of the Anglo-Saxons

Compiled by
ARTHUR H. HEUSINKVELD
and
EDWIN J. BASHE

PUBLISHED BY THE UNIVERSITY, IOWA CITY, IOWA

Issued semi-monthly throughout the year. Entered at the post office at Iowa City, Iowa, as second class matter under the Act of October 3, 1917.

UNIVERSITY OF IOWA HUMANISTIC STUDIES

Franklin H. Potter, A.M., Editor

VOLUME IV   NUMBER 5

A BIBLIOGRAPHICAL GUIDE TO OLD ENGLISH

A Selective Bibliography of the Language, Literature, and History of the Anglo-Saxons

Compiled by

Arthur H. Heusinkveld

State University of Iowa

and

Edwin J. Bashe

Saint Mary-of-the-Woods College

PUBLISHED BY THE UNIVERSITY, IOWA CITY

PREFACE

This *Bibliographical Guide to Old English* is planned to serve the following purposes: (1) to provide the student, especially the beginner, with a guide to the bibliographical tools most likely to prove necessary and useful in any more than a very superficial study of Old English; (2) to remind him that the language and the literature are but two of many phenomena in the Anglo-Saxon period, and that neither can be adequately understood without a knowledge of other major phenomena of that period; (3) to provide him with a list of the most important literary and linguistic monuments of the period so that he may not only gain a general notion of their number and variety, but also have the means whereby to make an intimate acquaintance with any particular author or work he may become interested in. It is the needs of the student which have led the authors to prepare this *Guide,* although they have not been unmindful of the fact that it may prove serviceable to the teacher as well. With it the teacher may be able, more easily than has hitherto been possible, (1) to familiarize the student with the bibliography of the subject, (2) to correlate the language and the literature with other major aspects of Anglo-Saxon civilization, and (3) to assign collateral reading on and the investigation of such subjects as his resourcefulness may devise and the needs of the students prompt. Both the student and the teacher, it is hoped, will find this *Guide* useful in many ways.

The present work owes its genesis, apart from the foregoing considerations, to the fact that the authors are aware of no bibliography of Old English literature more recent than the *Bibliographical Sketch of Anglo-Saxon Literature,* by Professor H. M. Ayres, which was published in 1910. This little work of twenty pages makes no pretense to completeness—nor does this *Guide,* for that matter—and is now hardly up to date. Brandl's *Angelsächsische Literatur* (1908) is doubtless the best account, bibliographical or descriptive, of Old English literature, that we have, being in both of the foregoing respects much more comprehensive than the chapters devoted to Old English in the *Cambridge History of English Literature* (1907). But Brandl's work is not easy for many English-speaking students to consult, and it, too, needs to be brought up to date.

Körting's *Grundriss der Geschichte der englischen Literatur* (5th ed., 1910) suffers from the same disadvantages that Brandl's does, in addition to having other defects. Only the *Grundriss* (1885) of the venerable Wülker, for whom we have deep respect, is left, but the passage of time has put limits to the usefulness of his work, at least for the beginner. Such are the predecessors of the present *Guide* and such are the considerations respecting them that have prompted its compilation.

The language of the period has fared better than the literature, having received exemplary bibliographical treatment at the hands of Professor A. G. Kennedy, in his *Bibliography of Writings on the English Language* (1927). The work that he has done—some of which we had done for the *Guide* before his book was published—has made it unnecessary for us to include any detailed enumeration of works pertaining to the language, and so we hereby gratefully acknowledge his services, contenting ourselves, for the most part, with referring the reader to his accurate and exhaustive bibliography.

Respecting the materials included in the present *Guide*, the authors have by no means aimed at completeness. We are aware that we have not listed all the extant monuments of the language and the literature, but we have endeavored to include the more important ones. It is quite possible that some monuments are not represented which deserve mention as well as, or rather than, some that are listed. We trust, however, that nothing of first importance has been omitted. The same is true of the bibliography. It is frankly and obviously selective, our aim being to list the more important contributions if materials were plentiful, and some of the less important if materials were scarce. Some things of relatively great importance have doubtless escaped our search, and others have not been included because they were inaccessible to us, but we feel that the materials actually listed will lead the student to all other works that have been deliberately or inadvertently omitted. The authors will be grateful if the users of the *Guide* will call to their attention all errors—which are hard to keep out of a work of this kind—and all omissions, so that in a second edition, which the serviceableness of the work may in the future justify, all necessary corrections and additions may be made.

TABLE OF CONTENTS

I. General Bibliography — 9
    A. Bibliography of Bibliographies — 9
    B. Bibliography of Old English Literature and Language — 9
    C. Bibliography of, and Treatises on, Germanic Antiquity — 10
    D. Annual Bibliographies — 11
    E. Periodicals Containing Current Bibliography — 11
    F. Bibliography of Dissertations — 12
    G. Indexes to Reviews — 12
II. Periodicals Containing Articles and Reviews — 13
    A. Periodicals Devoted Exclusively to English — 13
    B. Periodicals Devoted to English and Other (Chiefly Modern) Languages and Literatures — 13
III. Series of Studies — 17
IV. Anniversary Volumes (*Festschriften*) — 19
V. The People and Their Institutions — 21
    A. General Bibliography — 22
    B. Ethnology — 22
    C. Social History — 24
    D. Political History — 25
    E. Economic and Industrial History — 27
    F. Law — 28
    G. The Church — 29
    H. The Arts, Crafts, and Archaeology — 30
VI. Language — 32
    A. General Bibliography — 32
    B. History of the Language — 32
    C. Grammar — 33
        1. General grammars — 33
        2. Phonology — 34
        3. Syntax — 34
        4. Dialect — 35
    D. Vocabulary — 35
        1. Dictionaries — 35
        2. Studies of vocabulary — 35
VII. Palaeography — 36
    A. General Bibliography — 36
    B. Alphabet — 36
        1. Runic — 36
        2. Roman — 37
    C. Facsimiles — 39

VIII. Books of Selections _____ 40
 IX. Literature _____ 42
     A. History and Criticism _____ 42
     B. Mythology and Legend _____ 43
  X. Verse _____ 46
     A. Manuscript Collections _____ 46
        1. Junius XI. _____ 46
        2. Exeter Book _____ 47
        3. Vercelli Book _____ 47
        4. Cotton Vitellius A XV. (Beowulf MS.) ___ 47
     B. Modern Collections _____ 48
     C. Translations _____ 49
     D. History and Criticism _____ 49
     E. Versification _____ 52
     F. Authors and Monuments _____ 54
 XI. Prose _____ 95
     A. Modern Collections _____ 95
     B. Translations _____ 95
     C. History and Criticism _____ 95
     D. Authors and Monuments _____ 95
XII. Miscellaneous _____134
     Bewcastle Ross _____134
     Charters _____134
     Codex Aureus Inscription _____135
     "Festermen" of Aelfric, The _____135
     Franks Casket (Clermont or Runic Casket) __135
     Genealogies _____136
     Glosses _____136
     Liber Vitae _____137
     Mortain Casket _____137
     Ruthwell Cross _____137
     Urswick Inscription _____137
XIII. Index of Modern Authors and Publications __138
XIV. Index of Old English Writings _____147

LIST OF ABBREVIATIONS

A. f. N. F. — Arkiv för Nordisk Filologi.
Amer. Bibl. — American Bibliography.
Anglist. Forsch. — Anglistische Forschungen.
Anz. f. d. A. — Anzeiger für deutsches Altertum.
Archiv — Archiv für das Studium der neueren Sprachen.
Beitr. — Beiträge zur Geschichte der deutschen Sprache und Literatur.
Bo. Beitr. — Bonner Beiträge zur Anglistik.
Bo. Stud. — Bonner Studien zur englischen Philologie.
C. H. E. L. — Cambridge History of English Literature.
E. E. T. S. — Early English Text Society.
E. H. R. — English Historical Review.
E. St. — Englische Studien.
E. Studies — English Studies.
G.-R. Mon. — Germanisch-romanische Monatsschrift.
J. E. G. Ph. — Journal of English and Germanic Philology.
Jsb. G. Ph. — Jahresbericht über die Erscheinungen auf dem Gebiete der germanischen Philologie.
Literaturblatt — Literaturblatt für germanische und romanische Philologie.
M. H. R. A. — Modern Humanities Research Association. Annual Bibliography of English Language and Literature.
M. L. N. — Modern Language Notes.
M. L. R. — Modern Language Review.
M. Ph. — Modern Philology.
Ph. Q. — Philological Quarterly.
P. M. L. A. — Publications of the Modern Language Association.
Q. F. — Quellen und Forschungen.
R. E. S. — Review of English Studies.
St. E. Ph. — Studien zur englischen Philologie.
St. Ph. — Studies in Philology.
T. L. S. — Times [London] Literary Supplement.
Y. St. — Yale Studies in English.
Z. f. d. A. — Zeitschrift für deutsches Altertum.
Z. f. d. Ph. — Zeitschrift für deutsche Philologie.

NUMBERING

The various works listed in this Bibliography are numbered consecutively. A number immediately following names or titles and enclosed in parentheses is used to refer back or forward to a main entry. In almost all the subdivisions the references follow the chronological order.

SYMBOLS

In the Index of Old English Writings an asterisk distinguishes the prose writings from the verse. A dagger indicates miscellaneous items, such as the Bewcastle and Ruthwell crosses, the genealogies, and the Franks casket.

A BIBLIOGRAPHICAL GUIDE TO OLD ENGLISH

PART I

GENERAL BIBLIOGRAPHY

A. Bibliography of Bibliographies
B. Bibliography of Old English Literature and Language
C. Bibliography of, and Treatises on, Germanic Antiquity
D. Annual Bibliographies
E. Periodicals Containing Current Bibliography
F. Bibliography of Dissertations
G. Indexes to Reviews

Lists of bibliographical aids such as books and articles on bibliography, treatises on methods of research, universal bibliographies, bibliographies of bibliographies, and literary catalogues may be found in—

1. CROSS, T. P. A list of books and articles, chiefly bibliographical, designed to serve as an introduction to the bibliography and methods of English literary history. 5th ed. Chicago, 1928.

A. BIBLIOGRAPHY OF BIBLIOGRAPHIES

2. NORTHUP, C. S. A register of bibliographies of the English language and literature. New Haven, 1926.

B. BIBLIOGRAPHIES OF OLD ENGLISH LITERATURE AND LANGUAGE

3. WÜLKER, R. Grundriss zur geschichte der angelsächsischen literatur. Leipzig, 1885.

   Indispensable for its bibliographies up to 1885. Contains excellent critical summaries.

4. Cambridge History of English literature. Ed. by A. W. Ward and A. R. Waller. 14 vols. Cambridge [Eng.] and New York, 1907-17.

   Only Vol. I covers the Old English field. Bibliographies are selective and rather uneven, and the data incomplete. No mention of many of the smaller monuments.

5. BRANDL, A. Angelsächsische literatur. In Paul's Grundriss (9). 2d ed. Strassburg, 1900-9. Also published separately, Strassburg, 1908.

   Scholarly, comprehensive yet concise, and with excellent selective bibliographies. In several respects the most satisfactory history of Old English literature.

6. KÖRTING, G. Grundriss der geschichte der englischen literatur von ihren anfängen bis zur gegenwart. 5te verm. und verb. Aufl. Münster, 1910.

7. AYRES, H. M. Bibliographical sketch of Anglo-Saxon literature. New York, 1910.
"It is designed . . . to place before students . . . the most convenient titles for beginning their studies."—Preface. Useful guide (up to 1910) for the more important monuments of the literature.
8. KENNEDY, A. G. A bibliography of writings on the English language from the beginning of printing to the end of 1922. Cambridge [Mass.] and New Haven, 1927.
Bibliography of the Old English to about A. D. 1100 on pp. 115-58. Exhaustive to 1923 and minutely categorized; unannotated; chronological arrangement. Best bibliography of the language.
9. PAUL, H., ed. Grundriss der germanischen philologie. Strassburg. 2d ed. 1900-09; 3d ed. 1911—
Indispensable for the study of Old English literature and language. Rich in bibliography. See below (D and E) for current bibliography.

C. BIBLIOGRAPHY OF, AND TREATISES ON, GERMANIC ANTIQUITY

NOTE: Useful bibliographies on special topics may be found in most of the standard encyclopedias (see Cross (1), pp. 20-22, for a list of them). The following special encyclopedias and treatises contain valuable articles, with bibliographies, on many aspects of the Anglo-Saxons and their civilization.
10. MÜLLENHOFF, K. Deutsche altertumskunde. 5 vols. in 6 parts. Berlin, 1870-1900. Vols. I and II, 2d ed., 1890-1906. Vol. IV, 2d ed., 1920.
Valuable, especially Vol. IV. "Characterized by a wealth of material, incisive criticism, and brilliant combinations."—Saussaye.
11. GUMMERE, F. B. Germanic origins: a study in primitive culture. New York, 1892.
A good introduction to continental Germanic culture. Very suggestive. Republished (1930) as *Founders of England*, with notes by F. P. Magoun, Jr.
12. HOOPS, J. Reallexikon der germanischen altertumskunde. 4 vols. Strassburg, 1911-19.
A mine of useful material on practically all aspects of the civilization of the Germanic peoples.
13. GOETTE, R. Kulturgeschichte der urzeit germaniens. Bonn, 1920.
14. KAUFFMANN, F. Deutsche altertumskunde. 2 vols. Munich: Vol. I, 1913; Vol. II, 1923.
Extraordinarily rich in bibliography.
15. NECKEL, G. Altgermanische kultur. Leipzig, 1925.
See also his article "Die gemeingermanische Zeit", in *Zeitschrift für Deutschkunde* 39. 1925.

16. SCHRADER, O. Reallexikon der indogermanischen altertumskunde. Strassburg, 1901. 2d ed. by A. Nehring, Strassburg, 1917-29.
17. STEINHAUSEN, G. Germanische kultur in der urzeit. 4th ed. Leipzig, 1927.
    Contains an appraisal of recent literature on the subject.
18. KARSTEN, T. E. Die Germanen. Eine einführung in die geschichte ihrer sprache und kultur. Berlin and Leipzig, 1928. In Paul's *Grundriss* (9).
19. EBERT, M. Reallexikon der vorgeschichte. 14 vols. in 15. Berlin, 1924-29.
    Complete except *Register* (promised for 1930). Contains a 17-page article on *Germanen*.
20. SCHRÖDER, F. R. Neuere forschungen zur germanischen altertumskunde und religionsgeschichte. G.-R. Mon. (51), Vol. 17:177-92, 241-55. 1929.
    A good survey of recent literature on Germanic antiquity.
Paul's Grundriss (9). Indispensable for practically all phases of Germanic antiquity.

D. ANNUAL BIBLIOGRAPHIES

21. Modern Humanities Research Association. Annual bibliography of English language and literature. Cambridge [Eng.], 1920—
    The most valuable current bibliography in the field of English language and literature. Aims to be complete.
22. Jahresbericht über die erscheinungen auf dem gebiete der germanischen philologie. Berlin—Leipzig, 1879—
    Indispensable for the period preceding 1920. Wider in scope than either 21 or 23, but not so exhaustive as 21.
23. American bibliography for 1921—, in P.M.L.A. (69), I— English Language and Literature.
    Appears annually in the March number. Lists books and articles by American scholars. Before 1920 this bibliography appeared in the *American Year-Book*.

E. PERIODICALS CONTAINING CURRENT BIBLIOGRAPHY

24. Literaturblatt für germanische und romanische philologie. Heilbronn—Leipzig, 1880—
    Monthly. Contains valuable bi-monthly lists of books and articles, also reviews, and summaries of the contents of very many current periodicals.
25. Archiv für das studium der neueren sprachen und litteraturen. Brunswick, 1846—
    Often called *Herrig's Archiv*, after the founder. Contains articles, extensive lists of new publications, and some reviews.
26. Modern language notes. Baltimore, 1886—
    Each number contains a list of recent publications in the modern language field, besides reviews and articles. Eight numbers a year.

27. The modern language review. A quarterly journal devoted to the study of medieval and modern literature and philology. Cambridge [Eng.], 1905—. Has quarterly lists of new books.
28. The Cumulative book index. Minneapolis, New York, etc., 1898—. Monthly, cumulated annually.
29. Times (London) literary supplement. London, 1902—. Weekly. Contains also reviews.
30. International index to periodicals, devoted chiefly to the humanities and science. New York, 1913—

    Appears five times a year, cumulating four times; the January number being an annual cumulation. Published at first under the title *Readers' Guide Supplement.*
31. Readers' guide to periodical literature; being a consolidation of the Readers' guide to periodical literature and Cumulative index to a selected list of periodicals. Minneapolis, New York, 1901—. Monthly, cumulating quarterly and annually.
32. Subject index to periodicals. . . . Issued by the Library Association. . . . London, 1915—

    Covers many periodicals not covered by the American indexes.
33. Bibliographie der deutschen zeitschriften-literatur, mit einschluss von sammelwerken. Leipzig, 1896—

    Semi-annual. Important for German periodicals.
34. Bibliographischer monatsbericht über neuerschienene schul- und universitätsschriften. Hrsg. von der Zentralstelle für Dissertationen und Programme der Buchhandlung. Leipzig, 1889—. Of particular value for dissertations, etc.

F. BIBLIOGRAPHY OF DISSERTATIONS

The chief bibliographies of dissertations are listed in the following: CROSS (1), pp. 19-20, and KENNEDY (8), Nos. 6, 21, 25, 52-56, and 65.

G. INDEXES TO REVIEWS

35. Bibliographie der rezensionen und referate. Leipzig, 1900—. Semi-annual.

    NOTE: Many reviews are listed, under individual authors and works, in the following: M.H.R.A. (21); Jsb. G.Ph. (22); and KENNEDY (8).

PART II

PERIODICALS CONTAINING ARTICLES AND REVIEWS

A. Periodicals Devoted Exclusively to English
B. Periodicals Devoted to English and Other (chiefly modern) Languages and Literatures

A. PERIODICALS DEVOTED EXCLUSIVELY TO ENGLISH

36. Anglia. Zeitschrift für englische philologie. Halle, 1877—. Chiefly articles. Important.
37. Anglia beiblatt. Beiblatt zur Anglia. Mittheilungen aus dem gesammten gebiete der englischen sprache und litteratur; monatsschrift für den englischen unterricht. Halle, 1890—. Monthly. Contains valuable reviews.
    Archiv (25). Important.
38. Englische studien. Organ für englische philologie unter mitberücksichtigung des englischen unterrichts auf höheren schulen. Leipzig, 1877—. Important. *General-register zu Band 1-25*, Leipzig, 1902.
39. English studies. A journal of English letters and philology. Amsterdam, 1919—
    Bi-monthly. Bibliography fairly good for periodicals.
40. The Year's work in English studies. Oxford, 1921—
    Appears annually. Important.

B. PERIODICALS DEVOTED TO ENGLISH AND OTHER (CHIEFLY MODERN) LANGUAGES AND LITERATURES

41. Aarbøger for nordisk oldkyndighed og historie. Copenhagen, 1866—
    Contains articles on such matters as runes and Scandinavian archaeology.
42. The Academy; a weekly review of literature, science and art. London, 1869-1916.
    Contains reviews and short articles. For a time was called *Academy and Literature*.
43. Acta philologica scandinavica; tidsskrift for nordisk sprogforskning. Copenhagen, 1926—
44. American journal of philology. Baltimore, 1880—. Quarterly.
45. Anzeiger für deutsches altertum und deutsche litteratur. Leipzig—Berlin, 1876—
    Published in connection with Z. f. d. A. (79). Contains only reviews.
    Archiv (25). Important.

46. Arkiv för nordisk filologi. Oslo, etc., 1883—
    Incidentally useful for the Scandinavian background.
47. Athenaeum. A journal of literature, science, the fine arts, music and the drama. London, 1828-1921.
    Merged with *The Nation* (58) to form *Nation and the Athenaeum*. Weekly. Contains occasional reviews of the more general works, and short articles.
48. Beiträge zur geschichte der deutschen sprache und literatur. Halle, 1874—
    Generally called, from the founders, *Paul and Braune's Beiträge*. Contains only articles. Appears three times a year. Important.
49. Deutsche literaturzeitung. Berlin, 1880—
    Weekly. Contains short reviews and bibliography.
50. Germania. Vierteljahrsschrift für deutsche alterthumskunde. Stuttgart—Vienna, 1856-92. Contains articles, reviews, bibliography.
51. Germanisch-romanische monatsschrift. Heidelberg, 1909—. Bi-monthly. Of value only for the articles it contains.
52. Indogermanische forschungen. Zeitschrift für indogermanische sprach- und altertumskunde. Strasbourg, 1891—. Its supplement is *Anzeiger für Indogermanische Sprach- und Altertumskunde*. Strasbourg, 1891—
    The former contains chiefly articles, the latter chiefly reviews.
53. Journal of English and Germanic philology. Urbana, Ill., 1897—
    Quarterly. Before Vol. 5, known as *Journal of Germanic Philology*. 1897-1902. Important.
54. Literarisches zentralblatt für Deutschland. Leipzig, 1850—
    Until 1904 spelled *Centralblatt*. Contains only bibliography and short reviews. Bi-weekly.
    Literaturblatt für germanische und romanische philologie (24).
55. Litteris. An international critical review of the humanities. Lund, 1924—
    Modern language notes (26). Important.
    Modern language review (27). Important.
56. Modern philology; a journal devoted to research in modern languages. Chicago, 1903—
    Quarterly. Important.
57. Le Moyen âge; revue d'histoire et de philologie. Paris, 1888—
58. The Nation and the Athenaeum, a weekly journal devoted to politics, literature, science and art. London, 1907—. Absorbed **Athenaeum** (47) in 1921. In 1931 combined with *New Statesman* to form *New Statesman and Nation*.
59. Neophilologus. A quarterly dedicated to the study of modern languages and of classical languages in their relation to the present. Groningen; The Hague, 1915—
60. Neue philologische rundschau. Gotha, 1881-1908. **Bi-weekly.**

61. Die Neueren sprachen. Zeitschrift für den neusprachlichen unterricht. Marburg in Hessen, 1887—. Appears irregularly. Formerly contained reviews, but latterly is no value to students of Old English.
62. Neuphilologische mitteilungen. Helsingfors, 1899—
63. Nordisk tidsskrift for filologi. Copenhagen, 1860—1922.
64. Nordisk tidskrift för vetenskap, konst och industri. Stockholm, 1878—
65. Norsk tidsskrift for sprogvidenskap. Oslo, 1928—
66. Notes and queries. A medium of intercommunication for literary men, general readers, etc. London, 1849—
    Weekly.
67. Philologica: journal of comparative philology. London, 1921—
68. Philological quarterly. A journal devoted to scholarly investigation in the classical and modern languages and literatures. Iowa City, Iowa, 1922—. Contains occasional articles and reviews.
69. Publications of the Modern Language Association of America. Baltimore, 1884—
    Index to Vols. 1-33, Baltimore, 1919. Important.
70. Review of English studies; a quarterly journal of English literature and the English language. London, 1925—
71. Revue critique d'histoire et de littérature. Recueil hebdomadaire. Paris, 1866—
72. Revue germanique: Allemagne—Angleterre—États-Unis—Pays-Bas, Scandinavie. Paris, 1905—
    Contains bibliographical notes and many reviews of German works on English. Since 1923 of no particular importance for English.
73. Romania; recueil trimestriel consacré à l'étude des langues et des littératures romanes. Paris, 1872—
74. Romanische forschungen; organ für romanische sprachen, volks- und mittellatein. Erlangen, 1883—
75. The Speculum. A journal of mediaeval studies. Boston, 1926—
    Quarterly journal published by the Mediaeval Academy of America. Emphasis on Latin medieval literature. Articles and reviews.
76. Studia neophilologica. A journal of Germanic and Romanic philology. Uppsala, 1928—. Issued twice a year in three numbers.
77. Studies in philology—a quarterly journal published under the direction of the Philological Club of the University of North Carolina. Chapel Hill, N. C., 1906—

Times literary supplement (29).

78. Zeitschrift für deutsche philologie. Halle a. S., 1869—. Quarterly. Now useful only for occasional reviews.

79. Zeitschrift für deutsches altertum und deutsche litteratur. Leipzig-Berlin, 1841—. Three numbers a year in four parts. Its supplement is *Anzeiger für Deutsches Altertum und deutsche Litteratur.* Berlin, 1876—. Z. f. d. A. XIX = Anz. f. d. A. I. Recently of negligible value for Old English.
80. Zeitschrift für vergleichende sprachforschung auf dem gebiete der indogermanischen sprachen. Berlin, 1852—

　　Contains articles which bring O. E. into comparison with other languages.

PART III

SERIES OF STUDIES

81. Anglistische forschungen. Heidelberg, 1901—. Important.
81a. Beiträge zur englischen philologie. Leipzig, 1919—
82. Berliner beiträge zur germanischen und romanischen philologie. Berlin, 1893-1917.
83. Bonner beiträge zur anglistik. Bonn, 1898-1908. Important. Continued by Bo. Stud. (84).
84. Bonner studien zur englischen philologie. Bonn, 1909—
85. Breslauer beiträge zur literaturgeschichte. Leipzig, 1904—
    California publications (110).
    Cambridge Philological Society (108).
86. Columbia University studies in English and comparative literature. New York, 1912—. Continues *Studies in Comparative Literature* and *Studies in English*.
    Connecticut Academy (109).
87. Early English Text Society, Publications of the. London: Original series, 1864—; Extra series, 1867—
    A series of texts, frequently with valuable introductions. Important.
87a. Erlanger beiträge zur englischen philologie. Erlangen, 1889-1904.
88. Essays and studies by members of the English Association. Oxford, 1910—. Appears annually.
89. Harvard studies and notes in philology and literature. Boston. 1892-1907. Revived in 1930.
90. Hesperia: schriften zur englischen philologie. Göttingen-Baltimore, 1913—
    Illinois studies (111).
    Iowa studies (112).
91. Kieler studien zur englischen philologie. Heidelberg-Kiel, 1901-15.
92. Kölner anglistische arbeiten. Leipzig, 1927—
93. Königliche preussische akademie der wissenschaften. Philosophisch-historische Klasse. Abhandlungen. Berlin, 1908—
94. Königliche sächsische akademie der wissenschaften. Philologisch-historische Klasse. Abhandlungen. Leipzig, 1850—
95. Leipziger beiträge zur englischen philologie. Leipzig, 1919—
96. Lunds Universitets årsskrift. Lund, 1864-1904.
    Manchester publications (102).
97. Mémoires de la Société Neophilologique à Helsingfors. Helsingfors, 1893—
98. Münchener beiträge zur romanischen und englischen philologie. Erlangen-Leipzig, 1890-1912.

99. Neue anglistische arbeiten. Leipzig, 1918—
Supersedes *Anglistische Arbeiten*, Heidelberg, 1912-13.
100. Otia Merseiana. The publication of the arts faculty of University College, Liverpool, 1899-1904.
101. Palaestra. Untersuchungen und texte aus der deutschen und englischen philologie. Berlin, 1898—. Important.
Pennsylvania publications (113).
102. Publications of the Victoria University of Manchester. English series. Manchester, 1909—
103. Quellen und forschungen zur sprach- und kulturgeschichte der germanischen völker. Strassburg, 1874-1918. Important.
104. Stanford University. Publications. Language and literature. Stanford University, 1920—
105. Studier i modern sprakvetenskap. Stockholm, 1898—
106. Studien zur englischen philologie. Halle, 1897—
Often called *Morsbach's Studien*. Important.
107. Surtees Society, Publications of the. Durham, 1835—
Texts containing ecclesiastical material.
Toronto studies (114).
108. Transactions of the Cambridge [Eng.] Philological Society. Cambridge, 1872—
109. Transactions of the Connecticut Academy of Arts and Sciences. New Haven, 1866—
110. University of California publications in modern philology. Berkeley, 1909—
111. University of Illinois studies in language and literature. Urbana, Ill., 1915—
112. University of Iowa. Humanistic studies. Iowa City, Iowa, 1907—
113. University of Pennsylvania, Publications of the. Series in philology and literature. Philadelphia, 1891-1917.
114. University of Toronto studies. Philological series. Toronto, 1903—
115. University of Virginia monographs, School of Teutonic Languages. New York, 1899-1904.
116. University of Wisconsin studies in language and literature. Madison, Wis., 1918—
117. Uppsala Universitets årsskrift. Uppsala, 1861—
Virginia monographs (115).
118. Washington, State Univ. of, Publications in language and literature. Seattle, 1920—
Wisconsin studies (116).
119. Yale studies in English. New Haven, 1898—. Important.

PART IV

ANNIVERSARY VOLUMES (*FESTSCHRIFTEN*)

120. Philologische studien. Festgabe für Eduard Sievers. Halle, 1896.
121. An English miscellany presented to Dr. Furnivall in honour of his seventy-fifth birthday. Oxford, 1901.
122. Untersuchungen und quellen zur germanischen und romanischen philologie. Johann von Kelle dargebracht von seinen kollegen und schülern. Prague, 1908. Vols. 8 and 9 of *Prager Deutsche Studien*.
123. Festschrift Wilhelm Viëtor zum 25 Dezember 1910 dargebracht. Marburg, 1910.
124. Collected papers of Henry Sweet, arranged by H. C. Wyld. Oxford, 1913.
125. Festschrift für Lorenz Morsbach. Halle, 1913. St. E. Ph. (106), Vol. L.
126. Flügel memorial volume. Stanford University, 1916.
    Contains nothing of value for the student of Old English except possibly Flügel's address, "The History of English Philology," pp. 9-35.
127. Texte und forschungen zur englischen kulturgeschichte. Festgabe für Felix Liebermann. Halle, 1921.
128. Streitberg-festgabe. Leipzig, 1924.
129. Stand und aufgaben der sprachwissenschaft. Festschrift für Wilhelm Streitberg. Heidelberg, 1924.
    Valuable articles pointing out the problems still to be solved. Concerned with the Indo-European field.
130. Beiträge zur germanischen sprachwissenschaft. Festschrift für Otto Behagel. Heidelberg, 1924. Very specialized articles.
131. Festschrift zu Eugen Mogk. Halle, 1924.
132. Probleme der englischen sprache und kultur. Festschrift Johannes Hoops. Heidelberg, 1925.
133. Neusprachliche studien. Festgabe Karl Luick. Marburg, 1925. Beiheft 6 of Die Neueren Sprachen (61).
134. Anglica: Untersuchungen zur englischen philologie (Festschrift A. Brandl). Palaestra (101), Vols. 147, 148. Berlin, 1925.
135. Germanica. Eduard Sievers zum 75 geburtstage. Halle, 1925.
136. Festschrift F. Kluge zum 70 geburtstag. Tübingen, 1926.
137. Arnold Schröer. Zum siebzigsten geburtstag. E. St. (38), Vol. 62, Pts. 1, 2. 1927.

138. Britannica. Max Förster zum sechzigsten geburtstage. Leipzig, 1929.
139. Studies in English philology. A miscellany in honor of Frederick Klaeber. Ed. by K. Malone and M. B. Ruud. Minneapolis, 1929.
139a. Studies in honor of Hermann Collitz. Baltimore, 1930.
139b. A Grammatical miscellany offered to Otto Jespersen on his seventieth birthday. Copenhagen and London, 1930.

PART V

THE PEOPLE AND THEIR INSTITUTIONS

A. General Bibliography
B. Ethnology
C. Social History
   1. General
   2. Studies of Special Aspects
D. Political History
E. Economic and Industrial History
F. Law
G. The Church
H. The Arts, Crafts, and Archaeology

NOTE: Much information on various aspects of Anglo-Saxon history and culture is furnished by special studies of groups of Old English words, such as those used in agriculture, commerce, architecture, music, and so forth. A bibliography of such studies may be found in KENNEDY (8), pp. 140-1. Useful discussions of similar topics are to be found in the encyclopedic treatises of HOOPS (12), SCHRADER (16), and EBERT (19).

The works listed under subheads of Part V may in many cases be supplemented, for the respective counties of England, by use of 140.

140. The Victoria history of the counties of England, ed. by H. A. Doubleday, William Page, et al. Westminster, etc., 1900—
141. TRAILL, H. D., AND J. S. MANN (editors). The building of Britain and the empire; a record of the progress of the people in religion, laws, learning, art, industry, commerce, science, literature, and manners. 6 vols. in 12. London, 1912.
    First published as *Social England*. Contains chapters and bibliographies on many aspects of Anglo-Saxon culture.
142. Mediaeval England. A new edition of Barnard's Companion to English history. Edited by H. W. C. Davis. Oxford, 1924.
    Contains chapters and bibliographies on architecture, war, costume, trade and shipping, town and country life, the church, education and learning, handwriting, art, and coinage.
143. The Cambridge medieval history. Planned by J. B. Bury, and edited by H. M. Gwatkin (and others). Cambridge, 1911—
    This work, though not confined to English history, contains, in the first three volumes, authoritative chapters and useful bibliographies covering English history to the end of the Anglo-Saxon period.

144. TAYLOR, H. O. The mediaeval mind. 2 vols. 3d (American) ed., New York, 1919; 4th ed., 1925.

An excellent presentation of the development of thought and expression in medieval Europe.

NOTE: Valuable articles on persons, places, and institutions are to be found in the *Encyclopaedia Britannica*. Lists of references follow the articles.

The *Dictionary of National Biography* contains authoritative articles on persons and also gives lists of references.

A. GENERAL BIBLIOGRAPHY

145. GROSS, C. The sources and literature of English history from the earliest times to about 1485. 2d ed. London and New York, 1915.

Part III, "The Anglo-Saxon Period," pp. 233-324. The best bibliographical tool for the history of medieval England. See also such works as *The Cambridge Medieval History* (143), HODGKIN (193), and OMAN (197).

146. PAETOW, L. Guide to the study of medieval history. Berkeley, 1917.

Covers the Middle Ages in general. Not so detailed for England as GROSS (145).

147. SONNENSCHEIN, W. S. The best books. 2d ed. London, 1910—

To date four parts have appeared. Part III (1923), pp. 1141-67 (especially pp. 1161-7), lists the best sources and modern works for the Anglo-Saxon period, with some helpful annotation. Entries do not give complete bibliographical data.

148. A guide to historical literature. Compiled by G. M. Dutcher, H. R. Shipman, S. B. Fay, A. H. Shearer, W. H. Allison. New York, 1931.

149. English historical review. London and New York, 1886—

Quarterly. Each number contains reviews and short notices of recent books. The July number contains an annual bibliography of periodical literature. A general index to articles and reviews in the first twenty volumes was published (London, 1906).

150. Jahresberichte der geschichtswissenschaft. Berlin, 1880-1913.

Issued annually, two or three years after the year covered. Listed significant historical works published in Europe. Not all volumes treat the Anglo-Saxon period.

B. ETHNOLOGY

Bibliography

GROSS (145), pp. 226-31. Bibliography may be found also in several of the more recent works listed under the literature of ethnology.

Literature

151. ZEUSS, K. Die deutschen und die nachbarstämme. Heidelberg, 1925. (reprinted from the 1st ed., Munich, 1837).

The first comprehensive treatment of Germanic ethnology. Still indispensable.

152. BEDDOE. J. The races of Britain. Bristol, etc., 1885. A standard work.

MÜLLENHOFF (10). Deutsche altertumskunde.

153. BREMER, O. Ethnographie der germanischen stämme. 1904. (In Paul's Grundriss (9), Vol. III, pp. 735-950.)

Up to its time the best and most comprehensive treatment. Now somewhat antiquated.

154. SHORE, T. W. Origin of the Anglo-Saxon race. A study of the settlement of England and the tribal origin of the Old English people. Ed. by T. W. and L. E. Shore. London, 1906.

155. CHADWICK, H. M. The origin of the English nation. Cambridge, 1907. New ed., with negligible changes, 1924.

Supports the view that no racial distinction can be made between Angles and Saxons in the conquest of Britain.

156. RIPLEY, W. Z. The races of Europe. New York, 1899.

A standard work. Contains a bibliography of the anthropology and ethnology of Europe. Another vol. with the same title was published in London (1900) and again in 1913.

HOOPS (12), *passim* (in connection with pertinent articles). See the index to each volume s. v. Stammeskunde.

157. MUCH, R. Deutsche stammeskunde. 3d ed., Berlin, 1920.

An excellent introduction to the subject.

158. PEAKE, H. J. English villages. London, 1922.

See chapter IV. A brief but excellent discussion of the races of Europe in the light of recent information.

159. FLEURE, H. J. The races of Egland and Wales: a survey of recent research. London, 1923.

Contains much useful and suggestive information.

160. WADSTEIN, E. On the origin of the English. Uppsala: Skrifter Utgivna av K. Humanistiska Vetenskaps-Samfundet i Uppsala, XXIV. Uppsala, 1927.

Advances suggestive views regarding the early settlement of Britain by the Anglo-Saxons.

161. WELDON, B.DE W. The origin of the English. London, 1928.

KARSTEN (18). Die Germanen.

162. SCHÜTTE, G. Our forefathers: The Gothonic nations. An ethnographical manual comprising the Gothic, German, Dutch, Anglo-Saxon, Frisian and Scandinavian tribes. Vol. I. Translated from the Danish by Jean Young. Cambridge [Eng.] Univ. Press, 1929.

Aims to provide an ethnological description of northern peoples comparable with the textbooks of Zeuss, Bremer, Much, and Kauffmann. A mine of valuable information.

163. FEHRLE, E. Tacitus, Germania. Hrsg., übersetzt und mit Bemerken versehen. Munich, 1929.

Contains a bibliography of Germanic ethnology.

C. SOCIAL HISTORY
1. General
2. Special Aspects

1. General

Bibliography

TRAILL AND MANN (141), *passim*. Bibliography at the end of each chapter.

GROSS (145), pp. 304-14, 208-10.

KLAEBER (462). On pp. cxlix-clii and 254-7, and in the Supplement of the second edition, are listed many books and articles of value for social history.

SONNENSCHEIN (147), pp. 1146-8, 1164-6.

Mediaeval England (142). Bibliography at the end of each chapter.

NOTE: See also the more recent volumes under *Literature* and appropriate volumes under *2. Special Aspects*.

Literature

164. TURNER, S. History of the Anglo-Saxons. 7th ed. London, 1852.
  See Vol. IV of the first ed. (1799) for discussion of manners, institutions, literature, etc.

  GUMMERE (11). An excellent account of the culture of the continental Germanic tribes.

165. MAITLAND, F. W. Domesday book and beyond. Cambridge [Eng.], 1897 (reprinted 1907).
  Valuable discussions of land tenures, classes of society, and history of the manor.

166. STRUTT, J. Glig-gamena angel-ðeod: the sports and pastimes of the people of England. New ed., enlarged, by J. C. Cox. London, 1903.
  See also Hoops (12), *s. v. Spiele*.

167. VON INAMA-STERNEGG, K. Wirtschaft. In Paul's Grundriss (9), Vol. III, pp. 1-50. Section on *Soziale Ordnung* and *Landes-kultur*.

  TRAILL AND MANN (141), *passim*.

  CHADWICK (429). The heroic age.

168. QUENNELL, MARJORIE, AND C. H. B. Everyday life in Anglo-Saxon, Viking and Norman times. London, 1926.

169. WINGFIELD-STRATFORD, E. C. The history of British civilization. 2 vols. New York and London, 1928. See especially chapter II, pp. 36-82.

  NOTE: See also sections D and E below.

2. Special Aspects

170. WRIGHT, T. The homes of other days. A history of domestic manners and sentiments in England. New York and London, 1871.
  Chapters I-VI (pp. 1-92) treat the Anglo-Saxon period.

171. FISCHER, A. Aberglaube unter den angelsachsen. Meiningen, 1891.

172. FILES, G. T. The Anglo-Saxon house. Leipsic, 1893.

173. ROEDER, F. Die familie bei den Angelsachsen. Eine kultur-litterarhistorische studie auf grund gleichzeitiger quellen. I Hauptteil: Mann und frau. Halle, 1899. Also St. E. Ph. (106), Vol. IV.
174. PADELFORD, F. M. Old English musical terms. Bo. Beitr. (83), Vol. IV. Bonn, 1899.
175. PFÄNDLER, W. Die vergnügungen der angelsachsen. Anglia (36), Vol. 29: 417-522. 1906. Bibliography, pp. 522-6.
176. BUDDE, E. Die bedeutung der trinksitten in der kultur der angelsachsen. Jena, 1906.
177. ROEDER, F. Über die erziehung der vornehmen angelsächsischen jugend in fremden häusern. Halle, 1910.

Another article, "Neue Beiträge zur Erziehung der angelsächsischen adeligen Jugend," announced in (125) as forthcoming, appeared as a separate pamphlet.
178. LEACH, A. F. Educational charters and documents, A. D. 598-1909. Cambridge [Eng.], 1911.

HOOPS (12). See the index to each volume *s. v. Mythus, Aberglaube, Familie, Getränke, Hausbau, Hauswesen, Nahrungsmittel, Spiele, Totenbestattung.* The articles falling under these general heads are of considerable bibliographical value.
179. LEACH, A. F. The schools of medieval England. London, 1915.
180. RÖSLER, MARG. Erziehung in England vor der normannischen eroberung. E. St. (38), Vol. 48: 1-114. 1915. Important supplement to ROEDER (177).
181. BROWNE, G. F. The importance of women in Anglo-Saxon times; and other addresses. London, 1919.
182. ARON, A. Traces of matriarchy in Germanic hero-lore. Univ. of Wis. Studies in Lang. and Lit. (116), No. 9. 1920.
183. PARRY, A. W. Education in England in the Middle Ages. London, 1920.
184. KELLER, G. Tanz und gesang bei den alten Germanen. Bern, 1927.
185. PHILIPPSON, E. A. Germanisches heidentum bei den Angelsachsen. Kölner anglistische Arbeiten (92), Vol. IV. Leipzig, 1929.

An excellent work, with extensive bibliography.

D. POLITICAL HISTORY
Bibliography
GROSS (145), pp. 295-304.

Camb. Med. Hist. (143), Vol. II, pp. 788-800; Vol. III, pp. 621-2, 625-30.

SONNENSCHEIN (147), pp. 1164-6, 1146, 1153-7; OMAN (197), *passim.*

NOTE: See also the more recent volumes under *Literature.*

Literature
186. KEMBLE, J. M. The Saxons in England. 2d ed. by W. de Gray Birch. London, 1876.
187. FREEMAN, E. A. History of the Norman conquest; its causes and results. 6 vols. Oxford, 1867-79; 2d ed. of Vols. I-IV, 1870-6; 3d ed. of Vols. I and II, 1877.

The great authority on the conquest; valuable for the early 11th century also. Needs correction on some points.
188. LAPPENBERG, J. M. History of England under the Anglo-Saxon kings (transl. by B. Thorpe). Revised ed. 2 vols. London, 1881.
A good survey.
189. ELTON, C. J. Origins of English history. 2d ed. London, 1890.
Chapter XII contains Anglo-Saxon history to 597. Valuable.
190. STUBBS, W. The constitutional history of England. 3 vols. 6th ed. of Vol. I, 1897 (reprinted 1903).
Vol. I, chapters 1-8, deal with the Anglo-Saxon period. Additional material is found in C. Petit-Dutaillis: *Studies and Notes Supplementary to Stubbs' Constitutional History Down to the Great Charter* (transl. from the French by W. E. Rhodes). Manchester, 1908-14. 2d ed. of Vol. I, 1911.
See also Ch. Petit-Dutaillis and Georges Lefebvre, *Studies and Notes Supplementary to Stubbs' Constitutional History*, transl. by M. I. E. Robertson and R. F. Treharne. Manchester, 1929.
191. RAMSAY, J. H. The foundations of England, or twelve centuries of British history, B. C. 55—A. D. 1154. 2 vols. London, 1898.
Especially interesting in Vol. I are chapter 10, "Early Anglo-Saxon Life and Institutions"; chapter 25, "England under Cnut"; chapter 31, "Later Anglo-Saxon Society".
192. GREEN, J. R. History of the English people. 8 vols. London, 1905-8.
Two older works by the same author, *The Making of England* (449-829), 2 vols., London, 1897 (reprinted 1910), and *The Conquest of England* (829-1071), London, 1883 (reprinted 1899), together cover Anglo-Saxon history to 1071. Needs to be supplemented by more recent histories.
193. HODGKIN, T. The history of England from the earliest times to the Norman conquest. New York, 1906.
CHADWICK (155). Origin of the English nation.
194. COLLINGWOOD, W. G. Scandinavian Britain. London, 1908.
See also F. M. Stenton, "The Danes in England", in *Proceedings of the British Academy* 1927. Vol. 13: 203-46.
195. MAWER, A. The Vikings. Cambridge [Eng.] and New York, 1913.
Good summary of the Viking expansion. Gives bibliography.
HOOPS (12), *s. v. Englisches siedelungswesen*. Vol. I, pp. 593-613. A discussion of the settlement. See also Vol. IV, pp. 529-53, *s. v. Wikinger*, for an account (by A. Bugge) of the Vikings.
196. WILLIAMS, M. W. Social Scandinavia in the Viking age. New York, 1920.
Good account of the civilization of the Vikings.
197. OMAN, C. W. C. England before the Norman conquest. 5th ed. London, 1921. Pays much attention to wars.
198. CHAMBERS, R. W. England before the Norman Conquest. London and New York, 1926.

Contains extracts in translation from Latin, Old English, and Scandinavian works to illustrate the history of the English race from continental times to the Battle of Stamford Bridge.

199. ZACHRISSON, R. E. Romans, Kelts, and Saxons in ancient Britain, an investigation into the two dark centuries (400-600) of English history. Uppsala, 1927.

Supports the view that there was intimate fusion between the Romans and the more civilized of the Britons, and that the Celts in English territory were amalgamated with, or absorbed by, the Anglo-Saxons within a few generations after the settlement.

NOTE: See also sections C and F.

E. ECONOMIC AND INDUSTRIAL HISTORY

Bibliography

200. MOORE, M. F. Bibliography of manorial and agrarian history, in Two Select Bibliographies of Mediaeval Historical Study. London, 1912.
201. HALL, H. A select bibliography for the study, sources, and literature of English mediaeval economic history. London, 1914.

GROSS (145), pp. 203-8.

SONNENSCHEIN (147), Part II, pp. 589-91; Part III, p. 1146.

Mediaeval England (142), *passim*.

NOTE: See also the more recent volumes under *Literature*.

Literature

202. ASHLEY, W. J. An introduction to English economic history and theory. 2 vols. Vol. I, 3d ed. London, 1894.

A very useful work on the manor, gilds, and economic legislation. Many quotations from original authorities.

VON INAMA-STERNEGG (167). See the sections on *Landes-kultur, Gewerbe, Handel und verkehr.*

203. VINOGRADOFF, P. The growth of the manor. London, 1905. 2d ed., 1911.

A study of origins. See also his article in HOOPS, (12), Vol. I, pp. 50-2.

204. VINOGRADOFF, P. English society in the eleventh century. Oxford, 1908.

"Deals with military organization, taxation, land tenure, manors, social classes. Much of the material relates to the periods before and after the eleventh century."—Gross.

205. CUNNINGHAM, W. The growth of English industry and commerce during the early and middle ages. 2 vols. Vol. I, 5th ed., Cambridge, 1910.

Sound and scholarly.

HOOPS (12). See the index to each volume *s. v. Agrarwesen, Baukunst, Bergbau, Finanzwesen, Handel, Kunst, Lehnswesen, Masse, Münzwesen, Rechenkunst, Schiffswesen, Siedlungswesen, Verkehrswesen.*

206. CHEYNEY, E. P. An introduction to the industrial and social history of England. New York, 1920.

207. USHER, A. P. An introduction to the industrial history of England. Boston, 1920.
208. SALZMAN, L. F. English industries of the Middle Ages. Oxford, 1923.
209. SEEBOHM, (Mrs.) M. E. The evolution of the English farm. Cambridge [Mass.], Harvard Univ. Press, 1927.
> See chapter V, "The Saxon Period", pp. [98]-125.
210. LIPSON, E. An introduction to the economic history of England. Vol. I. The Middle Ages. 5th ed., London, 1930.
211. SALZMAN, L. F. English trade in the Middle Ages. Announced by the Oxford Univ. Press for publication in Nov., 1930.
NOTE: See also sections C and H.

F. LAW, etc.

Bibliography

GROSS (145), pp. 124-9, 257-67; SONNENSCHEIN (147), Part II, pp. 471-2.

WHITE (220), pp. xv-xxx; TASWELL-LANGMEAD (221), pp. xxiii-xxvi.

NOTE: See also the more recent volumes under *Literature*.

Literature

212. SCHMID, R. Die gesetze der angelsachsen. 2d ed. Leipzig, 1858.
> Valuable introduction.
213. ADAMS, H., ed. Essays in Anglo-Saxon law. New York, 1876.
> Law courts, land and family law, procedure.

STUBBS (190). A comprehensive survey. Now partly superseded by recent researches.

214. POLLOCK, F., AND F. W. MAITLAND. The history of English law before the time of Edward I. 2 vols. 2d ed. Cambridge, 1898.
> Supersedes previous works on English law for the period it covers.
215. CHADWICK, H. M. Studies on Anglo-Saxon institutions. Cambridge, 1905.
> Territorial divisions, administrative system, nobility, etc. Written chiefly for the advanced student.

HOOPS (12). See the index to each volume s. v. *Agrarwesen, Bergbau, Handel, Gefolgschaft, Kirchenverfassung, Lehnswesen, Familie, Rechtsdenkmäler, Rechtswesen, Staatsverfassung, Stamm, Ständewesen.*

VON INAMA-STERNEGG (167). See the sections on *Soziale ordnung* and *Stadtverfassung*.

216. VON AMIRA, K. Grundriss des germanischen rechts. In Paul's Grundriss (9), 3d ed. 1913.
217. LIEBERMANN, F. Die gesetze der angelsachsen. 3 vols. Halle, 1903-16.
> The best work on the laws of the Anglo-Saxons. See especially Vol. III for discussion.
218. ADAMS, G. B. Constitutional history of England. New York, 1921.
219. HOLDSWORTH, W. S. A history of English law. 3d ed. 9 vols. London, 1922-6.

220. WHITE, A. B. The making of the English constitution 449-1485. 2d ed. London and New York, 1925.
Excellent annotated bibliography, pp. xv-xxx.
221. TASWELL-LANGMEAD, T. P. English constitutional history (9th ed., by A. L. Poole). Boston, 1929. A standard work.
222. MORRIS, W. A. The constitutional history of England to 1216. New York, 1930.
Goes back to remote Germanic origins. Bibliography included.

G. THE CHURCH

Bibliography

GROSS (145), pp. 314-24; 138-49.
Camb. Med. Hist. (143), Vol. II, pp. 793-4.
SONNENSCHEIN (147), Part I, pp. 174-6.
NOTE: See also the more recent volumes under *Literature*.

Literature

223. LINGARD, J. The history and antiquities of the Anglo-Saxon church. 2 vols. London, 1845. Reprinted 1858. Very detailed discussion.
224. HADDAN, A. W., AND W. STUBBS. Councils and ecclesiastical documents relating to Great Britain and Ireland. 3 vols. Oxford, 1869-78.
225. PLUMMER, C. Venerabilis Baedae opera historica. 2 vols. Oxford, 1896. See especially Vol. II (notes).
226. BRIGHT, W. Chapters of early English church history. 3d ed. Oxford, 1897.
The best work on the early period (up to A. D. 709).
227. BROWNE, G. F. Augustine and his companions. London, 1897.
228. HUNT, W. The English church from its foundation to the Norman conquest, 597-1066. London, 1899.
A fair-minded and scholarly account of the whole period. Bibliographical references for each chapter. Forms the first volume of an eight volume *History of the English Church*, ed. by W. R. W. Stephens and W. Hunt. London, 1899-1910.
229. WAKEMAN, H. O. An introduction to the history of the Church of England. London, 1908.
The best one-volume history of the English Church. 10th ed. London, 1923.
230. PLUMMER, A. The churches in Britain before A. D. 1000. 2 vols. London, 1911-12.
HOOPS (12). See the index to each volume *s. v. Bekehrungsgeschichte, Bildungswesen, Kirche, Kirchenbau, Kircheneinrichtung, Kirchenverfassung, Kultus.*
231. BROWNE, G. F. The conversion of the Heptarchy. Revised ed. London, 1914.
232. ROBINSON, J. A. The Times of St. Dunstan. Oxford, 1923.
233. MEISSNER, J. L. G. The Celtic church in England. After the Synod at Whitby. London, 1929.

Stresses unduly the influence of the Celtic church. Must be used with great caution.
233a. ALLISON, T. English religious life in the eighth century.... New York, 1929.

H. THE ARTS, CRAFTS, AND ARCHAEOLOGY

Bibliography
TRAILL AND MANN (141), *passim.*
HALL (201), pp. 59-65; GROSS (145), pp. 66-76.
CHAMBERS (461), pp. 345-65, *passim.* A valuable chapter on archaeology, with abundant references.
SONNENSCHEIN (147), Part III, pp. 1578-83, especially p. 1580.
Mediaeval England (142), *passim.*
NOTE: See also the more recent volumes under *Literature.*

Literature
234. HODGETTS, J. F. Older England: illustrated by Anglo-Saxon antiquities in the British Museum. London, 1884-5.
235. DE BAYE, J. Industrial arts of the Anglo-Saxons (transl. from the French by T. B. Harbottle). London, 1893.
   Deals with the smaller remains, such as jewelry, arms, pottery, graves, etc.
236. HOOPS, J. Pflanzenaberglaube bei den Angelsachsen. Globus, 1893.
   See also his *Waldbäume und Kulturpflanzen im german. Altertum.* Strassburg, 1905.
237. ANDERSON, L. H. The Anglo-Saxon scop. University of Toronto Studies (114), Vol. I. Toronto, 1903.
   On the basis of poetic monuments. In readable essay style.
238. PAYNE, J. F. English medicine in the Anglo-Saxon times. Oxford, 1904.
   Rather complimentary to the Anglo-Saxons. With 23 illustrations and many excerpts in translation. References to other works which discuss Anglo-Saxon medicine are given on pp. 35-6 of Payne's work.
239. BROWN, G. B. The arts and crafts of our Teutonic forefathers. Chicago, 1911.
   Deals chiefly with the continental Germanic tribes, but throws light also on the Anglo-Saxons in England. Bibliography, pp. 232-8.
240. BROWN, G. B. The arts in early England (to 1066). 6 vols. London, 1903—
   Vol. I, *The Life of Saxon England in its Relation to the Arts;* Vol. II, *Ecclesiastical Architecture:* Vols. III and IV, *Saxon Art and Industry in the Pagan Period;* Vol. V, *Christian Art;* Vol. VI, Part 1, "concludes the treatment of the monuments of the great age of Northumbrian art" begun in Vol. V. The rest of Vol. VI "will furnish a treatment of the stone monuments of the middle and later Anglo-Saxon periods down to the Norman Conquest". A very valuable work.

HOOPS (12). See the index to each volume *s. v. Agrarwesen, Archäologie, Astronomie, Badewesen, Baukunst, Befestigungswesen, Bergbau, Fischerei, Gefässe, Geräte, Gesang, Handwerk, Hausbau, Hauswesen, Heerwesen, Jagd, Kirchenbau, Kleidung, Körperpflege, Kunst, Medizin, Metalle, Mineralien, Musik, Ornamentik, Schiffs- und Seewesen, Schmuck, Totenbestattung, Waffen, Werkzeuge.*

241. LEEDS, E. T. The archaeology of the Anglo-Saxon settlements. Oxford, 1913.

Presents very interesting archaeological evidence concerning the Anglo-Saxon conquest of England.

242. STJERNA, K. Essays on questions connected with the Old English poem of Beowulf (trans. and ed. by J. R. Clark Hall). Viking Club Publications, Extra Series, Vol. III. Coventry, 1912.

A study of Scandinavian archaeological material: armor, jewelry, dwellings, grave-mounds, etc. Throws light on early Anglo-Saxon culture.

243. SINGER, C. A review of the medical literature of the dark ages, with a new text of about 1110. (Reprinted from the Proceedings of the Royal Society of Medicine 10: 107-60.) London, 1917.

CHAMBERS (461). Appendix F: Beowulf and the archaeologists, pp. 345-65.

244. OMAN, C. W. C. A history of the art of war in the Middle Ages. 2 vols. 2d ed. Boston and New York, 1923.

Vol. I treats the Anglo-Saxon period.

244a. SMITH, R. A. A guide to the Anglo-Saxon and foreign Teutonic antiquities [British Museum]. London, 1923.

245. SINGER, C. Early English magic and medicine. Proceedings of the British Academy 1919-20. Vol. 9: 341-74. London, 1924.

246. PEERS, C. R. English ornament in the seventh and eighth centuries. Proceedings of the British Academy 1926. Vol. 12: 45-54.

247. SINGER, C. From magic to science: essays on the scientific twilight. New York, 1928.

See especially chapter II, "The Dark Ages and the Dawn of Science"; chapter III, "The Lorica of Gildas the Briton"; chapter IV, "Early English Magic and Medicine".

248. ÅBERG, N. The Anglo-Saxons in England during the early centuries after the invasion. Uppsala, 1926. (Also Cambridge, Leipzig, The Hague.)

Concerned wholly with Anglo-Saxon ornaments (brooches, pins, vases, buckles, rings, buttons, spoons, ewers, etc.). Profusely illustrated. Some bibliography in footnotes.

NOTE: See also sections C and E.

PART VI

LANGUAGE

A. General Bibliography
B. History of the Language
C. Grammar
   1. General grammars
   2. Phonology
   3. Syntax
   4. Dialect
D. Vocabulary
   1. Dictionaries
   2. Studies of vocabulary

A. GENERAL BIBLIOGRAPHY

WÜLKER (3), pp. 95-105. Lists only grammars, dictionaries, and readers. Linguistic studies are often included under the individual monuments.

KÖRTING (6), pp. 16-19; WYLD (253), pp. 11-14; KENNEDY (8), pp. 115-58.

B. HISTORY OF THE LANGUAGE

249. EMERSON, O. F. The history of the English language. New York, 1894 (reprinted 1924).

    A scholarly work, which emphasizes the development of the native element in English and the importance of phonetic changes.

250. KLUGE, F., et al. Geschichte der englischen sprache. In Paul's Grundriss (9).

251. HUCHON, R. Histoire de la langue anglaise. Tome I, Des origines à la conquête normande (450-1066). Paris, 1923.

    An attempt at a complete history of the language.

252. JESPERSEN, O. Growth and structure of the English language. 5th ed. Leipzig, 1926.

253. WYLD, H. C. A short history of English, with a bibliography of recent books on the subject. 3d ed. London, 1927.

    Omits discussion of vocabulary. Contains explanation of dialect differences in phonology.

254. LINDELÖF, U. Elements of the history of the English language (transl. from the Swedish by R. M. Garrett). State University of Washington Publications in English (118). 1911.

    An excellent introduction to the history of the language. The second edition of a German original, *Grundzüge der Geschichte der englischen Sprache*, appeared at Leipzig and Berlin, 1928.

C. GRAMMAR

1. General Grammars

Bibliography

WÜLKER (3), pp. 95-9; SIEVERS (255), pp. 363-71.
KENNEDY (8), pp. 115-18. Contains also a bibliography of studies of Old English grammar, pp. 151-3.

Textbooks

254a. COSIJN, P. Altwestsächsische grammatik. Haag, 1883-8.
Scientific, excellent. An abridged form, *Kurzgefasste altwestsächsische Grammatik*, 2d ed., appeared at Leiden, 1893.
254b. COOK, A. S. A first book in Old English.
Grammar, reader, notes, and vocabulary. 3d ed. Boston, 1903.
254c. WYATT, A. J. An elementary Old English grammar (early West-Saxon). Cambridge, 1897.
255. SIEVERS, E. An Old English grammar (transl. and ed. by A. S. Cook). 3d ed. Boston, 1903.
Lists a great number of dialect forms. In the phonology "an elementary knowledge of Gothic has been presupposed". Indispensable as a reference book.
256. DIETER, F. Laut- und formenlehre der altgermanischen dialekte. Leipzig, 1900.
See chapters 4, 10, 16, and 22.
257. SMITH, C. A. An Old English grammar and exercise book. 4th ed. Boston, 1903 (6th reprint, 1913).
258. WRIGHT, J., AND E. M. An elementary Old English grammar. Oxford, 1923. Dependable.
259. WRIGHT, J., AND E. M. An Old English grammar. 3d ed. London, 1925.
Helpful in the comparative study of O. E. and the related Germanic and Indo-European languages.
260. SIEVERS, E. Abriss der angelsächsischen grammatik. 6th ed. Halle, 1924; 8th ed., 1931.
261. WARDALE, E. E. An Old English grammar. 2d ed. Revised. London, 1926.
262. MOORE, S., AND T. A. KNOTT. The elements of Old English. 5th ed. Ann Arbor, 1927.
263. FLOM, G. T. Introductory Old English grammar and reader. Boston, 1930.

Outlines of Old English grammar may be found also in the following: SWEET (313); SWEET (323); BRIGHT (318); TURK (329); KRAPP AND KENNEDY (331).

The following historical grammars contain much material on Old English grammar:

264. KOCH, C. F. Historische grammatik der englischen sprache. 2d ed. 3 vols. Kassel, 1878-91.
Vol. I (1882) *Laut- und Flexionslehre;* Vol. II (1878) *Satzlehre;* Vol. III (1891) *Wortbildung.*

265. KALUZA, M. Historische grammatik der englischen sprache. 2 vols. 2d ed. Berlin, 1906-07.
266. LUICK, K. Historische grammatik der englischen sprache. Leipzig, 1914—
    When completed, this will be the best work on its subject.

2. Phonology

Bibliography: KENNEDY (8), pp. 132-4.

Literature
267. SWEET, H. History of English sounds. Oxford, 1888. Somewhat out of date.
268. POGATSCHER, A. Zur lautlehre der griechischen, lateinischen und romanischen lehnworte im altenglischen. Q. F. (103), Vol. LXIV, 1888.
269. MAYHEW, A. L. Synopsis of Old English phonology, being a systematic account of Old English vowels and consonants and their correspondence in the cognate languages. Oxford, 1891.
270. HEMPL, G. Old-English phonology. Revised ed. Boston, 1894.
271. BRENNER, O. Zur aussprache des angelsächsischen. Beitr. (48), Vol. 20: 554-9. 1895.
    DIETER (256). Laut- und formenlehre.
272. BÜLBRING, K. D. Altenglisches elementarbuch. Heidelberg, 1902.
    Still the standard work on Old English phonology. Rivalled only by LUICK (266).
    WYLD (253); LUICK (266).

3. Syntax

NOTE: Since there is no book treating Old English syntax as a whole, one must consult partial studies listed in the following:
273. CHASE, F. H. A bibliographical guide to Old English syntax. Leipzig, 1896. The most complete list up to its date.
274. WÜLFING, J. E. Die Syntax in den werken Alfreds des grossen. Bonn, 1894-1901.
    The only extensive work on Old English syntax, but not complete. Gives syntax of the parts of speech, but not of the whole sentence. Parts II and III make use of constructions from Aelfric, *Blickling Homilies, Chronicle*, Wulfstan, and the *Gospels*, in addition to Alfredian material.
275. CALLAWAY, M. Studies in the syntax of the Lindisfarne Gospels with appendices on some idioms in the Germanic languages. Baltimore, 1918.
    The bibliography contains about 400 entries.
276. SMALL, G. W. The comparison of inequality: The semantics and syntax of the comparative particle in English. Baltimore, 1924. Good bibliography.
    KENNEDY (8), pp. 153-7. The most extensive bibliography.

4. *Dialect*

KENNEDY (8), pp. 132-4; 157-8. First section lists many phonological studies involving determination of dialect; second section lists general and special studies of dialect proper.

D. VOCABULARY

1. Dictionaries

Bibliography: KENNEDY (8), pp. 121-3.

NOTE: The most useful dictionaries are the following (in order of their general importance):

277. BOSWORTH, J., AND T. N. TOLLER. An Anglo-Saxon dictionary based on the manuscript collections of the late Joseph Bosworth ... ed. and enl. by T. N. Toller. Oxford, 1882-98. Supplement by Toller, Oxford, 1908-21.
278. HALL, J. R. C. A concise Anglo-Saxon dictionary for the use of students. 2d ed. Cambridge and New York, 1916. The best portable dictionary.
279. SWEET, H. The student's dictionary of Anglo-Saxon. New York and London, 1897.
280. GREIN, C. W. M. Sprachschatz der angelsächsischen dichter. New ed. by J. Köhler and F. Holthausen. Heidelberg, 1912-14. Aims to be complete for the poetic vocabulary.

2. Studies of Vocabulary

a. For glossaries, glosses, individual words, and groups of words, see KENNEDY (8), pp. 128-9, 134-47. For glosses, see also Part XII of this *Guide*.
b. For word-formation (prefixes, suffixes, and compounds), see KENNEDY (8), pp. 147-8.
c. For names, see KENNEDY (8), pp. 148-50.
d. For component elements of the Old English vocabulary, and for special categories of words, see KENNEDY (8), p. 151.
e. For semasiological studies, see KENNEDY (8), p. 157.
f. For foreign elements and influences, see KENNEDY (8), p. 157.

PART VII

PALAEOGRAPHY

A. General Bibliography
B. Alphabet
   1. Runic
   2. Roman
C. Manuscripts
D. Facsimiles

A. GENERAL BIBLIOGRAPHY

KENNEDY (8), pp. 73-84. For bibliography of bibliographies of palaeography, see KENNEDY, p. 73, Nos. 2003-7.

HOOPS (12). See the index to each volume *s. v. Schriftwesen*, for special articles, with bibliography.

B, 1. ALPHABET—RUNIC

Bibliography

C. H. E. L. (4), pp. 475-8; BRANDL (5), pp. 951, 956.

281. DICKINS, B. Runic and heroic poems of the old Teutonic peoples. Cambridge [Eng.], 1915.

KENNEDY (8), pp. 75-8. For bibliography of bibliographies of writings on runes, see KENNEDY, p. 75.

Literature

282. STEPHENS, G. The old northern runic monuments of Scandinavia and England. 4 vols. London and Copenhagen, 1866-1901.
    With hunreds of illustrations of crosses and pillars, weapons, ornaments, etc., and colored plates. English translations in parallel columns with runic inscriptions. Some interpretations are unsound.

283. WIMMER, L. F. A. Die runenschrift . . . übersetzt von F. Holthausen. Berlin, 1887.
    Perhaps the best-known work on runes. Derives the runic alphabet from Latin capitals in imperial times. Wimmer's theory is discussed by G. Hempl in Philologische Studien (120), pp. 12-20.

284. SIEVERS, E. Runen und runeninschriften. In Paul's Grundriss (9), I, pp. 248-62.

C. H. E. L. (4), (Chapter by A. C. Paues), pp. 7-13. Satisfactory as far as it goes.

285. VON FRIESEN, O. Runenschrift. In HOOPS (12), Vol. IV, pp. 5-51. 1918-19.

An excellent introduction to the theories of the origin and history of the runic alphabet, accompanied by reproductions of runic monuments. Argues for a combined Greek and Latin origin of the runes.

286. BUCK, C. D. An ABC inscribed in Old English runes. M. Ph. (56), Vol. 17: 219-24. 1919.

Accepts an Italic (non-Latin) source for the runic alphabet: "Wimmer's theory ought to be definitely abandoned as contrary to all reason."

287. PEDERSEN, H. Runernes oprindelse. Aarbøger for Nordisk Oldkyndighed og Historie (41). 3d series, Vol. 13: 37-82. Copenhagen, 1923.

287a. CAHEN, M. Origine et développement de l'écriture runique. Mém. de la Soc. de Ling. de Paris, Vol. 25: 1-46. 1923. For runes in England, see pp. 37 ff.

288. BUGGE, E. S., AND M. OLSEN. Norges indskrifter med de aeldre runer. 3 vols. Christiania, 1891-1924. Vol. III by M. Olsen.

289. AGRELL, S. Der ursprung der runenschrift und die magie. A. f. N. F. (46), Vol. 43: 97-109. 1927.

The subject received more elaborate treatment in his book (290).

290. AGRELL, S. Runornas talmystik och dess antika förebild. Lund, 1927.

Contains an English summary of the contents. Supports the view that the runic alphabet was originally derived from the Romans.

290a. MARSTRANDER, C. J. S. Om runene og runenavnenes oprindelse. Norsk Tidsskrift for Sprogvidenskap (65), Vol. I: 85-179. 1928. Contains a résumé in French, pp. 180-88.

291. FEIST, S. Zum ursprung der germanischen runenschrift. Acta Philologica Scandinavica (43), Vol. 4: 1-25. 1929.

Contains a bibliographical survey, illustrations, and excellent discussion. Accepts a north Italian origin for runic script.

292. HAMMARSTRÖM, M. Om runskriftens härkomst. Helsingfors, 1929. Studier i Nordisk Filologi XX, nr. 19. Accepts a north Italian origin for runic script.

292a. VON FRIESEN, O. Runes. In Ency. Brit. Vol. 19, pp. 659-64. 1929.

B, 2. ALPHABET—ROMAN

Bibliography

293. KELLER, W. Angelsächsische palaeographie. Die schrift der angelsachsen mit besonderer rücksicht auf die denkmäler in der volkssprache. I Einleitung. Palaestra (101), Vol. 43. 1906.

Valuable annotations. See below also HOOPS (12).

GROSS (145), pp. 41-8; KENNEDY (8), pp. 73-4.

Literature
294. WATTENBACH, W. Das schriftwesen im mittelalter. 3d ed. Leipzig, 1896. The best work on the general history of medieval writing.
295. THOMPSON, E. M. The history of English handwriting, A. D. 700-1400. Transactions of the Bibliographical Society, Vol. V. London, 1901. Standard. Many facsimiles (about 20 of Old English manuscripts).
 KELLER (293). Angelsächsische palaeographie.
296. THOMPSON, E. M. Handbook of Greek and Latin palaeography. 3d ed. London, 1906.
 The best work of its kind. An enlarged edition, entitled *An Introduction to Greek and Latin Palaeography*, appeared at Oxford, 1912.
297. ARNDT, W. Lateinische schrift. Überarbeitet von H. Block. In Paul's Grundriss (9), Vol. I, pp. 274-82.
298. CAPPELLI, A. Lexicon abbreviaturarum quae in lapidibus, codicibus, et chartis praesertim medii-aevi occurrunt. 2d ed. Milan, 1912; 3d ed., 1929.
 Gives facsimiles and transcriptions of a very large number of abbreviations and contractions used in medieval Latin. Extremely useful.
 HOOPS (12), *s. v. Angelsächsische Schrift*, Vol. I, pp. 98-103. Article by W. Keller. With annotated bibliography.

C. MANUSCRIPTS (MATERIALS, SCRIBES, SCRIPTORIA, etc.)

Bibliography
299. MOORE, M. F. A classified list of works relating to the study of English palaeography and diplomatic, in Two select bibliographies of mediaeval historical study. London, 1912.
 Practically complete on English palaeography and diplomatic to 1911. See especially pp. 37-38.
 C. H. E. L. (4), pp. 477-8.

Literature
 WATTENBACH (294). Das schriftwesen im mittelalter.
300. JAMES, M. R. The ancient libraries of Canterbury and Dover. Cambridge [Eng.], 1903.
 ARNDT (297), pp. 265-74. Based on WATTENBACH (294).
 C. H. E. L. (4), (Chapter by A. C. Paues), pp. 16-20.
301. GASQUET, F. A. The Old English Bible and other essays. 2d ed. London, 1908.
 Essay I: "Notes on Medieval Monastic Libraries"; Essay II: "The Monastic Scriptorium".
302. KELLER, W. Über die akzente in den angelsächsischen handschriften. In Untersuchungen und Quellen (122), pp. 7-120.
303. SAVAGE, E. A. Old English libraries. London, [1911].

BIBLIOGRAPHY OF OLD ENGLISH 39

304. CRAIGIE, W. A. Interpolations and omissions in Anglo-Saxon poetic texts. In Philologica (67), Vol. 2: 5-19. 1925.
304a. RADEMACHER, M. Die worttrennung in angelsächsischen handschriften. Münster, 1926.
305. MILLAR, E. G. English illuminated manuscripts from the Xth to the XIIIth century. Paris and Brussels, 1926.
> Discusses illumination and contains some 30 plates of MSS. from the pre-Conquest period. See also J. A. Herbert, *Illuminated Manuscripts*, London, 1911, chapter VII, "English Illumination to A. D. 1200", pp. 122-42.
306. KELLER, W. Zur worttrennung in den angelsächsischen handschriften. In Britannica (138), pp. 89-105.

D. FACSIMILES

Bibliography
KELLER (293), pp. 2-6. See pp. 5-6 for a list of the facsimiles of Old English poetical and prose works.
MOORE (299), pp. 40-6; HOOPS (12), Vol. I, p. 103.
GROSS (145), pp. 45-8; KENNEDY (8), pp. 74-5.

Collections
307. WESTWOOD, J. O. Facsimiles of the miniatures and ornaments of Anglo-Saxon and Irish manuscripts. London, 1868.
> Valuable because the plates often show portions of text.
308. Facsimiles of ancient charters in the British Museum. [O.E. period ed. by E. A. Bond, with collaboration of E. M. Thompson.] 4 parts. London, 1873-8.
> With 144 plates. Indispensable for the study of the development of O.E. writing.

KELLER (293). Contains thirteen plates with text.
309. SKEAT, W. W. Twelve facsimiles of Old English manuscripts, with transcriptions and introduction. Oxford, 1892.
> Only three of them are properly Old English.
310. The Palaeographical Society. Facsimiles of manuscripts and inscriptions, ed. by E. A. Bond, E. M. Thompson. . . . First and second series. 5 vols. London, 1873-94.
> Many of the 455 plates are illustrative of Old English monuments. The most important collection.
311. The New Palaeographical Society. Publications. Facsimiles of ancient manuscripts, ed. by E. M. Thompson, E. A. Bond, *et al.* London, 1903.
> Highly important. Continuation of (310).

MILLAR (305). English illuminated manuscripts.
NOTE: For facsimiles of the chief poetical manuscripts, see Part X: A. Manuscripts.

PART VIII

BOOKS OF SELECTIONS

Bibliography

WÜLKER (3), pp. 101-5; KENNEDY (8), pp. 118-21.

Textbooks

312. SWEET, H. A second Anglo-Saxon reader. Archaic and dialectal. Oxford, 1887.
313. SWEET, H. An Anglo-Saxon primer, with grammar, notes and glossary. 8th ed. Oxford, 1896.
314. SWEET, H. First steps in Anglo-Saxon. Oxford, 1897.
315. WYATT, A. J. An elementary Old English reader (early West Saxon). Cambridge, 1901.
316. EARLE, J. A book for the beginner in Anglo-Saxon. 4th ed., newly revised throughout. Oxford, 1902.

COOK (254b). A first book in Old English.

317. KLUGE, F. Angelsächsisches lesebuch. 4th ed. Halle, 1915.

The fourth edition is not as rich in content as the third edition (1902).

318. BRIGHT, J. W. An Anglo-Saxon reader. With notes, a complete glossary, a chapter on versification and an outline of Anglo-Saxon grammar. 4th ed. New York, 1917.
319. SCHÜCKING, L. L. Kleines angelsächsisches dichterbuch—lyrik und heldenepos. Texte und textenproben mit kurzen einleitungen und ausführlichem wörterbuch. Cöthen, 1919.
320. WYATT, A. J. An Anglo-Saxon reader, edited with notes and glossary. Cambridge, 1919.

Good bibliographical summaries in the notes. The material consists of extracts not usually chosen, in order "to represent as many sides as we could of the life of our forefathers".

321. FÖRSTER, M. Altenglisches lesebuch für anfänger. 4th ed. Heidelberg, 1931. No grammar. Emphasis upon linguistic study.
322. SEDGEFIELD, W. J. An Anglo-Saxon verse-book. Manchester, London, and New York, 1922.
323. SWEET, H. An Anglo-Saxon reader in prose and verse, with grammatical introduction, notes and glossary. 9th ed., revised by C. T. Onions. Oxford, 1922.
324. CRAIGIE, W. A. Easy readings in Anglo-Saxon. 2d ed. Edinburgh, 1927.
325. ZUPITZA, J., AND J. SCHIPPER. Alt- und mittelenglisches übungsbuch. 13th ed., by A. Eichler. Wien, 1928.

326. CRAIGIE, W. A. Specimens of Anglo-Saxon prose. I. Biblical narratives and ancient history. Edinburgh, 1924. II. Early Christian lore and legend. Edinburgh, 1925. III. British and Anglo-Saxon history. Edinburgh, 1929.

327. CRAIGIE, W. A. Specimens of Anglo-Saxon poetry. I. Biblical and classical themes. Edinburgh, 1923. II. Early Christian lore and legend. Edinburgh, 1926. III. Germanic legend and Anglo-Saxon history. (Announced as in press, Oct., 1930.)

328. WYATT, A. J. The threshold of Anglo-Saxon. Cambridge [Eng.], 1926.

Selections chiefly from the *Chronicle* and *Beowulf*, in normalized text.

329. TURK, M. H. An Anglo-Saxon reader. New York, 1927.

Contains also about forty pages of selections from Middle English.

330. SEDGEFIELD, W. J. An Anglo-Saxon book of verse and prose. Manchester and London, 1928.

The prose portion is also published separately (1928).

331. KRAPP, G. P., AND A. G. KENNEDY. An Anglo-Saxon reader. New York, 1929.

FLOM (263). An introductory Old English grammar and reader.

NOTE: See also Part X, B. Modern Collections.

PART IX

LITERATURE

A. History and Criticism
B. Mythology and Legend

A. HISTORY AND CRITICISM

Bibliography
   WÜLKER (3), pp. 105-8; C. H. E. L. (4), pp. 469-71; 491-2.
   BRANDL (5), *passim;* KÖRTING (6), pp. 21-2.
331a. LAWRENCE, W. W. Selected bibliography of medieval literature in England. New York, 1930.

Works limited to the Old English period
332. EARLE, J. Anglo-Saxon literature. London. 1884.
   A rather brief but very pleasing sketch.
333. BROOKE, S. A. English literature from the beginning to the Norman conquest. New York, 1898 (reprinted 1921).
   BRANDL (5). The best descriptive and bibliographical account we have.
334. BROOKE, S. A. The history of early English literature. London and New York, 1892 (reprinted 1914).
   Contains much good criticism of Old English literature, and many bits of spirited translation. Not entirely trustworthy in scholarship.
334a. SNELL, F. J. The age of Alfred 664-1154. London, 1912. Rather elementary but useful.
335. CHAMBERS, R. W. The lost literature of medieval England. The Library, 4th Ser. 5: 293-321. London, 1925.
   An interesting summary of the sources of our knowledge of Old English literature.

Works including the Old English period
336. EBERT, A. Allgemeine geschichte der literatur des mittelalters im abendlande. 3 vols. Leipzig, 1874-87. Vol. I, 2d ed., 1889. Vols. I and especially III are important.
337. MORLEY, H. English writers. Vol. I, 3d ed. London, 1891. Vol. II. 1888.
338. TEN BRINK, B. Geschichte der englischen litteratur. Vol. I. 2d ed., revised by A. Brandl. Berlin, 1899.
   English translation (by H. M. Kennedy) of the first edition, London and New York, 1883. The work is substantial and scholarly, but now somewhat antiquated.
339. KER, W. P. The dark ages. London, 1904.

340. WÜLKER, R. Geschichte der englischen litteratur. 2d ed. Leipzig and Vienna, 1906-7.
"Descriptive presentation. Encyclopedic rather than organic. Some disproportional treatment."
C. H. E. L. (4). Only chapters 1-8.
341. KER, W. P. English literature: medieval. (Home Univ. Library XLIII.) New York, 1912. Brief treatment. Instructive comparisons between Old English and Scandinavian heroic poetry.
342. BALDWIN, C. S. An introduction to English medieval literature. New York, 1922.
Chapter I discusses Beowulf, Old English Christian poetry, and (briefly) Old English prose.
343. BENHAM, A. R. English literature from Widsith to the death of Chaucer. New Haven, 1916.
344. TRENEER, A. The sea in English literature. From Beowulf to Donne. London and Liverpool, 1926.
The first chapter (pp. 1-44)—"The Sea in Old English Literature"—contains discriminating criticism, though occasionally with too subjective interpretation, of Old English poetry, especially of *Beowulf, The Wanderer, The Seafarer,* some *Riddles, Genesis A, Elene, Andreas,* and *Guthlac.*
345. HECHT, H., AND L. L. SCHÜCKING. Die englische literatur im mittelalter. Wildpark-Potsdam, 1930.
Part I is by L. L. Schücking: *Die angelsächsische und frühmittelenglische Dichtung.* A rather brief sketch.
346. SCHRÖER, M. M. A. Grundzüge und haupttypen der englischen literatur-geschichte. Part I. (Sammlung Göschen, No. 286.) 3d ed., Leipzig, 1927.
NOTE: See also Part X, D. History and Criticism.

B. MYTHOLOGY AND LEGEND

Bibliography
WÜLKER (3), pp. 109-10.
347. SYMONS, B. Heldensage. In Paul's Grundriss (9), 2d ed., Vol. III, pp. 606-734, *passim.*
348. MOGK, E. Germanische mythologie. In Paul's Grundriss (9), 2d ed., Vol. III, pp. 230-406, *passim.*
See also Mogk's *Germanische Religionsgeschichte und Mythologie.* 3d ed. (Sammlung Göschen.) 1927.
BRANDL (5), pp. 954, 969.
349. CLARKE, M. G. Sidelights on Teutonic history during the migration period. Cambridge [Eng.], 1911. Bibliography pp. 275-83. Serviceable, but must be used with care.
CHAMBERS (661). Widsith.
350. GEROULD, G. H. Saints' legends. Boston and New York, 1916. Bibliography, pp. 351-8.
CHAMBERS (461), pp. 379-411, *passim.*
KLAEBER (462), pp. cxxx-cxxxviii; SCHNEIDER (370).

Treatises

351. GRIMM, J. Deutsche mythologie. 3 vols. 4th ed. Berlin, 1875-8. Transl. as *Teutonic Mythology*, by J. S. Stallybrass, 4 vols., London, 1880-8.

   A very valuable work, especially for the numerous references it contains. Obsolete in some details.

352. GRIMM, W. Die deutsche heldensage. 3d ed. Gütersloh, 1889.

   Mainly historical legends.

353. GOLTHER, W. Handbuch der germanischen mythologie. Leipzig, 1895.

   Under the influence of Bugge.

   SYMONS (347), pp. 606-734.

354. SAUSSAYE, P. D. CHANTEPIE DE LA. The religion of the Teutons. Boston and London, 1902. Transl. by B. J. Vos.

   A good survey. Extensive annotated bibliographies, pp. 418-63. Somewhat out of date.

   MOGK (348), pp. 230-406. A valuable treatise, with a section on sources.

355. KAUFFMANN, F. Northern mythology. Translated from the German by M. S. Smith. London, 1903.

   A good brief introduction to Germanic mythology.

   HEUSLER (427). Lied und epos.

356. CRAIGIE, W. A. The religion of ancient Scandinavia. London, 1906.

   A brief but good survey.

357. OLRIK, A. Nordisches geistesleben in heidnischer und frühchristlicher zeit. Transl. from the Danish by W. Ranisch. Heidelberg, 1908.

   CHADWICK (155). Origin of the English nation.

358. PANZER, F. Studien zur germanischen sagengeschichte. I Beowulf. Munich, 1910.

   Some of his conclusions regarding literary relationships must be taken with reserve.

   HOOPS (12). See the index to each volume *s. v. Heldensage*.

359. MEYER, R. M. Altgermanische religionsgeschichte. Leipzig, 1910.

   CHAMBERS (661). Widsith. See also CLARKE (349) and CHADWICK (429).

360. BRUINIER, J. W. Die germanische heldensage. Leipzig and Berlin, 1915.

   GEROULD (350). See especially chapter III, "The Epic Legend in Old English", and chapter IV, "Prose Legends Before the Conquest".

361. JIRICZEK, O. L. Die deutsche heldensage. 4th ed. Berlin and Leipzig, 1913. An earlier edition was transl. as *Northern Hero Legends*, by M. G. B. Smith, London and New York, 1902. The more recent German editions are to be preferred.

   A good brief introduction.

   HOOPS (12). See Vol. IV, p. 602, index *s. v. Mythus und Aberglaube*.

362. OLRIK, A. The Heroic legends of Denmark. Transl. and revised, in collaboration with the author, by L. M. Hollander. New York, 1919.

   Valuable, particularly for the legendary background of Beowulf. The original, *Danmarks Heltedigtning*, Copenhagen, 1903, 1910, comprises two vols., of which Vol. I is translated by Hollander.

363. WOLTERS, F., AND C. PETERSON. Die heldensagen der germanischen frühzeit. Breslau, 1921. Prose narratives.

   CHAMBERS (461). Introduction to Beowulf.

364. HERRMANN, P. Die heldensagen des Saxo Grammaticus. Part II. Leipzig, 1922.

   Part I, a translation of Saxo, was published in 1901. Part II is the commentary.

   HEUSLER (430); KLAEBER (462), pp. xii-xlviii.

365. VON DER LEYEN, F. Die götter und göttersagen der Germanen. 3d ed. Munich, 1924.

366. SCHNEIDER, H. Heldendichtung, geistliche dichtung, ritterdichtung. Heidelberg, 1925.

366a. MUNCH, P. A. Norse mythology: Legends of gods and heroes. Translated by S. B. Hustvedt from the revision by M. Olsen. New York, 1926.

   Valuable. Bibliography, pp. 279-80.

367. MOGK, E. Deutsche heldensage. 2d ed. Leipzig, 1926.

368. WOLFF, L. Die helden der völkerwanderungszeit. Jena, 1928.

369. PHILLPOTS, BERTHA. Wyrd and Providence in Anglo-Saxon thought. Essays and Studies (88), Vol. 13: 7-27. 1928.

370. SCHNEIDER, H. Germanische heldensage. 1. band: Einleitung: Ursprung und wesen der heldensage; 1. buch: Deutsche heldensage. Berlin and Leipzig, 1928.

   Also part of Paul's *Grundriss* (9), and published in concise résumé in Sammlung Göschen, Berlin, 1930, under the title *Deutsche Heldensage*.

   PHILIPPSON (185). A valuable collection of materials on the pre-Christian religion of the Anglo-Saxons. Professes to be the first attempt since KEMBLE (186) to portray comprehensively the beliefs of the Angles and Saxons.

PART X
VERSE

A. Manuscript Collections
  1. Junius XI
  2. Exeter Book
  3. Vercelli Book
  4. Cotton Vitellius A XV (Beowulf MS.)
B. Modern Collections
C. Translations
D. History and Criticism
E. Versification
F. Authors and Monuments

NOTE: A full concordance of O.E. poetry is being (1931) compiled by Messrs. Howard and Ehrensperger.

A. MANUSCRIPT COLLECTIONS

NOTE: A brief statement of the contents and a bibliography of the four chief poetical manuscripts (including chief editions and facsimile collections) may be found in BRANDL (5), pp. 946-7.

A brief history and description of the four chief manuscripts may be found in SPAETH (392), pp. 188-9.

NOTE: A series of volumes to include all extant records of Old English poetry—The Vercelli Book, The Exeter Book, the Beowulf Manuscript, The Meters of Boethius, The Psalms, and the minor records—is in course of publication by the Columbia University Press. No. 374a is the first volume.

1. *Junius XI*

KÖRTING (6), p. 25. Bibliography and list of contents.

371. KENNEDY, C. W. The Caedmon poems, translated into English prose. London, 1916.

  Reliable translations, useful introductions, facsimiles of the illustrations in the Junius MS., and discussion of facsimiles. Chronological bibliography, (selected, but full). Footnotes to introduction are valuable.

372. THORPE, B. Caedmon's metrical paraphrase of parts of the Holy Scriptures, in Anglo-Saxon; with an English translation, notes and a verbal index. London, 1832.

373. GOLLANCZ, I. The Caedmon manuscript of Anglo-Saxon Biblical poetry. Junius XI in the Bodleian Library. Published for the British Academy by ... Oxford University Press. Oxford, 1927.

  Useful introduction. Excellent facsimile of the whole manuscript.

374. CLUBB, M. D. The second book of the "Caedmonian" manuscript. M. L. N. (43), Vol. 43: 304-6. 1928.
    Chiefly a discussion of Gollancz's views as set forth in (373).
374a. KRAPP, G. P. The Junius manuscript. Genesis; Exodus; Daniel; Christ and Satan. The first volume of the Anglo-Saxon Poetic Records. A Collective Edition. New York, 1930.

2. Exeter Book

WÜLKER (3), pp. 218-24. Description of the manuscript, brief discussion, and list of contents.
KÖRTING (6), pp. 24-5. A briefer handling of the same material.
375. THORPE, B. Codex Exoniensis. A collection of Anglo-Saxon poetry, from a manuscript in the library of the Dean and Chapter of Exeter. With an English translation, notes, and indexes. London, 1842. The only complete text.
376. GOLLANCZ, I. The Exeter Book. E. E. T. S. (87), Vol. CIV. 1895.
    Part I: Text and translation of *Christ, Guthlac, Azarias, Phoenix, Juliana, Wanderer, Endowments of Men,* and *Father's Instruction.* Parts II and III not published.
376a. The Exeter Book of Anglo-Saxon poetry. London, 1931. A facsimile edition with two introductory chapters by R. W. Chambers and M. Förster.

3. Vercelli Book

WÜLKER (3), pp. [237]-242. Description, brief discussion, and list of contents. The same material, including also a list of editions, may be found in KÖRTING (6), pp. 23-4.
377. KEMBLE, J. M. The poetry of the Codex Vercellensis with an English translation. Published for the Aelfric Society. London, 1843-56. Edited, with a translation.
378. WÜLKER, R. Codex Vercellensis. Die angelsächsische handschrift zu Vercelli in getreuer nachbildung. Leipzig, 1894.
    Photographic reproductions of only the poetic sections of the MS. Excellently done.
379. FÖRSTER, M. Il codice vercellese con omelie e poesie in lingua anglosassone. Rome, 1913. A splendid facsimile volume.
380. FÖRSTER, M. Der Vercelli-Codex CXVII nebst abdruck einiger altenglischer homilien der handschrift. In Festschrift für Lorenz Morsbach (125), pp. 21-179. 1913. St. E. Ph. (106), Vol. L.

4. Cotton Vitellius A XV (Beowulf MS.)

ZUPITZA (499). Excellent facsimile.
381. SISAM, K. The Beowulf Manuscript. M. L. R. (27), Vol. 11: 335-7. 1916.
    Very useful.
382. FÖRSTER, M. Die Beowulf-handschrift. Berichte über die verhandlungen der Sächsischen Akademie der Wissenschaften. Vol.

71, No. 4. Leipzig, 1919. A very important study of the manuscript.

CHAMBERS (461), pp. 385-7.

383. RYPINS, S. I. A contribution to the study of the Beowulf codex. P. M. L. A. (69), Vol. 36: 167-85. 1921. See also his article, "The Beowulf Codex", in M. Ph. (56), Vol. 17: 173-9. 1920.

KLAEBER (462). Description, history, and bibliography (in footnotes), pp. xcvii-civ; general bibliography, pp. cxxiii, clv, and p. 413.

RYPINS (715). Includes two pages of facsimile.

384. HOOPS, J. Die foliierung der Beowulf-handschrift. E. St. (38), Vol. 63: 1-11. 1928.

A plea for consistency in references to the foliation of the MS. The author prefers the 18th century foliation, which has been used by most editors.

B. MODERN COLLECTIONS

385. GREIN, C. W. M. Bibliothek der angelsächsischen poesie. Neu bearbeitet, vermehrt und nach neuen lesungen der handschriften herausgegeben von R. P. Wül(c)ker. 3 vols. Cassel and Leipzig, 1883-98.

The only practically complete collection. Supplemented by HOLTHAUSEN (386). The new collective edition being published by the Columbia Univ. Press promises to be the standard modern edition of Old English poetry. See KRAPP (374a) and Note to A: Manuscript Collections.

386. HOLTHAUSEN, F. Kleinere altenglische dichtungen. Anglia (36), Vol. 41: 400-4. 1917.

Verses and small poems which are not contained in GREIN (385). Critical text and brief explanations.

387. ROBINSON, W. C. An introduction to our early English literature, from the earliest times to the Norman conquest. London, 1885.

Text and translation, including poems of the *Chronicle* and *Maldon*.

388. SWEET, H. The oldest English texts. E. E. T. S. (87), Vol. LXXXIII. 1885.

Includes "all the extant Old-English texts up to about 900 that are preserved in contemporary MSS., with the exception of the Chronicle and the works of Alfred".

DICKINS (281); SCHÜCKING (319); SEDGEFIELD (322).

389. KERSHAW, N. Anglo-Saxon and Norse poems. Cambridge [Eng.], 1922.

Includes text and translation of *Wanderer, Seafarer, Wife's Lament, Husband's Message, Ruin*, and *Battle of Brunanburh*.

SEDGEFIELD (330). An Anglo-Saxon book of verse and prose.

NOTE: See also section A, preceding.

C. Translations

Bibliography

390. THRELKELD, F. A. A bibliography of translations from Old English literature into Modern English and Modern German.
    Unpublished Stanford University A. M. thesis. 1921.

Collections

391. COOK, A. S., AND C. B. TINKER. Select translations from Old English poetry. Revised ed. Boston, 1926.
    Selected translations, with a few by the authors. Various metres.
392. SPAETH, J. D. Old English poetry. Princeton, 1922.
    Translations into alliterative verse of selections from epic, lyric, and gnomic poetry. Good notes.
393. GUMMERE, F. B. The oldest English epic: Beowulf, Finnsburg, Waldere, Deor, Widsith, and the German Hildebrand. New York, 1909.
    "Translated in the original metres." A very successful translation.
394. HALL, J. L. Judith, Phoenix and other Anglo-Saxon poems translated. New York, Boston, Chicago, [1902].
395. GARNETT, J. M. Elene; Judith; Athelstan, or, The fight at Brunanburh; Byrhtnoth, or, The fight at Maldon; and The Dream of the Rood: Anglo-Saxon poems translated. Boston, 1901.
396. GORDON, R. K. Anglo-Saxon poetry. Translations of English poetry composed between 650 and 1000 A. D. Everyman's Library 794. London, 1927.
    Contains prose translations of the most important poetic monuments.
397. FAUST, C., AND S. THOMPSON. Old English poems. Chicago and New York, 1918. A useful volume, with brief comments on each poem.
398. The Cambridge book of prose and verse. Ed. by G. Sampson. Cambridge, 1924. "A selection of passages to illustrate the first volume of *The Cambridge History of English Literature*."—Preface.

NOTE: Translations accompanying the Old English texts may be found in DICKINS (281), THORPE (372, 375), GOLLANCZ (376), KEMBLE (377), and KERSHAW (389). For translations of individual works, see below under the respective monuments.

D. History and Criticism

Bibliography

C. H. E. L. (4), pp. 469-71; KLAEBER (462), pp. cxxxviii-cxl; cxl-cxlvii; and pp. 415-22.

Works limited to Old English

399. MERBOT, R. Aesthetische studien zur angelsächsischen poesie. Breslau, 1883.
    MÖLLER (478). Das altenglische volksepos.

400. BODE, W. Die kenningar in der angelsächsischen dichtung. Darmstadt and Leipzig, 1886.
401. TOLMAN, A. H. The style of Anglo-Saxon poetry. P. M. L. A. (69), Vol. 3: 17-47. 1887.
402. ABEGG, D. Zur entwicklung der historischen dichtung bei den angelsachsen. Q. F. (103), Vol. LXXIII. Strassburg, 1894.
403. MEAD, W. E. Color in Old English poetry. P. M. L. A. (69), Vol. 14: 169-206. 1899.
404. HANSCOM, E. D. The feeling for nature in Old English poetry. J. E. G. Ph. (53), Vol. 5: 439-63. 1905.
405. SKEMP, A. R. The transformation of Scriptural story, motive, and conception in Anglo-Saxon poetry. M. Ph. (56), Vol. 4: 423-70. 1907.
    Discusses principally *Genesis, Exodus, Judith, Daniel, Christ, Dream of the Rood, Christ and Satan,* and the Exeter Book *Descent into Hell.*
405a. RICHTER, C. Chronologische studien zur angelsächsischen literatur auf grund sprachlich-metrischer kriterien. Halle, 1909. St. E. Ph. (106), Vol. XXIII.
406. BARNOUW, A. J. Anglo-Saxon Christian poetry, an address delivered ... at Leiden, October 12, 1907. Transl. by L. Dudley. The Hague, 1914.
407. IMELMANN, R. Die altenglische Odoaker-dichtung. Berlin, 1907.
    Proposes the theory that the "First *Riddle*", *Wife's Lament*, and *Husband's Message* form a trilogy connected with the Odoacer legend.
408. EHRISMANN, G. Religionsgeschichtliche beiträge zum germanischen frühchristentum. I. Der jenseitsgedanke in der ags. dichtung. ... III. Das himmlische heimweh. IV. Die elegischen motive in der ags. dichtung. V. Die ursprung der elegischen stimmung bei den angelsachsen. Beitr. (48), Vol. 35: 209-12, 218-39. 1909.
409. RANKIN, J. W. A study of the kennings in Anglo-Saxon poetry. J. E. G. Ph. (53), Vol. 8: 357-422; 9: 49-84. 1909-10.
    Discusses the sources of the kennings.
410. SMITHSON, G. A. The Old English Christian epic; a study of the plot technique of the Juliana, the Elene, the Andreas, and the Christ, in comparison with the Beowulf and with the Latin literature of the Middle Ages. Berkeley, 1910. Univ. of Cal. Pubs. in Mod. Phil. (110), Vol. I, No. 4.
411. SARRAZIN, G. Von Kädmon bis Kynewulf. Berlin, 1913.
    Attempts a chronological arrangement of *Genesis, Exodus, Daniel, Widsith, Beowulf, Riddles, Dream of the Rood, Guthlac A,* and *Christ.* Argues for attribution of *Genesis* to Caedmon. Considers *Christ* three poems. Believes *Beowulf* in its present form was written by Cynewulf.
411a. BARTELS, A. Rechtsaltertümer in der angelsächsischen dichtung. Kiel, 1913.

412. SIEPER, E. Die altenglische elegie. Strassburg, 1915.
   Gives many texts, with notes and a translation into German, and discusses the origin and development of the Old English elegy, its internal and external technique, Celtic influences, evidences from Old Norse, and the psychology of the ancient Germanic peoples.
413. IMELMANN, R. Forschungen zur altenglischen poesie. Berlin, 1920.
   Defends and expands the theory (proposed in part in 407) that the *Wife's Lament, Seafarer*, "First *Riddle*", *Wanderer*, and *Husband's Message* form parts of a handling of the Odoacer legend. Also discusses part of the *Franks Casket, Rhyming Poem, Finnsburh*, and sections of *Beowulf*.
   CHAMBERS (461). Beowulf. An introduction.
414. RICCI, H. L'elegia pagana anglosassone. Florence, 1923.
415. THOMAS, W. L'épopée anglo-saxonne. Paris, 1924.
416. PONS, E. Le thème et le sentiment de la nature dans la poésie anglo-saxonne. Strasbourg, 1925; New York, 1925.
   An interesting and suggestive contribution.
417. WYLD, H. C. Diction and imagery in Anglo-Saxon poetry. In Essays and Studies (88), Vol. 11: 49-91. 1925.
417a. RICCI, A. The Anglo-Saxon eleventh-century crisis. R.E.S. (70), Vol. 5: 1-11.
   The chronology of Anglo-Saxon poetry, *ibid.*, pp. 257-66. 1929.

Works Including Old English

418. WARTON, T. History of English poetry. Ed. by W. C. Hazlitt. London, 1871.
   Vol. II contains Sweet's sketch of the history of Anglo-Saxon poetry.
419. HEINZEL, R. Über den stil der altgermanischen poesie. Q. F. (103), Vol. X. Strassburg, 1875. A suggestive study.
420. MEYER, R. M. Die altgermanische poesie nach ihren formelhaften elementen beschrieben. Berlin, 1889. A valuable work.
421. BURTON, R. Literary likings. Boston, 1898.
   See pp. 175-245: "Old English Poetry". A discussion chiefly of nature in Old English poetry (pp. 183-221) and woman in Old English poetry, (pp. 222-45).
422. COURTHOPE, W. J. History of English poetry. 6 vols. London, 1895-1910. Vol. I covers the Old English period.
423. MOORMAN, F. W. The interpretation of nature in English poetry from Beowulf to Shakespeare. Q. F. (103), Vol. XCV. Strassburg, 1905. Pages 1-44 deal with Old English poetry.
424. HART, W. M. Ballad and epic. Harvard Studies and Notes (89), Vol. VI. Boston, 1907.
   Pays much attention to structure, motifs, and other aspects of early narrative verse.

425. KER, W. P. Epic and romance. London and New York, 1897. 2d ed., Oxford, 1908. Reprinted 1922.

    A stimulating, scholarly treatment of the heroic age and the conditions under which the popular epic arose.

426. HEUSLER, A. Der dialog in der altgermanischen erzählenden dichtung. Z. f. d. A. (79), Vol. 46: 189-284. 1902.

427. HEUSLER, A. Lied und epos in germanischer sagendichtung. Dortmund, 1905.

428. DIXON, W. M. English epic and heroic poetry. London and New York, 1912.

    Has chapters on *Beowulf,* other Old English heroic poetry, and the Old English Christian epic.

429. CHADWICK, H. M. The heroic age. Cambridge [Eng.], 1912.

    A very valuable comparison of the Germanic with the Greek and other heroic poetry. Describes the society which produced the popular epic.

430. HEUSLER, A. Die altgermanische dichtung. Wildpark—Potsdam, 1924.

    Comprehensive and thorough. Subsequently copyrighted in 1926. See also his article, "Dichtung", in HOOPS (12), Vol. I, pp. 439-62.

    EMERSON (570). Considers chiefly the *Phoenix* in relation to the Latin *Carmen de Phoenice.*

431. KISSACK, R. A. The sea in Anglo-Saxon and Middle English poetry. Washington Univ. Studies (118), Humanistic Series, Vol. XIII, pp. 371-81. 1926.

432. SCHOLZ, H. VAN DER MERWE. The kenning in Anglo-Saxon and Old Norse poetry. Utrecht and Nijmegen, 1927.

433. ROUTH, H. V. God, man, and epic poetry. 2 vols. Cambridge [Eng.], Univ. Press, 1927.

    Deals extensively with Old English literature, especially with *Beowulf.*

    NOTE: For general works which include discussions of Old English verse, see also Part IX, A. History and Criticism;B. Mythology and Legend.

E. VERSIFICATION

Bibliography

    C. H. E. L (4), pp. 532-3; BRANDL (5), pp. 1022-4.

    HOOPS (12), Vol. I, pp. 231-40, *passim;* KLAEBER (462), pp. cxlvii-cxlix and p. 422.

Works limited to Old English

434. KALUZA, M. Der altenglische vers: eine metrische untersuchung. Berlin, 1894. The first part discusses the various theories.

435. SETZLER, E. On Anglo-Saxon versification from the standpoint of modern-English versification. Baltimore, 1904. A simplified version of SIEVERS (437).

436. LUICK, K., AND J. SCHIPPER. See Paul's Grundriss (9), Vol. IIb, pp. 141-240. 1905. See especially pp. 141-60.

NOTE: Brief treatments of Old English versification may be found in BRIGHT (318), SWEET (323), SPAETH (392), KRAPP AND KENNEDY (331), and FLOM (263). Under the heading of *Works limited to Old English* belong also RANKIN (441), ROUTH (442), GREG (443), SCRIPTURE (445), and BAUM (446a).

Works including Old English

437. SIEVERS, E. Zur rhythmik des germanischen alliterationsverses. Beitr. (48), Vol. X, 209-314; 451-545. 1885. Anastatic reprint, New York, 1909. The great work on Germanic metrics.

438. SIEVERS, E. Altgermanische metrik. Halle, 1893.
Standard. A clear, useful abridgment in Paul's Grundriss (9), Vol. IIb, pp. 1-38. For Old English, see especially pp. 29-34.

439. SCHIPPER, J. Grundriss der englischen metrik. Vienna and Leipzig, 1895.
Translated as *History of English Versification*, Oxford, 1910.
Good description of metrical technique and copious enumeration of monuments.

440. KALUZA, M. A short history of English versification from the earliest times to the present day. Transl. by A. C. Dunstan. London, 1911.
About a third of the book is devoted to Old English.

HOOPS (12) Vol. IV, pp. 231-40. The article *Stabreim* is by A. Heusler.

441. RANKIN, J. W. Rhythm and rime before the Norman Conquest. P. M. L. A. (69), Vol. 36: 401-28. 1921.

442. ROUTH, J. Anglo-Saxon meter. M. Ph. (56), Vol. 21: 429-34. 1924.
Attempts to supply an explanation of Sievers' types.

443. GREG, W. W. The 'five types' in Anglo-Saxon verse. M. L. R. (27), Vol. 20: 12-17. 1925. Points out and attempts to correct "arbitrary and artificial" features of the Sievers types.

444. HEUSLER, A. Deutsche versgeschichte mit einschlusz des altenglischen und altnordischen stabreimverses. Vol. I, Part 1 and 2. Berlin and Leipzig. 1925. Part of Paul's *Grundriss* (9). Reviews the previous theories, pp. 116 ff.

445. SCRIPTURE, E. W. Die grundgesetze des altenglischen stabreimverses. Anglia (36), Vol. 52: 69-75. 1928.
Argues against the division of Old English poetry into half lines. Believes that the alliterating groups have a rhythm independent of line division.

446. LEONARD, W. E. Four footnotes to papers on Germanic metrics. In Studies in English Philology (139), pp. 1-13. 1929.

446a. BAUM, P. F. The character of Anglo-Saxon verse. M. Ph. (56), Vol. 28: 143-56. 1930. Concludes that "the only metrical pattern in Anglo-Saxon verse is the two stresses to the line [half-line], with light syllables variously placed."

F. AUTHORS AND MONUMENTS

NOTE: For linguistic studies of the following monuments, see KENNEDY (8), under the names of the poems.

Aldhelm, Praise of

Text
  HOLTHAUSEN (386), p. 403.
447. NAPIER, A. S. Old English glosses chiefly unpublished. Oxford, 1900. See pp. xiv-xv.

Discussion: BRANDL (5), p. 1079.

Alfred, Poems by (in his translation of the Pastoral Care)

NOTE: Other poems by King Alfred are treated under Boethius, Metra of, p. 62.

Bibliography
448. HOLTHAUSEN, F. Die gedichte in Alfreds übersetzung des Cura Pastoralis. Archiv (25), Vol. 106: 346-7. 1901.

Text
  SWEET (738). First poem, p. 8f.; second poem, p. 467 f. The poems are printed as prose. With translation.
  HOLTHAUSEN (448), pp. 346-7. Only the "closing poem" is printed.
449. EARLE, J. Alfred as a writer. In Alfred the Great (718), ed. by A. Bowker. London, 1899. Only the "prefatory poem" is given, pp. 194-5. With translation.
  ZUPITZA-SCHIPPER (325). Gives both poems, pp. 35-7, in the 11th ed.

Discussion: HOLTHAUSEN (448).

Alfred's Capture and Death

Bibliography: WÜLKER (3), p. 344; KÖRTING (6), p. 41; SEDGEFIELD (612), pp. 48-50.

Text
  GREIN-WÜLKER (385), Vol. I, p. 384.
  EARLE-PLUMMER (792), Vol. I, pp. 158-60. Reprinted in ZUPITZA-SCHIPPER (325), 11th ed.
  SEDGEFIELD (612), pp. 24-6.
  CLASSEN-HARMER (794), pp. 70-71.

Discussion
  ABEGG (402), pp. 63-73, 114-26.
  EARLE-PLUMMER (792), Vol. II, pp. 211-5.

Translation: THORPE (793), Vol. II, pp. 129-30; ROBINSON (387).

Alms

Bibliography: WÜLKER (3), pp. 235-6.
Text: THORPE (375), p. 467, with translation; GREIN-WÜLKER (385), Vol. IIIa, p. 181.
Discussion: WÜLKER (3), p. 236.

Azarias

Bibliography: WÜLKER (3), p. 143; SCHMIDT (450), p. 40.

Text
  THORPE (375), pp. 185-97. With translation.
  GREIN-WÜLKER (385), Vol. II, pp. 491-7, 516-20.
  GOLLANCZ (376), pp. 188-200. With translation.
450. SCHMIDT, W. Die altenglischen dichtungen Daniel und Azarias. Bo. Beitr. (83), Vol. XXIII: 41-6. 1907. Emended text, with notes and glossary.

Discussion
451. HOFER, O. Über die entstehung des angelsächsischen gedichtes Daniel. Anglia (36), Vol. 12: 158-204. 1889. See especially pp. 184-91.
  SCHMIDT (450), pp. 49-59.
  BRANDL (5), pp. 1034-5; SCHÜCKING (345), p. 17.

Bede's Death Song

Bibliography
  WÜLKER (3), p. 145.
452. BROTANEK, R. Texte und untersuchungen zur altenglischen literatur- und kirchengeschichte. Halle, 1913. See pp. 151-7.

Text
  SWEET (388), p. 149; SWEET (323), p. 175.
  BROTANEK (452), pp. 162-87, *passim*. Gives fourteen manuscript versions, and a facsimile from MS. St. Gall 254.
  SEDGEFIELD (322), p. 81.
Discussion: BROTANEK (452), pp. 150-1, 161-93; WILLIAMS (596), pp. 67-9.
Translation: BROOKE (334), p. 340; COOK AND TINKER (391), p. 78.

Be Dōmes Dæge (Doomsday)

Bibliography
  WÜLKER (3), pp. 371-2. Calls the poem *Gedicht vom jüngsten Gericht*.
  LÖHE (454), p. 4; BRANDL (5), p. 1096; KÖRTING (6), p. 60.

Text
453. LUMBY, J. R. Be dōmes dæge. E. E. T. S. (87), Vol. LXV. 1876. Gives text, English translation, and Latin *De Die Judicii*. No apparatus except glossary and notes.
  GREIN-WÜLKER (385), Vol. II, pp. 250-72. Calls the poem *Vom jüngsten Tage*.
454. LÖHE, H. Be dōmes dæge. Bo. Beitr. (83), Vol. XXII: 6-37. 1907. Text, German translation, Latin original, notes, and glossary.

Discussion
455. NÖLLE, G. Die legende von den fünfzehn zeichen vor dem jüngsten gerichte. Beitr. (48), Vol. 6: 413-76. 1879.
456. BRANDL, A. Be dōmes dæge. Anglia (36), Vol. 4: 97-104. 1881.

457. DEERING, R. W. The Anglo-Saxon poets on the judgment day. Halle, 1890.
LÖHE (454). See especially pp. 38-62.
458. GRAU, G. Quellen und verwandtschaften der älteren germanischen darstellungen des jüngsten gerichtes. Halle, 1908. St. E. Ph. (106), Vol. XXXI.
    See pp. 176-80. Pp. 15-198 discuss Old English literature. See also H. Hecht's review of Grau's book in Archiv (25), Vol. 130: 424-30. 1913.

Benedictine Office*

Bibliography: WÜLKER (3), pp. 380, 499.

Text
459. THOMSON, E. Godcunde lar and Þeodom. 2d ed. London, 1875. With translation.
460. FEILER, E. Das Bendicktiner-Offizium, ein altenglisches brevier aus dem 11. jahrhundert. Heidelberg, 1901. Part I appeared as a dissertation in 1900.

Discussion: FEILER (460), pp. 1-48; FEHR (694).

Beowulf

Bibliography
    WÜLKER (3), pp. 244-307. Contains also a useful survey of *Beowulf* criticism to 1885.
    BRANDL (5), pp. 1015-24.
461. CHAMBERS, R. W. Beowulf. An introduction to the study of the poem, with a discussion of the stories of Offa and Finn. Cambridge [Eng.], 1921; 2d ed., 1931.
    A thorough, scholarly work of great importance. Contents: the historical elements; the non-historical elements; theories as to origin, date, and structure of the poem; parallels and illustrations (originals and translations given); the fight at Finnsburh; appendices; a full, slightly annotated bibliography.
462. KLAEBER, F. Beowulf. Boston, 1922. 2d ed., 1928.
    Supersedes all previous editions of the poem. The bibliography, pp. cxxiii-clxii and 413-24, is selective but very full to 1928.
463. LAWRENCE, W. W. Beowulf and epic tradition. Cambridge [Mass.], 1928.
    "This volume . . . makes its appeal to those who wish to gain a sound knowledge of *Beowulf* so far as it may be done without an understanding of Anglo-Saxon, and to those who are just beginning a reading of the poem in that language."—Pref.
    Contents: I Intro.; II Peoples and Social Organization; III The Tragedies of the Royal Houses; IV The Tale of Finnsburg; V Scyld and Breca; VI Grendel and his Dam; VII The Dragon; VIII Development and Composition of the Epic. Bibliography, Notes, Appendices.

---

*See also Part XI: *Benedictine Rule*, p. 109.

Text
464. WÜLKER, R. P. Das Beowulfslied, nebst den kleineren epischen, lyrischen, didaktischen und geschichtlichen stücken. Vol. I, pp. 149-277, of GREIN-WÜLKER (385). Cassel, 1883.
    Diplomatic edition, pp. 18-148. Much critical apparatus in footnotes. Anastatic reprint, Hamburg, 1922.
465. SEDGEFIELD, W. J. Beowulf, edited with introduction, bibliography, notes, glossary, and appendices. 2d ed. Manchester, 1913.
    Contains also the *Finnsburh* Fragment, *Deor, Waldhere,* and *Widsith.* Good introduction and excellent glossary.
466. WYATT, A. J. Beowulf, with the Finnsburg fragment. Revised with introduction and notes by R. W. Chambers. Cambridge [Eng.], 1914 (2d impression 1920).
    A very good edition, with excellent notes at foot of page. Valuable index of persons and places. Contains one page of the MS. in facsimile (with transliteration) and two pages of Thorkelin's transcript. Glossary does not contain complete references to occurrences of forms. The reprint contains additional textual notes, pp. 255-57.
467. HEYNE, M. Beowulf. Mit ausführlichem glossar hrsg. Bearbeitet von L. L. Schücking. 13th ed. Paderborn, 1929.
    Good conservative edition.
468. HOLTHAUSEN, F. Beowulf nebst den kleineren denkmälern der heldensage, mit einleitung, glossar und anmerkungen. I teil: texte und namenverzeichnis, 6. verbesserte auflage. II teil: einleitung, glossar, und anmerkungen, 5. verbesserte auflage. Heidelberg, 1929.
    Brief introduction, but good glossary. The notes are rather condensed for ordinary use. Gives 4 plates. Rather inclined to needless emendations.
KLAEBER (462). Includes the text of the *Finnsburh* Fragment, *Waldhere, Deor,* passages from *Widsith,* and OHG.*Lay of Hildebrand.* From its wealth of information concerning the poem, the book has been called a "*Beowulf*-encyclopaedia." Generally considered the best edition.

Discussion—General
KER (425), pp. 182-202.
C. H. E. L. (4), pp. 24-34 (chapter by Chadwick). Advances theories which are open to challenge.
BRANDL (5), pp. 988-1014. An excellent summary.
CHADWICK (429), especially pp. 47-57. Compares Germanic with Greek heroic poetry.
STJERNA (242). Important for archaeological background.
CHAMBERS (461). Of first importance.
KLAEBER (462). The Christian coloring (pp. xlviii-lii); structure (lii-lix); tone, style, meter (pp. lix-lxxii, 421-2). Contains also a bibliography of general discussions (pp. cxxix-cxxx, 415-6).

CHAMBERS (494). Foreword (pp. vi-xxxii) to Strong's translation.
ROUTH (433). See especially Vol. II, chapter 1, pp. 1-24.
LAWRENCE (463). Beowulf and epic tradition.
469. BRADLEY, H. Beowulf, in *Ency. Brit.* (14th ed.), Vol. III, pp. 424-6.
470. SCHÜCKING, L. L. Das königsideal im Beowulf. Bulletin of the Mod. Hum. Res. Ass'n. Vol. VIII, no. 8, pp. 143-54. 1929.

Discussion—Mythical Elements
GRIMM (352). Die deutsche heldensage.
471. MÜLLENHOFF, K. Beowulf: Untersuchungen über das angelsächsische epos und die älteste geschichte der germanischen seevölker. Berlin, 1889. Still important.
SYMONS (347). Heldensage.
472. BOER, R. C. Die Beowulfsage. A. f. N. F. (46), Vol. 19: 19-88. 1902. See also BOER (480).
473. LAWRENCE, W. W. Some disputed questions in Beowulf criticism. P. M. L. A. (69), Vol. 24: 220-73. 1909.
   Criticism of mythological interpretation.
PANZER (358). Important investigation of folk-tale elements. Gives Norse parallels.
OLRIK (362); CHAMBERS (461), pp. 41-97; LAWRENCE (463), *passim.*
473a. DEHMER, H. Die Grendelkämpfe Beowulfs im lichte moderner märchen forschung. G.-R. Mon. (51), Vol. 16: 202-18. 1928.
KLAEBER (462), pp. xii-xxvii. Contains also a bibliography of discussions (pp. cxxxi-cxxxiv, 416-9), and page references for most of the foregoing authors.

Discussion—Historical Elements
GRIMM (352); CHADWICK (155).
CHAMBERS (661). Contains a wealth of information on the tribes and heroes mentioned in the poem.
JIRICZEK (361); CHAMBERS (461), pp. 1-40.
474. MALONE, K. The literary history of Hamlet. I. The early tradition. Angl. Forsch. (81), Vol. LIX. Heidelberg, 1923.
   Ingenious, but not entirely convincing, reconstruction and interpretation of the Scandinavian historical conditions.
KLAEBER (462), pp. xxix-xlviii. Contains also (pp. cxxxiv-cxxxviii, 416-9) bibliography of discussions, and page references for the foregoing.
475. WESSÉN, E. De Nordiska folkstammarna i Beowulf. Stockholm, 1927.
   An important study.
476. MALONE, K. Hrethric. P. M. L. A. (69), Vol. 42: 268-313. 1927.
   Collection and interpretation of traditions concerning the Scylding dynasty.
LAWRENCE (463), *passim.*

Discussion—Composition; Authorship; Date

477. MÜLLENHOFF, K. Die innere geschichte des Beovulfs. Z. f. d. A. (79), Vol. 14: 193-244. 1869.

 The well known article on the "ballad theory."

478. MÖLLER, H. Das altenglische volksepos in der ursprünglichen strophischen form. Kiel, 1883.

 Favors multiple authorship; gives the so-called original parts in four-line stanzas. Important review by Heinzel in Anz. f. d. A. (45), Vol. 10: 215-33. 1884.

WÜLKER (3), pp. 244-307. Useful summary.

479. TEN BRINK, B. Beowulf: Untersuchungen. Q. F. (103), Vol. LXXII. 1888.

 See Heinzel's review in Anz. f. d. A. (45), Vol. 15: 153-82. 1889.

480. BOER, R. C. Die altenglische heldendichtung. I. Beowulf. Halle, 1912.

 Argues that the poem is a composite. Gives Scandinavian parallels. Some of his conclusions are open to question.

HART (424), pp. 150-226.

SARRAZIN (411). Genesis, relations, and date of the poem. Ascribes it to Cynewulf.

481. SCHÜCKING, L. L. Wann enstand der Beowulf? Beitr. (48), Vol. 42: 347-410. 1917.

 Suggests composition about 900. See also his article, "Die Beowulfdatierung", in Beitr. (48), Vol. 47: 293-311. 1923.

482. LIEBERMANN, F. Ort und zeit der Beowulfdichtung. Nachrichten von der königl. Gesellschaft der Wissenschaften zu Göttingen, Philol. hist. Klasse, pp. 255-76. 1920.

 Argues for date about 725. Proposes theory that a southern poet went to Northumberland about 690, and there composed the poem. Cf. COOK (483).

CHAMBERS (461), pp. 98-128, 322-32.

KLAEBER (462), civ-cxxii (genesis of the poem). See also the Supplement—"A note concerning the genesis of Beowulf", pp. 437-40.

483. COOK, A. S. The possible begetter of the Old English Beowulf and Widsith. Trans. Conn. Acad. (109), Vol. 25: 281-346. 1922.

 Carries further the theory of LIEBERMANN (482).

484. COOK, A. S. Cynewulf's part in our Beowulf. Trans. Conn. Acad. (109), Vol. 27: 385-406. 1925.

 Argues that the author of *Beowulf* drew inspiration and material from Gregory directly, without the mediation of Cynewulf.

485. KLAEBER, F. Attila's and Beowulf's funeral. P. M. L. A. (69), Vol. 42: 255-67. 1927.

 Interesting discussion of possible influences on the *Beowulf* poet's handling of the funeral. Cites parallels but does not attempt to settle the question.

ROUTH (433); LAWRENCE (463), pp. 244-91.

Bibliography of translations

486. TINKER, C. B. The translations of Beowulf: a critical bibliography. Y. St. (119), Vol. XVI. 1903.
    CHAMBERS (461), pp. 390-5.
    KLAEBER (462), pp. cxxvi-cxxix, and Supplement, pp. 414-5.
    LAWRENCE (463), pp. 296-7.

Complete Translations

487. HALL, J. L. Beowulf. An Anglo-Saxon epic poem, translated from the Heyne-Socin text. Boston, 1892 (reprinted 1900).
    Alliterative verse.
488. GARNETT, J. M. Beowulf, an Anglo-Saxon poem, and the Fight at Finnsburg. 4th ed. Boston, 1900.
    A literal translation in metre imitative of the original.
488a. CHILD, C. G. Beowulf and the Finnesburh fragment. Boston, 1904. With an introductory sketch and notes.
    GUMMERE (393). Perhaps the most satisfactory verse translation. Conveys the spirit and movement of the original.
489. TINKER, C. B. Beowulf. 2d ed. New York, 1910.
    A good prose version. Episodes are printed in smaller type.
490. HALL, J. R. C. Beowulf and the Finnsburg fragment: a translation into modern English prose. 2d ed. London, 1911.
    Literal. Valuable introduction and appendices. Episodes are printed in smaller type.
491. HALL, J. R. C. Beowulf. A metrical translation into modern English. Cambridge [Eng.], 1914.
    Four-stress lines, without alliteration; as literal as possible. Not so good as HALL (490).
492. MONCRIEFF, C. K. S. Widsith, Beowulf, Finnsburgh, Waldere, Deor, done into common English after the old manner. With an introduction by Viscount Northcliffe. New York, 1921.
    Alliterative verse, as literal as possible.
493. LEONARD, W. E. Beowulf. A new verse translation for fireside and classroom. New York and London, 1923.
    An attractive translation in the "Nibelungen couplet".
494. STRONG, A. Beowulf, translated into modern English rhyming verse, with introduction and notes; with a foreword on 'Beowulf and the heroic age' by R. W. Chambers. London, 1925.
    Uses the metre of Morris's *Sigurd the Volsung*.
495. BAUGH, A. C., in *Century Types of English Literature*, ed. by G. W. McClelland and A. C. Baugh. New York, 1925.
496. MUNN, J. B., in *Ideas and Forms in English and American Literature*. Chicago, 1925.
497. CRAWFORD, D. H. Beowulf, translated into English verse, with an introduction, notes and appendices. London, 1926.
    Not a very great improvement upon its numerous predecessors. Much useful apparatus for an understanding of the poem.

Concordance
498. COOK, A. S.   A concordance to Beowulf.   Halle, 1911.
Facsimile
499. ZUPITZA, J.   Beowulf.   Autotypes of the unique Cotton MS.   Vitellius A XV in the British Museum, transliteration and notes. E. E. T. S. (87), Vol. LXXVII.   London, 1882.
   The facsimile is of the greatest value. The transliteration must be used with care, for it "contains more than can be read in the Facsimile or even in the MS., inasmuch as it has been my endeavor to give the text as far as possible in that condition in which it stood in the MS. a century ago".

Bi Monna Cræftum ("The Gifts of Men")
Bibliography: WÜLKER (3), p. 196; KÖRTING (6), p. 59.
Text
   THORPE (375), pp. 293-300.   With translation.
   GREIN-WÜLKER (385), Vol. IIIa, pp. 140-3.
   GOLLANCZ (376), pp. 292-9.   With translation.
   SEDGEFIELD (322), pp. 106-9.
Discussion
500. RIEGER, M.   Über Cynewulf.   Z. f. d. Ph. (78), Vol. I: 323.   1869.
   WÜLKER (3), pp. 197-9; BRANDL (5), p. 1036.
   BROOKE (334), pp. 435-6; SCHÜCKING (345), pp. 30-1.
Translations: GORDON (396), pp. 348-9.   See also *Text* above.

Bi Manna Lease ("The Falsehood of Men")
Bibliography
   WÜLKER (3), p. 200.
   BRANDL (5), p. 1048.   Mistakenly called "Predigtbruchstück über Psalm 23", instead of "Psalm 28".
   KÖRTING (6), p. 60.
   FÖRSTER (380), in Festschrift . . . Morsbach (125), pp. 79-80.
Text
   KEMBLE (377), Part II, pp. 73-82.   With translation.
   GREIN-WÜLKER (385), Vol. IIa, pp. 108-10.   Calls the poem—"Predigtbruchstück über Psalm 28".
Discussion
   WÜLKER (3), pp. 200-1.
   FÖRSTER, M. (380), in Festschrift . . . Morsbach (125), pp. 79-80.

Bi Manna Mode ("The Mind of Men")
Bibliography: WÜLKER (3), p. 200; KÖRTING (6), p. 60.
Text
   THORPE (375), pp. 313-18.   Calls the poem—"Monitory Poem".   With translation.
   GREIN-WÜLKER (385), Vol. IIIa, pp. 144-7.

Discussion
  WÜLKER (3), p. 200; BRANDL (5), p. 1047.

Bi Manna Wyrdum ("The Fates of Men")

Bibliography
  WÜLKER (3), p. 199; KÖRTING (6), p. 59.
Text
  THORPE (375), pp. 327-33. With translation.
  GREIN-WÜLKER (385), Vol. IIIa, pp. 148-51; SEDGEFIELD (322), pp. 45-8.
Discussion
  RIEGER (500), p. 324; WÜLKER (3), pp. 199-200; BRANDL (5), pp. 1036-7; SCHÜCKING (345), p. 30.

Translation (See also Text)
501. MORLEY, H. The library of English literature. London, Paris, New York [n. d.], pp. 8-11. Morley's translation is found also in English Writers (337), Vol. II, pp. 32-7.
  GORDON (396), pp. 350-1; FAUST AND THOMPSON (397), pp. 58-61.

Boethius, Metra (Metres) of*

Bibliography
  WÜLKER (3), pp. 413, 420-35.
502. KRÄMER, E. Die altenglischen Metra des Boetius herausgegeben und mit einleitung und vollständigem wörterbuch versehen. Bo. Beitr. (83), Vol. VIII: 1-149. 1902.
  BRANDL (5), p. 1066.
503. FEHLAUER, F. Die englischen übersetzungen von Boethius' De consolatione philosophiae. Berlin, 1909. Bibliography in footnotes, pp. 9-31.
Text
  GREIN-WÜLKER (385), Vol. IIIb, pp. 1-57.
  SEDGEFIELD (733), pp. 151-204.
  KRÄMER (502), pp. 44-101.

Discussion
  WÜLKER (3), pp. 420-35.
  SEDGEFIELD (733), pp. xxxviii-xli. See discussion in SEDGEFIELD (737), pp. xxvii-xxxi.
  KRÄMER (502), pp. 1-43.
  FEHLAUER (503), especially pp. 20-31.

Translation
  The whole works of King Alfred the Great (727). Text and metrical translation by M. F. Tupper: Vol. I, pp. 164-249. Prose version by S. Fox: Vol. II, pp. 426-537, *passim*.
  SEDGEFIELD (737), pp. 177-240.

---

*See also Part XI, Alfred: (c) Boethius, p. 105.

Brunanburh, Battle of

Bibliography
WÜLKER, pp. 339-42.
504. CROW, C. L. Maldon and Brunnanburh. Boston, 1897. Bibliography, pp. xxxv-xxxvii.
SEDGEFIELD (612), pp. 45-8; KÖRTING (6), p. 40.

Text
GREIN-WÜLKER (385), Vol. I, pp. 374-9; CROW (504), pp. 13-17.
SEDGEFIELD (612), pp. 1-15; KERSHAW (389), pp. 66-70. With translation.
NOTE: The text is found also in many books of selections, *e. g.*, BRIGHT (318), WYATT (320), SEDGEFIELD (322), and FLOM (263).

Discussion
ABEGG (402), pp. 27-39; CROW (504), pp. vi-xxi, *passim*.
SEDGEFIELD (432), pp. v-xx; KERSHAW (389), pp. 59-65.
505. KLAEBER, F. A note on the Battle of Brunanburh. Palaestra (101), Vol. 150: 1-7. 1925.
   Interesting criticism of the spirit of the poem. Considers it less sincerely Germanic than *Maldon*. "It is not a fair specimen of Anglo-Saxon, or Old Germanic, poetry of the heroic order." Believes the author was influenced by the *Book of Joshua*.

Translation (See also Text)
GARNETT (395), pp. 57-9; HALL (394), pp. 57-9.
COOK AND TINKER (391), pp. 26-30. Tennyson's verse translation. In Appendix iia is a prose translation by Hallam Tennyson.
GORDON (396), pp. 359-60.

Caedmonian Poems
a) Caedmon's Hymn
b) Christ and Satan
c) Daniel
d) Exodus
e) Genesis

Bibliography
WÜLKER (3), pp. 111-17. General survey of discussion of Caedmonian works, pp. 117-34, 139-40.
KÖRTING (6), pp. 42-5.
506. KENNEDY, C. W. The Caedmon poems, translated into English prose. London, 1916. General bibliography, pp. 251-5.
Facsimiles: GOLLANCZ (373), pp. 1-229.
   NOTE: KRAPP (374a) will be found indispensable for all the Caedmonian poems, except the Hymn.

a. Caedmon's Hymn
Bibliography
WÜLKER (3), pp. 117-20; C. H. E. L. (4), pp. 479-80; BRANDL (5), p. 1028.
KÖRTING (6), p. 45; KENNEDY (506), pp. 251-5, *passim*.

Text
    SWEET (388), p. 149; GREIN-WÜLKER (385), Vol. IIb, pp. 316-7.
507. FRAMPTON, M. G. Cadmon's Hymn. M. Ph. (56), Vol. 22: 1-15. 1924.
    A study of all the versions, with the conclusion that the Cambridge Moore MS. contains the oldest and most nearly original version. All MS. readings are given.
508. SIEVERS, E. Caedmon und Genesis. In Britannica (138), pp. 57-84. 1929.
    Gives a restoration of the *Hymn*. The text may be found also in several books of selections, *e. g.*, BRIGHT (318), SEDGEFIELD (322), ZUPITZA-SCHIPPER (325), SWEET (323), KRAPP AND KENNEDY (331), FLOM (263), and GOLLANCZ (373).

Discussion
509. WÜLKER, R. Über den hymnus Caedmons. Beitr. (48), Vol. 3: 348-57. 1876.
    Gives Latin, West-Saxon, and Northumbrian versions. Argues against accepting Northumbrian version as Caedmon's actual work.
510. ZUPITZA, J. Über den hymnus Cädmons. Z. f. d. A. (79), Vol. 22: 210-23. 1878.
    Believes the Northumbrian version was Caedmon's, and that the West-Saxon version was a translation of the Latin of Bede.
TEN BRINK (338), pp. 371 ff.; SARRAZIN (411), pp. 17 ff.
FRAMPTON (507). Cadmon's Hymn.
511. POUND, LOUISE. Caedmon's Dream Song. In Studies in Eng. Philology (139), pp. 232-9. 1929.
SIEVERS, E. (508), in Britannica (138).

Translation
KENNEDY (506), p. 3; COOK AND TINKER (391), p. 77.
FAUST AND THOMPSON (397), pp. 83-4.

Facsimile
Palaeographical Society (310). Facsimiles. Part 9, plate 140. 1879.

b. Christ and Satan

Bibliography
WÜLKER (3), pp. 120-34, *passim;* KÖRTING (6), p. 47.
512. FRINGS, T. Christ und Satan. Z. f. d. Ph. (78), Vol. 45: 216-36. 1913. Gives a summary of preceding work on this poem.
KENNEDY (506), p. 258.
513. CLUBB, M. D. Christ and Satan: an Old English poem. Y. St. (119), Vol. 70. 1925. This bibliography (pp. 139-42) supersedes all others, up to 1925.
KRAPP (374a). Indispensable for bibliography, text, and discussion.

Text
THORPE (372), pp. 265-310. With translation.
GREIN-WÜLKER (385), Vol. IIb, pp. 521-62.
CLUBB (513), pp. 5-40. Aims to be a complete edition. Contains an extensive introduction, critical text, notes, and glossary.

Discussion
  WÜLKER (3), pp. 120-34, *passim;* FRINGS (512), pp. 216-20, 232-6.
  KENNEDY (506), pp. lxiv-lxx; CLUBB (513), pp. ix-lx.
  GOLLANCZ (373), pp. xcviii-cvi.
514. GREENE, R. L. A re-arrangement of Christ and Satan. M. L. N. (26), Vol. 43: 108-10. 1928. Argues for the transposing of parts II and III in the interests of chronology and logical structure.
Translation (See also Text)
  KENNEDY (506), pp. 149-73; GORDON (396), pp. 140-6.
Facsimile: GOLLANCZ (373), pp. 213-29.

c. Daniel

Bibliography
  WÜLKER (3), pp. 120-30, *passim.*
515. BLACKBURN, F. A. Exodus and Daniel: two Old English poems preserved in MS. Junius XI in the Bodleian Library of the University of Oxford, England. Boston, 1907. Bibliography, pp. 128-30.
  SCHMIDT (450), p. 506; KÖRTING (6), p. 47; KENNEDY (506), pp. 257-8.
  KRAPP (374a). Indispensable for bibliography, text, and discussion.
Text
  THORPE (372), pp. 216-63. With translation.
  GREIN-WÜLKER (385), Vol. II, pp. 476-515.
  BLACKBURN (515), pp. 67-106. Up-to-date, careful text.
  SCHMIDT (450), pp. 5-39.
Discussion
  HOFER (451). A study of the genesis and structure of the poem.
  BLACKBURN (515), pp. vii-xxxvi; SCHMIDT (450), pp. 49-59.
  BRANDL (5), p. 1038; KENNEDY (506), pp. lx-lxiv.
  GOLLANCZ (373), pp. lxxxv-xcvii.
Translation (See also Text)
  KENNEDY (506), pp. 121-45; GORDON (396), pp. 133-9.
Facsimile: GOLLANCZ (373), pp. 173-212.

d. Exodus

Bibliography
  WÜLKER (3), pp. 120-30, *passim;* 133-4.
  BLACKBURN (515), pp. 128-30; KÖRTING (6), pp. 46-7.
516. MOORE, S. On the sources of the Old-English Exodus. M. Ph. (56), Vol. 9: 83-108. 1911. Bibliography in footnotes.
  KENNEDY (506), pp. 256-7.
  KRAPP (374a). Indispensable for bibliography, text, and discussion.
Text
  THORPE (372), pp. 177-216. With translation.
  GREIN-WÜLKER (385), Vol. IIb, pp. 445-75.
  BLACKBURN (515), pp. 3-32.

Discussion
517. GROTH, E. Composition und alter der altenglischen Exodus. Berlin, 1883.
518. MÜRKENS, G. Untersuchungen über das altenglische Exoduslied. Bo. Beitr. (83), Vol. II: 62-117. 1899.
   BLACKBURN (515), pp. vii-xxvi; MOORE (516).
   KENNEDY (506), pp. l-lx; GOLLANCZ (373), pp. lxviii-lxxix.
Translation (See also Text)
519. JOHNSON, W. S. Translation of the Old English Exodus. J. E. G. Ph. (53), Vol. 5: 44-57. 1903. Prose.
   KENNEDY (506), pp. 99-118; GORDON (396), pp. 123-32.
Facsimile: GOLLANCZ (373), pp. 143-72.

e. Genesis

Bibliography
   WÜLKER (3), pp. 120-30, *passim;* 131-3.
   KÖRTING (6), pp. 45-6.
520. KLAEBER, F. The later Genesis and other Old English and Old Saxon texts relating to the fall of man. Heidelberg, 1913.
521. HOLTHAUSEN, F. Die ältere Genesis. Heidelberg, 1914. Bibliography, pp. vii-x. Additions in Anglia (36), Vol. 46: 60-2. 1922.
   KENNEDY (506), pp. 255-6.
522. BRADLEY, H. The 'Caedmonian' Genesis. In Essays and Studies (88), Vol. VI: 7-29. 1920.
523. KLAEBER, F. Zur jüngeren Genesis. Anglia (36), Vol. 49: 361-75. 1926. Valuable recent bibliography, pp. 372-4.
   KRAPP (374a). Indispensable for bibliography, text, and discussion.
Text
   THORPE (372), pp. 1-177. With translation.
   GREIN-WÜLKER (385), Vol. IIb, pp. 318-444.
   KLAEBER (520). Additional notes to text and glossary appear in KLAEBER (523) above.
   HOLTHAUSEN (521), pp. 1-88. Contains also introduction, notes, glossary, and Latin sources, and one page of facsimile.
Discussion
524. JOVY, H. Untersuchungen zur altenglischen Genesisdichtung. Bo. Beitr. (83), Vol. 5: 1-32. 1900.
   KLAEBER (520); HOLTHAUSEN (521), pp. vii-x.
   KENNEDY (506), pp. xxiii-l.
525. BERTHOLD, L. Die quellen für die grundgedanken von v. 235-851 der altsächsisch-angelsächsischen Genesis. In Germanica (135), pp. 380-401. 1925.
   GOLLANCZ (373), pp. l-lxii.
526. SIEVERS, E. Caedmon und Genesis. In Britannica (138), pp. 57-84. 1929.

   An important study of the authorship. Through application of metrical tests, Sievers attempts an ascription of certain lines to Caedmon, and deals with other aspects of the poem.

Translation (See also Text)
527. MASON, L. Genesis A (sometimes attributed to Caedmon) translated from the Old English. Y. St. (119), Vol. XLVIII. 1915.
    Prose translation, based on Grein-Wülker's text. Free from willful archaisms.
KENNEDY (506), pp. 7-96; GORDON (396), pp. 105-22.
Facsimile: GOLLANCZ (373), pp. 1-42.

Charms*

Bibliography
WÜLKER (3), pp. 347-55; BRANDL (5), pp. 957-8.
528. GRENDON, F. The Anglo-Saxon Charms. Journal of American Folk-Lore, Vol. 22: 105-237. 1909.
    Contains a selected bibliography (pp. 106-9, 160-2) which is expanded by G. Binz in Anglia Beibl. (37), Vol. 27: 162. 1916.
HOOPS (12). Vol. IV, pp. 381-2, *s.v. Zauber*.
GRENDON (531a). See note on Klaeber's article.

Text
COCKAYNE (674), Vol. I, pp. 384-405; Vol. III, pp. 286-91; 294-5. With translation.
GREIN-WÜLKER (385), Vol. I, pp. 312-30.
GRENDON (528), pp. 164-213. With translation. On pp. 162-4 is a list, with latest edition indicated, of the charms not printed in his article. Very full treatment of the charms.

Discussion
COCKAYNE (674), Vol. I, pp. xxviii-liv.
GRIMM-STALLYBRASS (351), Vol. III, chapter 38.
BROOKE (334), chapter IX. A very readable chapter.
SAUSSAYE (354); PAYNE (238), especially pp. 114-42.
529. BRIE, M. Der germanische, insbesondere der englische zauberspruch. Mitteilungen der Schlesischen Gesellschaft für Volkskunde, XVI. 1906.
BRANDL (5), pp. 955-7.
GRENDON (528), pp. 105-59. Notes, pp. 214-37.
530. HÄLSIG, F. Zauberspruch bei den Germanen . . . Leipzig, 1910.
531. SKEMP, A. R. The Old English Charms. M. L. R. (27), Vol. 6: 289-301. 1911.
HEUSLER (430), pp. 44-64. An excellent discussion of Germanic *Ritualdichtung* and *Zauberdichtung*.
SINGER (245); SINGER (247).
531a. GRENDON, F. Anglo-Saxon Charms. New York, 1930. A reprint of GRENDON (528) with introduction and critical apparatus. Bibliography of Charms brought to date by Klaeber in Anglia Beibl. (37), Vol. 42: 6-7. 1931.

---

*See also Part XI, Lacnunga, p. 120.

Translation (See also Text)
    Translations of various charms may be found also in BROOKE (334), COOK AND TINKER (391), GORDON (396), GRIMM-STALLYBRASS (351), KEMBLE (186), GUMMERE (11).

Chronicle, Poems of the Anglo-Saxon
    See *Alfred's Capture and Death; Brunanburh; Edgar's Coronation; Edgar's Death; Edward the Confessor's Death; Edward the Martyr's Death; Five Cities; William the Conqueror.*
    NOTE: Several portions of the *Chronicle* in quasi-poetic form are discussed in BRANDL (5), pp. 1082-4. For further discussion see SEDGEFIELD (612), pp. xx-xxi, and for bibliography *Ibid.*, p. 50.

Creed
Bibliography: WÜLKER (3), pp. 375-6.
Text
    THOMSON (459), pp. 142-53. With translation.
    GREIN-WÜLKER (385), Vol. IIb, pp. 245-9.
Discussion: THOMSON (459); FEILER (460), pp. 63 ff.

Curse of Urse, The
Text and Discussion: BRANDL (5), p. 1096; TUPPER (610a), 2. The Curse of Urse, pp. 100-3.

Cynewulfian Poems
   a) Andreas
   b) Christ
   c) Dream of the Rood (Vision of the Cross)
   d) Elene
   e) Fates of the Apostles
   f) Guthlac
   g) Juliana
   h) Phoenix
   i) Physiologus
   j) Riddles

Bibliography (with general discussion)
    WÜLKER (3), pp. 147-96, 201-4.
532. TRAUTMANN, M. Kynewulf. Der bischof und dichter. Bo. Beitr. (83), Vol. I: 1-123. 1898.
533. BROWN, C. F. Cynewulf and Alcuin. P. M. L. A. (69), Vol. 18: 308-34. 1903.
534. SARRAZIN, G. Zur chronologie und verfasserfrage angelsächsischer dichtungen. E. St. (38), Vol. 38: 145-95. 1907. (See especially pp. 145-58.)
535. BROWN, C. F. The autobiographical element in the Cynewulfian rune passages. E. St. (38), Vol. 38: 196-233. 1907.
    Not especially bibliographical, but important for Cynewulf in general.
BRANDL (5), pp. 1043-4. Bibliography for only the four signed poems.

536. JANSEN, K. Die Cynewulf-forschung vor ihren anfängen bis zur gegenwart. Bo. Beitr (83), Vol. XXIV: 1-123. 1908.
    Almost complete to 1908. For additions and corrections, see SCHMITZ (537) and BROWN (539). Besides giving bibliography, Jansen discusses problems concerned with the canon.
537. SCHMITZ, T. Review of JANSEN (536): Anglia Beibl. (37), Vol. 22: 6-8. 1911.
    Adds titles omitted by JANSEN (536). In the same volume (pp. 337-41) Schmitz lists Cynewulf bibliography for 1908-9.
538. BROWN, C. F. Irish-Latin influence in Cynewulfian texts. E. St. (38), Vol. 40: 1-29. 1909.
539. BROWN, C. F. Review of JANSEN (536): E. St. (38), Vol. 45: 98-101. 1910.
    Makes additions and corrections to JANSEN (536) and SCHMITZ (537).
    KÖRTING (6), pp. 49-52.
540. KENNEDY, C. W. The poems of Cynewulf. Translated into English prose. London, 1910. See pp. 335-47.
540a. TUPPER, F. The philological legend of Cynewulf. P. M. L. A. (69), Vol. 26: 235-79. 1911.
541. HOLTHAUSEN, F. Cynewulf's Elene. 3d ed. Heidelberg, 1914. General bibliography, pp. xiv-xv.
Facsimiles: Facsimiles of *Andreas, Elene, Dream of the Rood,* and *Fates of the Apostles* are found in WÜLKER (378) and FÖRSTER (379).

a. Andreas

Bibliography
    KRAPP (544), pp. lxxiii-lxxviii.
    KÖRTING (6), pp. 56-7; FÖRSTER (380), p. 68.
542. COOK, A. S. The Old English Andreas and Bishop Acca of Hexham. Trans. Conn. Acad. (109), Vol. 26: 245-322. 1924. Bibliography in footnotes.
    See also general bibliography of Cynewulfian Poems.

Text
543. BASKERVILLE, W. M. Andreas: A legend of St. Andrew. Edited with critical notes. Boston, 1885.
    GREIN-WÜLKER (385), Vol. IIa, pp. 1-86.
544. KRAPP, G. P. Andreas and the Fates of the Apostles. Boston, 1906. The standard text.

Discussion
545. BOURAUEL, J. Zur Quellen-und verfasserfrage von Andreas, Crist und Fata. Bo. Beitr. (83), Vol. 9: 65-132. 1901.
    KRAPP (544), pp. ix-lxxii; GRAU (548), pp. 131-45. See also SARRAZIN (534), pp. 158-70.
    KENNEDY (540), pp. 42-51; SMITHSON (410), *passim.*

546. HAMILTON, G. L. The sources of the Fates of the Apostles and Andreas. M. L. N. (26), Vol. 35: 385-95. 1920. Argues for an Anglo-Irish source.
  COOK (542). Full of valuable information.
547. OLIVERO, F. Andreas e i Fati degli Apostoli. Traduzione dall' anglosassone con introduzione e note. Torino, 1927.

Translation
  KEMBLE (377). The poetry of the Codex Vercellensis . . .
548. ROOT, R. K. Andreas: The legend of St. Andrew, translated from the Old English, with an introduction. Y. St. (119), Vol. VII. 1899.
  HALL (394), pp. 62-119; KENNEDY (540), pp. 211-63; GORDON (396), pp. 200-33.

b. Christ

Bibliography
549. COOK, A. S. The Christ of Cynewulf. Boston, 1900 (second impression, 1909). Bibliography, p. 295 and Introduction, *passim*.
  KÖRTING (6), p. 55.
  See also general bibliography of Cynewulfian Poems.

Text
  THORPE (375), pp. 1-107. With translation.
550. GOLLANCZ, I. Cynewulf's Christ. London, 1892. Based on the then unpublished edition of GOLLANCZ (376). With translation.
  GREIN-WÜLKER (385), Vol. IIIa, pp. 1-54.
  COOK (549), pp. 1-64. The standard text.

Discussion
  COOK (549), pp. xvi-xlvi. Valuable.
551. BINZ, G. Untersuchungen zum altenglischen sogenannten Christ. Festschrift zur 49ten Versammlung deutscher Philologen und Schulmänner, pp. 181-97. Basel, 1907. Argues that the *Christ* is three poems. See also G. H. Gerould's article in E. St. (38), Vol. 41: 1-19 (1909), and S. Moore's in J. E. G. Ph. (53), Vol. 14: 550-67. 1915.
  GRAU (458), pp. 29-88; JANSEN (536), pp. 70-7.
  KENNEDY (540), pp. 27-34; SMITHSON (410), *passim*.
551a. HOWARD, E. J. Cynewulf's *Christ* 1665-1693. P. M. L. A. (69), Vol. 45: 354-67. 1930. Ascribes to Cynewulf the lines in question, on the basis of internal evidence.

Translation (See also Text)
552. WHITMAN, C. H. The Christ of Cynewulf. A poem in three parts: the advent, the ascension, and the last judgment. Translated into English prose. Boston, 1900. It "closely conforms in reading and punctuation to [Cook's] recent edition of the *Christ*."
  KENNEDY (540), pp. 153-204; GORDON (396), pp. 147-81.

c. Dream of the Rood ("Vision of the Cross")*

See also Part XII: Ruthwell Cross, p. 137.

Bibliography

553. COOK, A. S. The Dream of the Rood. An Old English poem attributed to Cynewulf. Oxford, 1905. See pp. viii-ix, lix-lx.
KÖRTING (6), pp. 48-9.
KENNEDY (540), pp. 335-47, *passim;* FÖRSTER (380), p. 81.
See also general bibliography of Cynewulfian Poems.

Text
GREIN-WÜLKER (385), Vol. IIa, pp. 116-25.

554. VIËTOR, W. Die nordhumbrischen runensteine. Marburg, 1895. Good text.
COOK (553), pp. 1-10. The standard text.

555. HEWISON, J. K. The Runic roods of Ruthwell and Bewcastle, with a short history of the cross and crucifix in Scotland. Glasgow, 1914. With translation.

556. RICCI, A. Il Sogno della Croce (Dream of the Rood) riveduto nel testo, con versione, introduzione e note, a cura di A. Ricci. Florence, 1926.

Discussion

557. STEVENS, W. O. The cross in the life and literature of the Anglo-Saxons. Y. St. (119), Vol. XXIII. 1904.
COOK (553) pp. ix-lvii. Introduction discusses the problem of authorship very fully; the author concludes that Cynewulf probably wrote it. Appendix gives specimens of all translations of lines 1-12.

558. BRANDL, A. Zum angelsächsischen gedicht 'Traumgesicht vom kreuze Christi.' Sitzungsberichte der Berliner Akademie der Wissenschaften, 1905. Pp. 716-23.
GRAU (458), p. 175; KENNEDY (504), pp. 62-8; SARRAZIN (411), pp. 113-33.
HEWISON (555); RICCI (556).

Translation (See also *Text*)
MORLEY (337), Vol. II, pp. 237-41.
GARNETT (395), pp. 71-7; KENNEDY (540), pp. 306-11.
COOK AND TINKER (391), pp. 93-9. Translation by Iddings.
GORDON (396), pp. 261-4.

d. Elene

Bibliography
KÖRTING (6), pp. 54-5; FÖRSTER (380), pp. 84-5.
HOLTHAUSEN (541), pp. ix-xv.

559. COOK, A. S. The Old English Elene, Phoenix and Physiologus. New Haven, 1919.
See pp. 141-5. Additional bibliography may be found in reviews by H. R. Patch, J. E. G. Ph. (53), Vol. 19: 418-22 (1920) and E. Ekwall, Anglia Beibl. (37), Vol. 33: 62 (1922).
See also general bibliography of Cynewulfian Poems.

Text
560. KENT, C.W. Elene. 2d ed. Boston, 1902. Edited with introduction,
Latin original, notes, glossary, and a bibliography.
GREIN-WÜLKER (385), Vol. IIa, pp. 126-201.
HOLTHAUSEN (541). Very good edition. Gives one page of facsimile,
and Latin sources.
COOK (559), pp. 1-46. Excellent texts and useful apparatus.

Discussion
GRAU (458), pp. 15-29; SMITHSON (410), *passim.*
HOLTHAUSEN (541), pp. ix-xvi. See also his article, "Zur Quelle von
Cynewulf's Elene," in Z. f. d. Ph. (78), Vol. 37: 1-19. 1905.
COOK (559), pp. vii-xxiv. The introduction contains much valuable
material.

Translation
GARNETT (395), pp. 1-43.
561. HOLT, L. H. The Elene of Cynewulf, translated into English prose.
Y. St. (119), Vol. XXI. 1904.
"The aim .... is to give an accurate and readable modern
English prose rendering."
KENNEDY (540), pp. 87-128; GORDON (396), pp. 234-60.

e. *Fates of the Apostles*

Bibliography
KRAPP (544), pp. lxxiii-lxxviii.
KENNEDY (540), pp. 335-47, *passim;* FÖRSTER (380), pp. 69-70.
See also general bibliography of Cynewulfian Poems.

Text
KEMBLE (377), Vol. II, pp. 94-9. With translation.
GREIN-WÜLKER (385), Vol. IIa, pp. 87-91; Vol. IIb, pp. 566-7.
KRAPP (544), pp. 69-73. Standard text.

Discussion
562. NAPIER, A. S. The Old English poem "The Fates of the Apostles."
Academy (42), Sept. 8, 1888.
BOURAUEL (545), *passim.*
KRAPP (544), pp. ix-lxxii. Valuable introduction and notes.
JANSEN (536), pp. 77-90; HAMILTON (546); OLIVERO (547).
563. SIEVERS, E., in Neusprachliche studien (133). On the basis of a
metrical study Sievers attempts a reconstruction of the *Fates of
the Apostles.* See "Zu Cynewulf," pp. 60-81, especially pp. 66-9.

Translation (See also Text)
KENNEDY (540), pp. 205-8; GORDON (396), pp. 197-9.

f. **Guthlac***

Bibliography
KÖRTING (6), pp. 55-6.

---

*See also Part XI, Guthlac, p. 116.

KENNEDY (540), pp. 335-47, *passim;* KURTZ (566), *passim.*
See also general bibliography of Cynewulfian Poems.
Text
THORPE (375), pp. 107-84. With translation.
GOLLANCZ (376), pp. 104-88. With translation.
GREIN-WÜLKER (385), Vol. IIIa, pp. 55-94.
Discussion
564. FORSTMANN, H. Untersuchungen zur Guthlac-legende. Bo. Beitr. (83), Vol. XII: 1-40. 1902. Discusses the Latin life of St. Guthlac, the Old English *Guthlac* A, and Middle English versions.
JANSEN (536)., pp. 99-105; KENNEDY (540), pp. 51-6.
565. GEROULD, G. H. The Old English poems on St. Guthlac and their Latin source. M. L. N. (26), Vol. 32: 77-89. 1917.
Disagrees with conclusions of FORSTMANN (564) regarding the source of *Guthlac* A; attributes *Guthlac* B either to Cynewulf or to a poet equally great.
566. KURTZ, B. P. From St. Anthony to St. Guthlac. A study in biography. Univ. of Cal. Publi. (110), Vol. 12: 103-46. 1925-6. See especially pp. 143-6.
Translation (See also Text)
KENNEDY (540), pp. 264-305; GORDON (396), pp. 284-309.

g. Juliana
Bibliography
567. STRUNK, W. Juliana. Boston, 1904.
See pp. 61-6.
KENNEDY (540), pp. 335-47, *passim.*
See also general bibliography of Cynewulfian Poems.
Text
THORPE (375), pp. 242-86. With translation.
GOLLANCZ (376), pp. 242-4. With translation.
GREIN-WÜLKER (385), Vol. IIIa, pp. 117-39.
STRUNK (567), pp. 1-32. Satisfactory text, introduction, notes, and glossary. Includes the Latin *Acta S. Julianae.*
Discussion
STRUNK (567), pp. v-xliv; GRAU (458), pp. 157-73.
SMITHSON (410), *passim.*
Translation (See also Text)
568. MURCH, H. S. Translation of Cynewulf's Juliana. J. E. G. Ph. (53), Vol. 5: 303-19. 1904.
KENNEDY (540), pp. 129-52; GORDON (396), pp. 182-96.

h. Phoenix
Bibliography
MANN (571), Anglia Beibl. (37), Vol. 10: 282-3; Vol. 12: p. 19; Vol. 13: 237-8 (the latter by A. L. Jellinek).

KÖRTING (6), pp. 57-8.
SCHLOTTEROSE (569), pp. 3-7; COOK (559), pp. 145-9.
See also general bibliography of Cynewulfian Poems.

Text

THORPE (375), pp. 197-242. With translation.
GOLLANCZ (376), pp. 200-40. With translation.
GREIN-WÜLKER (385), Vol. IIIa, pp. 95-116.

569. SCHLOTTEROSE, O. Die altenglische dichtung 'Phoenix.' Bo. Beitr. (83), Vol. 25. 1908. Translated into German.
BRIGHT (318), pp. 165-88; COOK (559), pp. 47-73.

Discussion

GRAU (458), pp. 99-131; JANSEN (536), pp. 105-8.
SCHLOTTEROSE (569), pp. 78-92. Believes the poem was written not by Cynewulf but by some person under his influence. Gives also the Latin original.
COOK (559), pp. xxv-lvi.

570. EMERSON, O. F. Originality in Old English poetry. R. E. S. (70), Vol. 2: 18-31. 1926. Traces "with some fullness the originality of the Old English Fenix poet." Careful comparison of the poem and its source.

Translation (See also Text)

HALL (394) pp. 19-42; KENNEDY (540), pp. 312-32.
COOK AND TINKER (391), pp. 144-63; FAUST AND THOMPSON (397), pp. 132-56.
GORDON, (396) pp. 265-79.

i. Physiologus

Bibliography

571. MANN, M. F. Zur bibliographie des Physiologus. Anglia Beibl. (37), Vol. 10: 274-87; Vol. 12: 13-23; Vol. 13: 18-21, 236-9. 1900-03.

The last instalment (Vol. 13: 236-9) is contributed by A. L. Jellinek. Additional notes by F. Holthausen in Anglia Beibl. (37), Vol. 12: 338-9.
PEEBLES (572), pp. 571-2 (footnotes); COOK (559), pp. 149-50.
See also general bibliography of Cynewulfian Poems.

Text

THORPE (375), pp. 355-66. With translation.
GREIN-WÜLKER (385), Vol. IIIa, pp. 164-70.
COOK (559), pp. 75-81; COOK (574). With translation.

Discussion

572. PEEBLES, R. J. The Anglo-Saxon Physiologus. M. Ph. (56), Vol. 8: 571-9. 1911.

573. TUPPER, F. The Physiologus of the Exeter Book. J. E. G. Ph. (53), Vol. 11:89-91. 1912.
COOK (559), pp. lvii-lxxxix.

573a. WELLMANN, M. Der Physiologus. Eine religionsgeschichtlich-naturwissenschaftliche untersuchung. Leipzig, 1930. Excellent for the classical background.

Translation (See also Text)
574. COOK, A. S. The Old English Physiologus. Text and prose translation. Verse translation by J. H. Pitman. Y. St. (119), Vol. LXIII. 1921.
GORDON (396), pp. 280-3.

j. Riddles

Bibliography
KÖRTING (6), pp. 52-3.
575. TUPPER, F. The Riddles of the Exeter book, edited with introduction, notes, and glossary. Boston, 1910. See pp. ci-cviii for bibliography.
576. TRAUTMANN, M. Die altenglischen rätsel (Die rätsel des Exeterbuchs). Heidelberg, 1915.

See also general bibliography of Cynewulfian Poems.

Text
THORPE (375), pp. 380-441, 470-3, 479-500. With translation.
TUPPER (575), pp. 1-67. Both this edition and that of TRAUTMANN (576) are good.
577. WYATT, A. J. Old English Riddles. Boston, 1912. A good edition. The apparatus is not as complete as in TUPPER (575).
TRAUTMANN (576), *passim*.

Discussion
BRANDL (5), pp. 969-72; JANSEN (536), pp. 93-9.
TUPPER (575), pp. xi-c. Excellent discussion of all phases of the subject. Very full notes.
WYATT (577). Good introduction. SARRAZIN (411), pp. 95-113.
578. TRAUTMANN, M. Quellen der altenglischen rätsel. Sprache und versbau der altenglischen rätsel. Zeit, heimat und verfasser der altenglischen rätsel. Anglia (36), Vol. 38: 349-73. 1914.
TRAUTMANN (576). A useful survey of the investigation of the *Riddles*, pp. 57-64. Sixteen pages of facsimiles.
SIEPER (412), pp. 169-82. Discussion of the first Exeter *Riddle*.
IMELMANN (413), *passim*.
HEUSLER (430), pp. 74-76. Discusses Germanic Riddles in general along with Old English.

Translation (See also Text)
BROOKE (334), *passim*. Some thirty-five Riddles are translated or paraphrased.
FAUST AND THOMPSON (397), pp. 44-55. Only thirteen Riddles are given.
COOK AND TINKER (391), pp. 70-5. Gives only eight Riddles.
GORDON (396), pp. 320-40.

Deor's Lament

Bibliography
   WÜLKER (3), pp. 330-4;   KÖRTING (6), p. 39.
   DICKINS (28), pp. 53-4;   HOLTHAUSEN (468).

Text
   THORPE (375), pp. 377-9. With translation.
   GREIN-WÜLKER (385), Vol. I, pp. 278-80.
   DICKINS (281), pp. 70-6. With translation.
   HOLTHAUSEN (468). Beowulf.
   SEDGEFIELD (322) pp. 8-9.
   A text is given also in SEDGEFIELD (465), pp. 107-8.
   KLAEBER (462), pp. 268-9.

Discussion
579. TUPPER, J. W. Deor's Complaint. M. L. N. (26), Vol. 10: 125-7. 1895.
   JIRICZEK (361).   See especially the discussion of the Theodoric legend. (1913).
580. LAWRENCE, W. W. The Song of Deor. M. Ph. (56), Vol. 9: 23-45. 1911. "A review of the whole poem, with certain suggestions not hitherto made . . ."
   CLARKE (349), pp. 188-208.
   CHAMBERS (661), *passim.* Comments on the resemblance of *Deor* to *Widsith*, and on Theodoric and Heorrenda.
   DICKINS (281), pp. 45-6.
   SIEPER (412), pp. 149-68. Gives a text also, p. 125.
580a. GRIENBERGER, T. Déor. Anglia (36), Vol. 45: 393-407. 1921.
   HOLTHAUSEN (468). Beowulf.

Translation (See also Text)
   GUMMERE (393), pp. 186-8.
   COOK AND TINKER (391), pp. 58-60. Translation by C. M. Lewis.
   FAUST AND THOMPSON (397), pp. 26-8;   GORDON (396), pp. 79-80.

Descent into Hell, Christ's ("Harrowing of Hell")

NOTE: The theme of this poem is treated also in the Caedmonian *Christ and Satan.*

Bibliography
   WÜLKER (3), pp. 186-7;   BRANDL (5), p. 1045.

Text
   THORPE (375), pp. 459-67. With translation.
   CRAMER (582), pp. 170-4;   GREIN-WÜLKER (385), Vol. IIIa, pp. 175-80.

Discussion
581. KIRKLAND, J. H. A study of the Anglo-Saxon poem, The Harrowing of Hell. Leipzig, 1885.
582. CRAMER, J. Quelle, verfasser und text des altenglischen gedichtes Christi Höllenfahrt. Anglia (36), Vol. 19: 137-74. 1896.
   SKEMP (405).

Didactic (Monitory) Poem

Bibliography: WÜLKER (3), p. 370.
Text
    THORPE (375), p. 469ff. With translation.
    GREIN-WÜLKER (385), Vol. IIb, pp. 280-1.
Discussion: WÜLKER (3), p. 370; BRANDL (5), p. 1048.

Durham, On the City of

Bibliography
    WÜLKER (3), pp. 344-5, 515-6; BRANDL (5), pp. 1079-80; KÖRTING (6), pp. 41-2.
Text: GREIN-WÜLKER (385), Vol. I, pp. 389-92.
Discussion: WÜLKER (3), pp. 345-6; BRANDL (5), pp. 1079-80.
Translation
583. WILLICH, A. F. M. Three philological essays, chiefly translated from the German of John Christopher Adelung. London, 1798.

Edgar's Coronation

Bibliography
    WÜLKER (3), pp. 343-4; BRANDL (5), p. 1079.
    KÖRTING (6), p. 41; SEDGEFIELD (612), pp. 49-50.
Text
    GREIN-WÜLKER (385), Vol. I, pp. 381-2.
    EARLE-PLUMMER (792), Vol. I, p. 973.
    SEDGEFIELD (612), pp. 21-2.
Discussion
    ABEGG (402), pp. 42-53. For *Edgar's Death* see pp. 42-53, 62-4.
    KELLER (919); BRANDL (5), p. 1078; NEUENDORFF (585), pp. 53-4.
    JOST (927a) gives a text also.
Translation
584. GILES, J. A. The Venerable Beda's Ecclesiastical History of England. Also the Anglo-Saxon Chronicle. London, 1847.
    THORPE (793), Vol. II, pp. 96-7; ROBINSON (387).

Edgar's Death

Bibliography: See *Edgar's Coronation*, p. 77.
Text
    GREIN-WÜLKER (385), Vol. I, pp. 382-4.
    EARLE-PLUMMER (792), Vol. I, pp. 118-22.
    SEDGEFIELD (612), pp. 22-4; CLASSEN-HARMER (794), p. 50.
Discussion and Translation: See *Edgar's Coronation*, p. 77.

Edward the Confessor's Death

Bibliography
    WÜLKER (3), p. 344; BRANDL (5), p. 1079.
    KÖRTING (6), p. 41; SEDGEFIELD (612), pp. 49-50.

Text
  GREIN-WÜLKER (385), Vol. I, pp. 386-8.
  EARLE-PLUMMER (792), Vol. I, pp. 192-5.
  SEDGEFIELD (612), pp. 26-7; SEDGEFIELD (322), pp. 121-2.
  CLASSEN-HARMER (794), pp. 84-5.
Discussion
  ABEGG (402), pp. 53-7; BRANDL (5), pp. 1078-9.
Translation
  GILES (584); THORPE (793), Vol. II, p. 164.
  GUEST (634), pp. 366-9. Gives text also. ROBINSON (387).

Edward the Martyr's Death

Bibliography
  KÖRTING (6), p. 41.
585. NEUENDORFF, B. Das gedicht auf den tod Eadweards des Märtyrers, 979, und einige verwandte gedichte. Archiv (25), Vol. 128: 45-54. 1912. Reviews opinions as to its prose or poetic nature. Gives also Earle-Plummer text.
Text
  EARLE-PLUMMER (792), Vol. I, p. 123; CLASSEN-HARMER (794), p. 51.
Discussion: ABEGG (402), pp. 93-5; NEUENDORFF (585), pp. 45-6.
Translation: THORPE (793), Vol. II, p. 100.

Exhortation to Christian Living (Lār)

Bibliography
  WÜLKER (3), pp. 368-70; KÖRTING (6), p. 60.
Text
  LUMBY (453), pp. 28-33. With translation.
  GREIN-WÜLKER (385), Vol. IIb, p. 273.
Discussion
  LUMBY (453), pp. 67-8; WÜLKER (3), pp. 368-70; BRANDL (5), p. 1095.

Father's Instruction, A (Fœder Lārcwidas)

Bibliography
  WÜLKER (3), pp. 230-1; BRANDL (5), p. 963; KÖRTING (6), p. 60.
Text
  THORPE (375), pp. 300-5. With translation.
  GREIN-WÜLKER (385), Vol. I, pp. 353-7.
  GOLLANCZ (376), pp. 300-4. With translation.
  SEDGEFIELD (322), pp. 109-11.
Discussion: BRANDL (5), p. 962.

Finnsburh, Fight at

Bibliography
  WÜLKER (3), pp. 307-15; DICKINS (281), pp. 51-3.
586. AURNER, NELLIE S. An analysis of the interpretations of the

Finnsburg documents. Univ. of Iowa Stud. (112), Vol. I, No. 6, 1917. Historical survey of *Finnsburh* scholarship; practically complete bibliography to 1916.
CHAMBERS (461), pp. 387-413, *passim.*
CRAWFORD (497), pp. 146-8.
KLAEBER (462), pp. 227-230 and Supplement, p. 424; LAWRENCE (463).

Text
GREIN-WÜLKER (385), Vol. I, pp. 14-17.
WYATT-CHAMBERS (466), pp. 158-62.
DICKINS (281), pp. 64-8. With translation.

587. MACKIE, W. S. The fight at Finnsburg. J. E. G. Ph. (53), Vol. 16: 250-73. 1917.
Believes "that no modern editor has treated the text of the Fragment with sufficient conservatism" and "that the commonly accepted conclusions about the original date and the original home rest upon uncertain evidence and find hardly any support from the poem itself". Critical text with many notes.
KLAEBER (462), pp. 231-5. Gives also Hickes' text.
NOTE: Many O. E. readers and almost all editions of *Beowulf* contain the text.

Discussion
MÖLLER (478), pp. 46-100, 151-6. Extended discussion of the *Finnsburh* fragment, the Finn episode in *Beowulf,* and the Finn legend. In Pt. 2, pp. vii-ix, he prints the *Finnsburh* fragment in strophic form.

588. TRAUTMANN, M. Finn und Hildebrand. Bo. Beitr. (83), Vol. 7: 1-64. 1903.
BRANDL (5), pp. 983-6. Important interpretation.

589. LAWRENCE, W. W. Beowulf and the tragedy of Finnsburg. P. M. L. A. (69), Vol. 30: 372-431. 1915. Excellent survey of the problems.
AURNER (586), pp. 3-29.

590. AYRES, H. M. The tragedy of Hengest in Beowulf. J. E. G. Ph. (53), Vol. 16: 282-95. 1917. An excellent analysis.
MACKIE (587). The fight at Finnsburg.
IMELMANN (413). Text of the *Finnsburh* Fragment and Episode, with commentary.
CHAMBERS (461), pp. 245-89. Indispensable.

591. SCHREINER, K. Die sage von Hengest und Horsa. Entwicklung und nachleben bei den dichtern und geschichtsschreibern Englands. Berlin, 1921.
KLAEBER (462), pp. 219-26.

592. WILLIAMS, R. A. The Finn episode in Beowulf. An essay in interpretation. Cambridge [Eng.], 1924.
New interpretation of the episode. "A notably ingenious but unwarranted reconstruction."—Klaeber.

593. MALONE, K. The Finn episode in Beowulf. J. E. G. Ph. (53), Vol. 25: 157-72. 1926.
    Believes the author of the "episode" was interested primarily in the tragic experiences of Hengest and Hildeburh.
594. KLAEBER, F. Beowulfiana. Anglia (36), Vol. 50: 107-22, 195-244. 1926.
    See 2. "Finnsburg", pp. 224-33.

Translation (See also Text)
    GARNETT (488). (Metrical); GUMMERE (393), pp. 160-3. Metrical.
    HALL (491), pp. 156-9. Verse and prose renderings.
    FAUST AND THOMPSON (397), pp. 35-37.
    GORDON (396), pp. 71-2 (Prose); MONCRIEFF (492); LEONARD (493).

Five Cities (Boroughs), Edmund's Freeing of

Bibliography
    WÜLKER (3), pp. 342-3; SEDGEFIELD (612), pp. 49-50.
    BRANDL (5), p. 1079; KÖRTING (6), pp. 40-1.

Text
    GREIN-WÜLKER (385), Vol. I, pp. 380-1.
    EARLE-PLUMMER (792), Vol. I, p. 110.
    SEDGEFIELD (612), pp. 20-1.
    MAWER (595), p. 551. Earle-Plummer text. With translation.
    CLASSEN-HARMER (794), pp. 46-7.

Discussion
    ABEGG (402), pp. 39-42; BRANDL (5), p. 1078.
595. MAWER, A. The redemption of the five boroughs. E. H. R. (149), Vol. 38: 551-7. 1923. See also F. Liebermann's article in Archiv (25), Vol. 148: 96. 1925.

Translation (See also Text)
    GILES (584); THORPE (793), Vol. II, p. 89.
    ROBINSON (387); CHAMBERS (198), p. 240.

Gloria

Bibliography: WÜLKER (3), pp. 372-4.

Text
    LUMBY (453), pp. 52-5. With translation.
    GREIN-WÜLKER (385), Vol. IIb, pp. 239-44. A three-line fragment of another version is printed in HOLTHAUSEN (386), p. 401.

Discussion: WÜLKER (3), p. 374; FEILER (460), pp. 46-7.

Gnomic Verses

Bibliography
    WÜLKER (3), pp. 228-30, 515.
596. WILLIAMS, B. C. Gnomic poetry in Anglo-Saxon. New York, 1914. Standard for gnomic poetry.
    KRÜGER (600).

Text
 THORPE (375), pp. 333-46. With translation.
 GREIN-WÜLKER (385), Vol. I, pp. 338-52.
 WILLIAMS (596). Contains general introduction, careful discussion of Exeter and Cotton gnomes, and a critical text.

Discussion
 597. STROBL, J. Zur spruchdichtung bei den angelsachsen. Z. f. d. A. (79), Vol. 31: 54-64. 1887.
 598. MÜLLER, H. Über die angelsächsischen versus gnomici. Jena, 1893.
 599. KELLNER, L. Altenglische spruchweisheit. Vienna, 1897.
 BRANDL (5), pp. 959-63.
 WILLIAMS (596). The most complete discussion up to its time.
 HEUSLER (430), pp. 64-74. A good discussion of Germanic *"Spruchdichtung"*.
 600. KRÜGER, C. Beiträge zur gnomischen dichtung der angelsachsen. Diss. Halle, 1924.

Translation (See also Text)
 NOTE: There is no complete translation of both the Cotton and the Exeter gnomes. Selections are translated in the following: BROOKE (334), *passim;* SPAETH (392), pp. 155-9; FAUST AND THOMPSON (397), pp. 58-61; COOK AND TINKER (391), pp. 67-9; GORDON (396), pp. 341-7.

Grave, The

Bibliography: FAUST AND THOMPSON (397), p. 157.

Text
 601. THORPE, B. Analecta Anglo-Saxonica. A selection in prose and verse from Anglo-Saxon authors of various ages. London, 1868.
 602. SCHRÖER, A. The Grave. Anglia (36), Vol. 5: 289-90. 1882. Diplomatic text. Little apparatus.
 GUEST (634), pp. 368-71. With translation.

Discussion
 603. MÜLLER, E. Zwei angelsächsische gedichte. I. The Grave. Archiv (25), Vol. 29: 205-11. 1861. Some discussion of the vocabulary. Gives also Thorpe's text and Longfellow's translation.
 BRANDL (5), p. 1096.
 603a. DUDLEY, L. "The Grave." M. Ph. (56), Vol. 11: 429-42. 1914. Bibliography in footnotes.

Translation (See also Text)
 MORLEY (337), Vol. II, pp. 33-4; FAUST AND THOMPSON (397), pp. 157-8.
 NOTE: Longfellow also has a translation, which is discussed in MÜLLER (603).

Hālgung-bōc

HOLTHAUSEN (386), p. 404. Gives a text. Another text is given by BIRCH (846), Appendix, p. xxii.

604. NAPIER, A. Contributions to Old English lexicography. Trans. Phil. Soc. (108), 1906, p. 35.

Husband's Message

Bibliography
    WÜLKER (3), p. 227.

605. TRAUTMANN, M. Zur Botschaft des gemahls. Anglia (36), Vol. 16: 207-25. 1894. Good critical bibliography to 1894.
    C. H. E. L. (4), p. 475; KERSHAW (389), pp. 37-43.

Text
    THORPE, pp. 472-5. With translation.
    GREIN-WÜLKER (385), Vol. I, pp. 306-11. Diplomatic and emended texts.
    TRAUTMANN (605). Grein-Wülker's and diplomatic texts.

606. BLACKBURN, F. A. The Husband's Message, and the accompanying Riddles of the Exeter Book. J. [E.] G. Ph. (53), Vol. 3: 1-13. 1901. With translation.
    KERSHAW (389), pp. 44-8. With translation.
    SEDGEFIELD (322), pp. 37-9.

Discussion
607. HICKETIER, F. Klage der frau, Botschaft des gemahls und Ruine. Anglia (36), Vol. 11: 363-8. 1889.
    Believes it possible that the three poems are riddles, but does not attempt to solve them. For discussion of his views, see TRAUTMANN (605).
    TRAUTMANN (605). Connects this poem with the *Wife's Complaint* as parts of a longer narrative poem, which has been lost or which was never finished.
    ROEDER (173), pp. 119 ff.
    BLACKBURN (606). Connects the "First *Riddle*" with this poem.
    C. H. E. L. (4), pp. 42-3.
    SIEPER (412), pp. 209-16. Gives a text also, p. 134.
    IMELMANN (413), pp. 1-38; KERSHAW (389), pp. 37-43.

Translation (See also Text)
    SPAETH (392), pp. 147-8; GORDON (396), pp. 89-90.

Hymns and Prayers*

Bibliography: WÜLKER (3), pp. 376-9.

Text
    THORPE (375), pp. 452-9. With translation.

---

*See also Creed, Gloria, and Pater Noster.

608. STEVENSON, J. The Latin hymns of the Anglo-Saxon church, with an interlinear Anglo-Saxon gloss. Surtees Soc. Publ. (107), Vol. XXIII. Durham and London, 1851.
    THOMSON (459), pp. 213-25. Three prayers. With translation.
    LUMBY (453), pp. 36-7. Oratio poetica. With translation. Published also in ZUPITZA-SCHIPPER (325) (11th ed.) and KLUGE (317) (3d ed.).
    GREIN-WÜLKER (385), Vol. IIb, pp. 211-26. One hymn and four prayers.
    SWEET (323), pp. 177-88. Thirteen hymns (Vespasian).

Discussion
    BRANDL (5), pp. 1047-9, 1093.
    SIEPER (412), pp. 253-7. Discusses the prayer beginning on p. 452 in THORPE (375) (*Exeter Book*, fol. 117b). Sieper gives a text on p. 143.

Judith

Bibliography
    WÜLKER (3), pp. 140-1, 513-4; COOK (609), pp. 71-3.
    C. H. E. L. (4), p. 496; BRANDL (5), p. 1091; KÖRTING (6), p. 49.
    TUPPER (610a), *passim*.

Text
    GREIN-WÜLKER (385), Vol. IIb, pp. 294-314.
609. COOK, A. S. Judith, an Old English epic fragment. Boston, 1904. With introduction, facsimile, notes, and glossary. Good text. With translation.

Discussion
610. FOSTER, J. G. Judith. Studies in metre, language and style. Q. F. (103), Vol. LXXI. Strassburg, 1892.
    COOK (609), pp. xv-lxxiii; BRANDL (5), p. 1091.
610a. TUPPER, F. Notes on Old English poems. 1. The home of the Judith. J. E. G. Ph. (53), Vol. 11: 82-9. 1912.
611. PURDIE, EDNA. The story of Judith in German and English literature. Bangor [Wales] and Paris, 1927. To be used with caution.

Translation (See also Text)
    GARNETT (395), pp. 44-56; HALL (394), pp. 5-17.
    FAUST AND THOMPSON (397), pp. 116-31.
    COOK AND TINKER (391), pp. 121-32. Morley's verse translation. Also found in *English Writers* (337), Vol. II, pp. 180-88.
    GORDON (396), pp. 352-8.

Last Judgment, The (Doomsday)

Bibliography: WÜLKER (3), p. 234; KÖRTING (6), p. 60.

Text
    THORPE (375), pp. 445-52. With translation.
    GREIN-WÜLKER (385), Vol. IIIa, pp. 171-4. Poem entitled *Bi Domes Daege*.

Discussion
    NÖLLE (455); DEERING (457), *passim;* GRAU (458), pp. 176-80.
Translation (See also Text): GORDON (396), pp. 314-9. Entitled "Doomsday".

Maldon, Battle of

Bibliography
    WÜLKER (3), pp. 334-8, 515; CROW (504), pp. xxxiii-xxxiv.
    SEDGEFIELD (612), pp. 45-8; C. H. E. L. (4), p. 494.
    KÖRTING (6), pp. 39-40; COOK AND TINKER (391), p. 31.
    ASHDOWN (617a).

Text
    GREIN-WÜLKER (385), Vol. I, pp. 358-73; CROW (504), pp. 1-12.
612. SEDGEFIELD, W. J. The Battle of Maldon and short poems from the Saxon Chronicle. Boston and London, 1904. With introduction, notes, and glossary. Standard edition.
    ASHDOWN (617a).
    NOTE: The text may be found also in many books of selections, *e. g.*, BRIGHT (318), WYATT (320), SEDGEFIELD (322), SWEET (323), KRAPP AND KENNEDY (331), FLOM (263).

Discussion
613. ZERNIAL, U. Das lied von Byrhtnoths fall. Berlin, 1882.
    ABEGG (402), pp. 1-26; CROW (504), pp. vi-xxxi, *passim*.
614. LIEBERMANN, F. Zur geschichte Byrhtnoths, des Helden von Maldon. Archiv (25), Vol. 101: 15-28. 1898.
    SEDGEFIELD (612), pp. v-xvi.
    C. H. E. L. (4), pp. 158-60; BRANDL (5), pp. 1076-7.
615. LABORDE, E. D. The style of The Battle of Maldon. M. L. R. (27), Vol. 19: 401-17. 1924.
616. LABORDE, E. D. The site of the Battle of Maldon. E. H. R. (149), Vol. 40: 161-73. 1925.
617. PHILLPOTTS, B. S. 'The Battle of Maldon': some Danish affinities. M. L. R. (27), Vol. 24: 172-90. 1929. Argues for a strong Scandinavian influence on the poet.
617a. ASHDOWN, M. English and Norse documents relating to the reign of Ethelred the Unready. Cambridge [Eng.], 1930.

Translation
    GARNETT (395), pp. 60-70; HALL (394), pp. 44-55.
618. SIMS, W. R. The Battle of Maldon. M. L. N. (26), Vol. 7: 275-86. 1892. An excellent verse translation.
    FAUST AND THOMPSON (397), pp. 163-75.
    COOK AND TINKER (391), pp. 32-43. Lumsden's translation.
    GORDON (396), pp. 361-7.
619. KER, in CHAMBERS (198), pp. 260-7.

Menologium (Calendcwide)

Bibliography
    WÜLKER (3), pp. 367-8, 516.
    EARLE-PLUMMER (792), Vol. I, p. 273.
620. IMELMANN, R. Das altenglische Menologium. Berlin, 1902.
    See also the review by E. Sokoll in Anglia Beibl. (37), Vol. 14: 307-15. 1903.
    C. H. E. L. (4), p. 497; KÖRTING (6), p. 62.

Text
621. Fox, S. Menologium, seu Calendarium Poeticum. . . . or, The Poetical Calendar of the Anglo-Saxons, with an English translation and notes. London, 1830.
    GREIN-WÜLKER (385), Vol. IIb, pp. 282-93.
    EARLE-PLUMMER (792), Vol. I, Appendix A, pp. 273-82.
    IMELMANN (620), pp. 56-64. Based on Grein-Wülker.

Discussion
622. PIPER, F. Die kalendarien und martyrologien der angelsachsen. Berlin, 1862.
    MORLEY (337), Vol. II, p. 204; TEN BRINK (338).
    IMELMANN (620), pp. 1-55. Authorship, locality, sources, purpose, language, and style.
    BRANDL (5), p. 1093.

Translation (See also Text)
    MORLEY (337), Vol. II, p. 204. Only for May.

Pater Noster

NOTE: There are three versions, beginning respectively (1) Halig fæder, (2) Fæder mancynnes, and (3) þu eart ure fæder.
Bibliography: WÜLKER (3), pp. 374-5.

Text
    THORPE (375), pp. 468-9. Text only of No. 1. With translation.
    THOMSON (459). Text of No. 2. With translation.
    LUMBY (453), pp. 40-9. Poetical paraphrase of No. 3.
    GREIN-WÜLKER (385), Vol. IIb, pp. 227-38; FEILER (460).

Discussion
    THOMSON (459). Only of No. 2.
    FEILER (460); BRANDL (5), pp. 1050, 1093-4.

Pharaoh

Bibliography: WÜLKER (3), p. 236.
Text
    THORPE (375), p. 468. With translation.
    GREIN-WÜLKER (385), Vol. IIIa, p. 182.
Discussion: WÜLKER (3), p. 236.

Proverbs*

Bibliography
WÜLKER (3), pp. 145-6.
623. HOLTHAUSEN, F. Der altenglische Spruch aus Winfrids Zeit. Archiv (25), Vol. 106: 347-8. 1901.

Text
THORPE (375), pp. 469-70. With translation.
624. ZUPITZA, J. Lateinisch-Englische spruECHE. Anglia (36), Vol. 1: 285-6. 1878.
625. WÜLCKER, R. P. Aus englischen bibliotheken. Anglia (36), Vol. 2: 354-87. 1879. Pp. 373-4.
GREIN-WÜLKER (385), Vol. IIb, p. 315. Only the *Proverb from Winfrid's Time.*
ROEDER (894), p. xii; HOLTHAUSEN (386), pp. 400-1.

Discussion
WÜLCKER (625); WÜLKER (3), pp. 145-6; HOLTHAUSEN (623); WILLIAMS (596).
NOTE: The last three of the foregoing discussions deal only with the *Proverb from Winfrid's Time.*

Psalms, Metrical (Paris Psalter and Kentish Psalm)

NOTE: Fragments of metrical versions are found in some of the prose psalters, *q. v.* See also *Benedictine Office.*

Bibliography
WÜLKER (3), pp. 379--84.
BRIGHT AND RAMSAY (895), pp. 149-56.
BRANDL (5), p. 1049 (Kentish Psalm); p. 1094.

Text
626. THORPE, B. Libri psalmorum versio antiqua Latina, cum paraphrasi Anglo-Saxonica. Oxford, 1835. Paris Psalter on pp. 129 ff.
GREIN-WÜLKER (385), Vol. IIIb, pp. 83-230 (Paris Psalter); pp. 231-6 (Kentish Psalm).
SWEET (323), pp. 196-201. Kentish Psalm.

Discussion
WÜLKER (3), pp. 381-4.
627. BRUCE, J. D. The Anglo-Saxon version of the Book of Psalms. Baltimore, 1894.
628. BARTLETT, H. The metrical division of the Paris Psalter. Baltimore, 1896.
629. COOK, A. S. Biblical quotations in Old English prose writers. London and New York, 1898. Excellent discussion of the psalms.
TEN BRINK (338); BRANDL (5), pp. 1048-9 (Kentish Psalm).
629a. RAMSAY, R. L. The Latin text of the Paris Psalter: a collation and some conclusions. Am. Jour. of Phil. (44), Vol. 41: 147-76. 1920.

---

*See also Gnomic Verses, p. 80.

630. BRÜNING, E. Die altenglischen metrischen psalmen in ihrem verhältnis zur lateinischen vorlage. Königsberg, 1921.

Rhyming Poem

Bibliography

WÜLKER (3), pp. 215-7, 515.

631. HOLTHAUSEN F. Das altenglische Reimlied. In Festschrift ... Morsbach (125).
Bibliography, pp. 191-2.

SIEPER (412), pp. 38 ff., 234 ff.; IMELMANN (413), p. 433.

632. MACKIE, W. S. The Old English Rhymed Poem. J. E. G. Ph. (53), Vol. 21: 507-19. 1922. Bibliography, p. 509.

Text

THORPE (375), pp. 352-5. With translation.

GREIN-WÜLKER (385), Vol. IIIa, pp. 156-63. Diplomatic and emended texts.

HOLTHAUSEN (631), pp. 192-9. With notes and German translation.

IMELMANN (413), pp. 426-32. With German translation.

MACKIE (632). With translation and notes.

SEDGEFIELD (322), pp. 120-1.

632a. HOLTHAUSEN, F. Das altenglische Reimlied. E. St. (38), Vol. 65: 181-9. 1931. A new edition with emendations.

Discussion

RIEGER (500), pp. 321-2. This poem is contrasted with Cynewulfian poems.

633. KLUGE, F. Zur geschichte des reimes im altgermanischen. Beitr. (48), Vol. IX: 422-50. 1884. See pp. 440-2, 450.

HOLTHAUSEN (631). A very brief introduction.

SIEPER (412), pp. 234-52. Gives a text also, p. 140, and a German translation.

IMELMANN (413), pp. 421-55; MACKIE (632).

Translation (See also Text)

634. GUEST, E. A history of English rhythms. London, 1838. New edition by W. W. Skeat. London, 1882. Gives a translation (and text), pp. 388-95.

Ruin, The

Bibliography

WÜLKER (3), pp. 211-5; 515; KÖRTING (6), p. 63; KERSHAW (389), pp. 51-3.

Text

THORPE (375), pp. 476-8. With translation.

GREIN-WÜLKER (385), Vol. I, pp. 296-301. Diplomatic and emended texts.

KERSHAW (389), pp. 54-6. With translation.

Discussion

635. EARLE, J. An ancient Saxon poem of a city in ruins. Supposed to be Bath. Bath, 1872.

WÜLKER (625), pp. 376-81. Gives a survey of opinions as to whether the poem refers to a ruined city or a ruined castle.
HICKETIER (607); SIEPER (412), pp. 226-33. Gives a text also, p. 138.
KERSHAW (389), pp. 51-3.

Translation (See also Text)
FAUST AND THOMPSON (397), pp. 78-80.
COOK AND TINKER (391), pp. 56-7. Almost complete.
GORDON (396), pp. 92-3.

Runic Poem, The (Rune Song)

Bibliography
WÜLKER (3), pp. 355-6; KÖRTING (6), pp. 62-3; DICKINS (281), pp. 10-11.

Text
GREIN-WÜLKER (385), Vol. I, pp. 331-7.
DICKINS (281), pp. 12-22. With translation.

Discussion
BRANDL (5), pp. 964-5; DICKINS (281), p. 6; HEUSLER (430), pp. 85-6.
636. GRIENBERGER, T. Das angelsächsische Runengedicht. Anglia (36), Vol. 45; 201-20. 1921.

Salomon and Saturn

Bibliography
WÜLKER (3), pp. 360-7.
637. VON VINCENTI, A. R. Die altenglischen dialoge von Salomon und Saturn. Mit historischer einleitung, kommentar und glossar. I. Leipzig, 1904. Münchener Beitr. (98), Vol. XXXI.
C. H. E. L. (4), pp. 482-3; BRANDL (5), p. 1092; KÖRTING (6), p. 62.
638. MENNER, R. J. The *Vasa Mortis* passage in the Old English *Saloman and Saturn*. In Studies in English Philology (139), pp. 240-57. 1929. Bibliography in footnotes.

Text
639. KEMBLE, J. M. The dialogue of Salomon and Saturnus. London, 1848. With translation. Contains also *Adrian and Ritheus*.
640. SCHIPPER, J. Salomo und Saturn. Germania (50), Vol. 22: 50-70. 1877. Includes the prose inserted after line 169. With translation.
GREIN-WÜLKER (385), Vol. IIIb, pp. 58-82.
VON VINCENTI (637), pp. 103-5.

Discussion
KEMBLE (639); EARLE (332), pp. 210-2; WÜLKER (3), pp. 361-7. MORLEY (337), Vol. II, p. 205; TEN BRINK (338), pp. 88-9.
VON VINCENTI (637); BRANDL (5), p. 1092; MENNER (638), pp. 240-57; SCHÜCKING (345), pp. 31-2.

Seafarer, The

Bibliography
  WÜLKER (3), pp. 207-11; C. H. E. L. (4), p. 474; BRANDL (5), p. 980.
  KÖRTING (6), p. 63; KERSHAW (389), pp. 16-19.

Text
  THORPE (375), pp. 306-13. With translation.
  GREIN-WÜLKER (385), Vol. I, pp. 290-5.
  KERSHAW (389), pp. 20-6. With translation.
  SEDGEFIELD (322), pp. 32-4.
  NOTE: The text is found also in several books of selections, *e.g.*,
  SCHÜCKING (319) and SWEET (323).

Discussion
  RIEGER (500), pp. 331-9.
641. KLUGE, F. Zu altenglischen dichtungen. 1. Der Seefahrer. E. St. (38), Vol. 6: 322-7; 2: Nochmals der Seefahrer. S. St. (38), Vol. 8: 472-4. 1883, 1885.
642. FERRELL, C. C. Old Germanic life in the Anglo-Saxon 'Wanderer' and 'Seafarer.' M. L. N. (26), Vol. 9: 402-7. 1894.
643. BOER, R. C. Wanderer und Seefahrer. Z. f. d. Ph. (78), Vol. 35: 1-28. 1903.
644. LAWRENCE, W. W. The Wanderer and the Seafarer. J. [E.] G. Ph. (53), Vol. 4: 460-80. 1902. Opposes interpretation of BOER (643).
645. EHRISMANN, G. Das gedicht vom Seefahrer. Beitr. (48), Vol. XXXV: 213-18. 1909. Believes the poem didactic—the picture of man striving to leave this world and to gain the heavenly home.
  SIEPER (412), pp. 183-95, 202-8. Gives a text also, p. 127.
  IMELMANN (413), pp. 39-72; KERSHAW (389), pp. 16-19.

Translation (See also Text)
  SPAETH (392), pp. 144-6; COOK AND TINKER (391), pp. 44-9. Iddings' translation.
  GORDON (396), pp. 84-6.

Soul to the Body, Address of the

Bibliography
  WÜLKER (3), pp. 231-3.
646. BATIOUCHKOF, T. Le débat de l'âme et du corps. Romania (73), Vol. 20: 1-55. 1891.
647. ZUPITZA, J. Zu Seele und Leib. Archiv (25), Vol. 91: 369-81. 1893. Survey of the work of preceding critics.
  C. H. E. L. (4), pp. 482-3, 510-11; BRANDL (5), p. 1096.
648. DUDLEY, L. An early homily on the 'Body and Soul' theme. J. E. G. Ph. (53), Vol. 8: 225-53. 1909.
  See pp. 239-42. See also her book *The Egyptian Element in the Legend of the Body and Soul.* Baltimore, 1911.

KÖRTING (6), p. 61; FÖRSTER (380), p. 79.
  NOTE: C. S. Northup has compiled "a full bibliography of the subject, which will be published soon". (Announced in 1925.)

Text
  THORPE (375), pp. 367-74. With translation. Gives also the version from the Vercelli MS., pp. 374-7 (*"A Blessed Soul"*).
  KEMBLE (377), pp. 100-10. With translation.
  GREIN-WÜLKER (385), Vol. IIa, pp. 92-107. Both Exeter and Vercelli texts.

Discussion
649. KLEINERT, G. Über den streit zwischen leib und seele. Halle, 1880.
650. BRUCE, J. D. "A contribution to the study of 'The Body and the Soul': Poems in English." M. L. N. (26), Vol. 5: 385-401. 1890.
650a. BUCHHOLZ, R. Die fragmente der Rede der Seele an den Leichnam. Erlanger Beiträge zur englischen Philologie, Vol. VI. Erlangen and Leipzig, 1890. Gives two late texts and much discussion.
  BATIOUCHKOF (646); ZUPITZA (647); DEERING (457), *passim*.
  GRAU (458), pp. 174-5; DUDLEY (648).
650b. KURTZ, B. P. Gifer the worm. An essay toward the history of an idea. Univ. of Cal. Pub. in Eng. (110), Vol. II, no. 1, pp. 235-61. 1929.

Translation (*See also Text*): GORDON (396), pp. 310-13.

Thureth, Praise of

Bibliography: BRANDL (5), p. 1080.

Text
651. NAPIER, A. S. Contributions to Old English lexicography. Trans. Philol. Soc. (108). 1906. See p. 35.

Discussion: BRANDL (5), p. 1079.

Waldhere

Bibliography
  WÜLKER (3), pp. 315-17; C. H. E. L. (4), p. 474; BRANDL (5), p. 988.
  KÖRTING (6), pp. 38-9; DICKINS (281), pp. 50-1; HOLTHAUSEN (468).
  SCHÜCKING (657), *passim;* SCHNEIDER (370), pp. 343-4.

Text
  GREIN-WÜLKER (385), Vol. I, pp. 7-13.
  SEDGEFIELD (465), pp. 105-7.
  DICKINS (281), pp. 52-62. With translation.
  HOLTHAUSEN (468); KLAEBER (462), pp. 266-8.

Discussion
652. HEINZEL, R. Über die Walthersage. Vienna, 1888.
653. LEARNED, M. D. The saga of Walter of Aquitaine. Baltimore, 1892.
654. ALTHOF, H. Waltharii poesis. Leipzig, 1899-1905.
  SYMONS (347), pp. 703-9.

655. TRAUTMANN, M. Zur berichtigung und erklärung der Waldere-
bruchstücke. Bo. Beitr. (83), Vol. V: 162 ff. 1900. Zum zweiten
Waldere-bruchstück. Bo. Beitr. (83), Vol. XI: 133-8. 1901.
BRANDL (5), pp. 986-8; CLARKE (349), pp. 209-31.
CHAMBERS (661), pp. 40-8, 60-3. On Theodoric, Attila, Guthhere.
DICKINS (281), pp. 37-43.
656. LEITZMANN, A. Walther und Hildegunde bei den Angelsachsen.
Halle, 1917.
HEUSLER, in HOOPS (12), Vol. IV, 476.
657. SCHÜCKING, L. L. Waldere und Waltherius. E. St. (38), Vol. 60:
17-36. 1925.
Schücking believes that Waldere was the entirely conscious
creation of an Anglo-Saxon cleric court-poet.

Translation (See also Text)
GUMMERE (393), pp. 167-70; FAUST AND THOMPSON (397), pp. 30-3.
GORDON (396), pp. 73-4.

Facsimile
658. HOLTHAUSEN, F. Die altenglischen Waldere-bruchstücke. Mit 4
autotypien. Göteborg, 1899.

Wanderer, The

Bibliography
WÜLKER (3), pp. 205-7; C. H. E. L. (4), p. 474; BRANDL (5), p. 980.

Text
THORPE (375), pp. 286-93. With translation.
GREIN-WÜLKER (385), Vol. I, pp. 284-9.
GOLLANCZ (376), pp. 286-92. With translation.
KERSHAW (389), pp. 8-14. With translation.
SEDGEFIELD (322), pp. 28-31; FLOM (263), pp. 272-5.
NOTE: The text is found also in other books of selections.

Discussion
RIEGER (500), pp. 324-31; FERRELL (642).
BOER, R. C. (643). Wanderer und Seefahrer. Z. f. d. Ph. (78), Vol.
35: 1-28. 1903.
LAWRENCE (644); SIEPER (412), pp. 196-201, 202-8. Gives a text
also, p. 130.
IMELMANN (413), pp. 118-44; KERSHAW (389), pp. 1-7.

Translation (See also Text)
SPAETH (392), pp. 140-4; COOK AND TINKER (391), pp. 50-5. E. H.
Hickey's translation.
GORDON (396), pp. 81-3.

Werferth's Preface to Gregory's Dialogues*

Bibliography
659. HOLTHAUSEN, F. Die alliterierende vorrede zur altenglischen über-

---

*See also Part XI: Werferth.

setzung von Gregors Dialogen. Archiv (25), Vol. 105: 367-9. 1900.
HOLTHAUSEN (386), p. 402.

Text
HOLTHAUSEN (659), pp. 367-8.
660. COOK, A. S. An unsuspected bit of Old English verse. M.L.N. (26), Vol. 17: 13-20. 1902. With translation.
HOLTHAUSEN (386), p. 402.

Discussion
KELLER (919), pp. 6 ff., 92 ff.; HOLTHAUSEN (659), pp. 368-9.
COOK (660); BRANDL (5), p. 1063.

Widsith

Bibliography
WÜLKER (3), pp. 318-30; BRANDL (5), p. 969.
661. CHAMBERS, R. W. Widsith: A study in Old English heroic legend. Cambridge [Eng.], 1912. An indispensable work for students of Germanic legend. Bibliography, pp. 225-35.
HOLTHAUSEN (468). Beowulf.

Text
THORPE (375), pp. 318-27. With translation.
GREIN-WÜLKER (385), Vol. I, pp. 1-6.
CHAMBERS (661), pp. 188-224. With translation and very copious notes. The standard edition.
HOLTHAUSEN (468). Beowulf.
SEDGEFIELD (322), pp. 2-5. A text is given also in SEDGEFIELD (465), pp. 101-5.

Discussion
MÖLLER (478), pp. 1-39. Prints the text in strophic form, part 2, pp. i-vi.
C. H. E. L. (4), (chapter by Chadwick) pp. 37-40.
662. LAWRENCE, W. W. Structure and interpretation of Widsith. M. Ph. (56), Vol. 4: 329-74. 1906.
BRANDL (5), pp. 966-9. SARRAZIN (411), pp. 52-61.
CHAMBERS (661). Full discussion of the legends. Critical survey of work to 1912.
663. SIEBS, T. Widsith. In Festschrift Wilhelm Viëtor (123), pp. 296-309.
664. JORDAN, R. in HOOPS (12), Reallexikon, Vol. IV, pp. 520-6. 1918.
665. SIEVERS, E. Zum Widsith. In Texte und Forschungen (127), pp. 1-19.
Application of his latest views on metrics, melody, etc. Contains a text as Sievers prefers it, followed by a discussion of the old and the added sections of the poem. His decisions are based largely on metrical grounds.
666. GRIENBERGER, T. Widsith. Anglia (36), Vol. 46: 347-82. 1922. Notes on many lines of the poem.
COOK (483); HEUSLER (430), pp. 86-9. A penetrating analysis.

667. MUCH, R. Widsith. Beiträge zu einem commentar. Z. f. d. A. (79), Vol. 62: 113-50. 1925.

Translation (See also Text)
  GUEST (634), pp. 374-87; GUMMERE (393), p. 191-200.
  COOK AND TINKER (391), pp. 3-8. Morley's translation.
  GORDON (396), pp. 75-8.

Wife's Complaint, The

Bibliography
  WÜLKER (3), pp. 224-6.
668. SCHÜCKING, L. L. Das angelsächsische gedicht von der Klage der Frau. Z. f. d. A. (79), Vol. 48: 436-49. 1906. Valuable critical discussion of previous work on the poem.
669. STEFANOVIČ, S. Das angelsächsische gedicht Die Klage der Frau. Anglia (36), Vol. 32: 399-433. 1909. Critical summary of previous work. Valuable.
  C. H. E. L. (4), p. 475; KERSHAW (389), pp. 28-30.

Text
  THORPE (375), pp. 441-4. With translation.
  GREIN-WÜLKER (385), Vol. I, pp. 302-5.
  STEFANOVIČ (669), pp. 419-20. The text is arranged in strophes.
  SEDGEFIELD (322), pp. 35-6; KERSHAW (389), pp. 32-4. With translation.

Discussion
  HICKETIER (607); TRAUTMANN (605); ROEDER (173), pp. 112-19.
  SCHÜCKING (668). See also SCHÜCKING (319), pp. 18-19.
  IMELMANN (407). Regards the first *Riddle* of the *Exeter Book, The Husband's Message,* and this poem as a trilogy and connected with the Odoacer story.
670. LAWRENCE, W. W. The Banished Wife's Lament. M. Ph. (56), Vol. 5:387-405. 1908.
  STEFANOVIČ (669); SIEPER (412), pp. 215-16, 217-25. Gives a text also, p. 136.
  IMELMANN (413), pp. 1-38. See also pp. 73-117, *passim.*
  KERSHAW (389), pp. 28-31.

Translation (See also Text)
  FAUST AND THOMPSON (397), pp. 72-4.
  COOK AND TINKER (391), pp. 64-6. A. Henry's translation.
  GORDON (396), pp. 87-8.

William the Conqueror

Bibliography: SEDGEFIELD (612), p. 50.

Text
  EARLE-PLUMMER (792), Vol. I, pp. 220-1.
  SEDGEFIELD (612), pp. 30-1; SEDGEFIELD (322), pp. 123-4.

Discussion
  ABEGG (402), pp. 99-101; SEDGEFIELD (612), pp. lx-x, xxi.

671. HOLTHAUSEN, F. Das altenglische gedict auf Wilhelm den Eroberer. Anglia Beibl. (37), Vol. 36:110-11. 1925.
Translation: THORPE (793), Vol. II, pp. 189-90.

Wonders of Creation, The
Bibliography: WÜLKER (3), pp. 234-5; BRANDL (5), p. 1047.
Text
  THORPE (375), pp. 346-52. With translation.
  GREIN-WÜLKER (385), Vol. IIIa, pp. 152-5.
Discussion: WÜLKER (3), pp. 234-5; BRANDL (5), p. 1047.

Worcester Fragment
BRANDL (5), p. 1133. Gives text, bibliography, and brief discussion.

PART XI

PROSE

A. Modern Collections
B. Translations
C. History and Criticism
D. Authors and Monuments

A. Modern Collections

672. GREIN, C. W. M., AND R. WÜLKER. Bibliothek der angelsächsischen prosa. Cassel and Göttingen, 1872—
    To date eleven volumes have appeared in this excellent series of Old English texts.

NOTE: Most of the modern collections are restricted in scope and are therefore listed subsequently in connection with the monuments which they include. The following collections are listed here for convenience:

673. COCKAYNE, O. Narratiunculae anglice conscriptae. London, 1861.
674. COCKAYNE, O. Leechdoms, wortcunning, and starcraft of early England. Being a collection of documents . . . illustrating the history of science in this country before the Norman conquest. 3 vols. London, 1864-6.
675. COCKAYNE, O. The shrine. A collection of occasional papers on dry subjects. 13 numbers. London, 1864-9.

B. Translations

676. COOK, A. S., AND C. B. TINKER. Select translations from Old English prose. Boston, 1908.
The Cambridge book of prose and verse (398).

C. History and Criticism

677. TUPPER, J. W. Tropes and figures in Anglo-Saxon prose. Baltimore, 1897.
677a. SAINTSBURY, G. A history of English prose rhythm. London, 1912. Reprinted 1922.
    See ch. II "Old English Prose Rhythm", pp. 10-42. See also pp. 102-5.
NOTE: See also Part IX: A. HISTORY AND CRITICISM.

D. Authors and Monuments

NOTE: Linguistic studies for many of the following prose monuments are listed in KENNEDY (8), pp. 123-31, under the names of the monuments.

Adrian and Ritheus

Bibliography
WÜLKER (3), p. 501; BRANDL (5), p. 1128.

Text
678. WRIGHT T. Adrian and Ritheus, in Altdeutsche Blätter (ed. by Haupt and Hoffman), Vol. II, pp. 189-93. Leipzig, 1840.
KEMBLE (639), pp. 198-207. With translation.

Discussion
KEMBLE (639), pp. 198 ff. and 206-11.
678a. FÖRSTER, M. Zu Adrian und Ritheus. E. St. (38), Vol. 23: 431-6. 1897.

Aelfric

a) Abgarus—*See* (q) Lives of the Saints
b) Admonitio ad Filium Spiritualem, St. Basil's—*See* (m) Homilies
c) Bible, Translations of the
d) Canons
e) Colloquy
f) De Consuetudine Monachorum, Excerpts from Aethelwold's
g) De Temporibus, Bede's
h) Esther
i) Glossary
j) Grammar
k) Heptateuch
l) Hexameron of St. Basil (*Exameron Anglice*)
m) Homilies
n) Interrogations of Sigewulf
o) Job
p) Judith
q) Lives of the Saints
r) Old and New Testaments, On the
s) Pastoral Letters

Bibliography (and General Discussion)
WÜLKER (3), pp. 452-6.

679. WHITE, C. L. Aelfric: A new study of his life and writings. Y. St. (119), Vol. II. 1898.
   Excellent classified and chronological bibliography. Valuable discussions of Aelfric's works and of those works sometimes attributed to him. Appendices contain convenient summaries of important studies concerned with Aelfric.
SKEAT (706); C. H. E. L. (4), pp. 492-4; KÖRTING (6), p. 71.

680. GEM, S. H. An Anglo-Saxon Abbott: Aelfric of Eynsham. Edinburgh, 1912.
   Not of much bibliographical value, but a useful survey of Aelfric's life and writings.

680a. JOST, K. Unechte Aelfrictexte. Anglia (36), Vol. 51: 81-103, 177-219. 1927. See also G. H. GEROULD. Abbot Aelfric's rhythmic prose. M. Ph. (56), Vol. 22: 353-66. 1925.
NOTE: See also the article on Aelfric in the *Encyclopaedia Britannica* and *The Dictionary of National Biography*.
  a. Abgarus—*See* (*q*) Lives of the Saints.
  b. Admonitio ad Filium Spiritualem, St. Basil's—*See* (*m*) Homilies.

  c. Bible, Translations of the
NOTE: Aelfric translated or gave homiletic renderings of the Pentateuch, Joshua, Kings, Esther, Judith, Job, and Maccabees.

Bibliography
  WÜLKER (3), pp. 467-71; WHITE (679), p. 212.
  BRANDL (5), p. 1109; FÖRSTER (829), *passim*.
681. CRAWFORD, S. J. The Old English version of the Heptateuch, etc. E. E. T. S. (87), Vol. CLX. 1922.
  Contains also Aelfric's *Treatise on the Old and New Testament*, his preface to *Genesis*, and the Vulgate text of the *Heptateuch*. Bibliography, pp. 12-14.

Text
  GREIN-WÜLKER (672), Vol. 1 (ed. by Grein) : Alfrik de vetere et novo testamento, Pentateuch, Iosua, Buch der Richter und Hiob. 1872. (Anastatic reprint, Hamburg, 1921.)
  SKEAT (706). Vol. LXXXII, pp. 384-413 (Kings); Vol. XCIV, pp. 66-125 (Maccabees). With translation.
682. GREIN-WÜLKER (672), Vol. 3 (ed by Assmann) : Angelsächsische homilien und heiligenleben. 1889.
  Contains *Esther* and *Judith*. Assmann also printed *Esther* in metrical form in Anglia (36), Vol. 9: 27-38 (1886) and *Judith* in Anglia (36), Vol. 10: 87-104. (1888.)
683. CHASE, F. H. A new text of the Old English prose Genesis. Archiv (25), Vol. 100: 241-66. 1898.
  Gives some six chapters of two MSS.
  CRAWFORD (687), pp. 2-6 (Lincoln fragment); CRAWFORD (681).

Discussion
684. ASSMANN, B. Abt Aelfrics angelsächsische bearbeitung des buches Esther. Herausgegeben und mit einer einleitung über überlieferung und verfasserschaft versehen. Halle, 1885.
685. ASSMANN, B. Abt Aelfric's angelsächsische homilie über das buch Judith. Anglia (36), Vol. 10: 76-104. 1888.
  I. Einleitung. II. Ueberlieferung. III. Verfasserschaft. IV. Text.
686. FÖRSTER, M. Aelfric's sogenannte Hiob-Übersetzung. Anglia (36), Vol. 15: 473-7. 1893. See also FÖRSTER (829), p. 57.
  WHITE (679), especially pp. 146-51.
  COOK (609), pp. lxxi-lxxiii. Aelfric's homily on Judith.
  BRANDL (5), pp. 1107-9.

687. CRAWFORD, S. J. The Lincoln fragment of the Old English version of the Heptateuch. M. L. R. (27), Vol. 15: 1-6. 1920.
CRAWFORD (681), pp. 1-12.
NOTE: *See also* (*m*) Homilies, for *Esther, Judith, Job*, and *Maccabees*.
Translation: See SKEAT (706) (*Text* above), and AELFRIC: (*m*) Homilies: *Translation*.
  d. Canons—*See* (*s*) Pastoral Letters.

      e. Colloquy

Bibliography
WÜLKER (3), pp. 476-7; WHITE (679), p. 212.
BRANDL (5), p. 1107; FÖRSTER (883), p. 39; KÖRTING (6), p. 71.

Text
THORPE (601), pp. 18-36.
688. WRIGHT, T. Anglo-Saxon and Old English vocabularies. I: 89-101. 2d edition by R. Wülker. London, 1884.
688a. STEVENSON, W. H. Early scholastic colloquies. Anecdota Oxoniensia, Medieval and Modern Series, Part XV. Oxford, 1929. Gives the Old English glosses from Codex Cott. Tib. A III, and, at the foot of the page, occasional Old English glosses found in the St. John's College MS.

Discussion
689. DIETRICH, E. Abt Aelfrik. Zur literaturgeschichte der angelsächsischen kirche. Zeitschrift für die historische Theologie, Vol. 25: 487-594 (1855); Vol. 26: 163-256 (1856). Gotha. Much of it is translated in WHITE (679).
WÜLKER (3), pp. 476-7.
690. ZUPITZA, J. Die ursprüngliche gestalt von Älfrics Colloquium. Z. f. d. A. (79), Vol. 31:32-45. 1887.
WHITE (679), pp. 41-2, 121-4.
691. SCHRÖDER, E. Colloquium Aelfrici. Z. f. d. A. (79), Vol. 41: 283-90. 1897.

  f. De Consuetudine Monachorum, Excerpts from Aethelwold's*

Bibliography
BRANDL (5), p. 1099; GROSS (145) pp. 275-6.

Text
692. SCHRÖER, A. De Consuetudine Monachorum. E. St. (38), Vol. 9: 294-6. 1886.
693. BRECK, E. A fragment of Aelfric's translation of Aethelwold's De Consuetudine Monachorum and its relation to other manuscripts. Leipzig, 1887.

Discussion
DIETRICH (689), Vol. 25, p. 541; SCHRÖER (692), pp. 290-4.
BRECK (693), pp. 3-15; BATESON (771), pp. 700-7.
WHITE (679), pp. 159-64; FEILER (460).

See also Aethelwold.

694. FEHR, B. Das Benedictiner—Offizium und die beziehungen zwischen Aelfric und Wulfstan. E. St. (38), Vol. 46: 337-46. 1913.

g. *De Temporibus*, Bede's

Bibliography
WÜLKER (3), pp. 477-8; WHITE (679), p. 211.

Text
695. WRIGHT, T. Popular treatises on science. London, 1841. See pp. 1-19. With translation.
COCKAYNE (674), Vol. III, pp. 232-81. Contains also some discussion.

Discussion
DIETRICH (689), Vol. 25, pp. 493-5.

696. REUM, A. De Temporibus, ein echtes werk des Abtes Aelfric. Anglia (36), Vol. 10: 457-98. 1888. Resumé in WHITE (679), pp. 188-92.
WHITE (679), pp. 124-5.

h. Esther—*See* (c) Bible.

i. Glossary

Bibliography
WÜLKER (3), pp. 461-2; WHITE (679), p. 211; BRANDL (5), p. 1107.

Text
697. ZUPITZA, J. Aelfrics grammatik und glossar. Berlin, 1880. Preferred text.
WRIGHT-WÜLKER (688), Vol. I, pp. 104-91.

Discussion
WHITE (679), pp. 120-1; BRANDL (5), pp. 1106-7. See also KENNEDY (8), pp. 123-4.

j. Grammar

Bibliography
WÜLKER (3), pp. 461-2; WHITE (679), p. 211.
BRANDL (5), p. 1107; KÖRTING (6), p. 73.

Text: ZUPITZA (697).

Discussion
WHITE (679), pp. 119-20; BRANDL (5), pp. 1106-7.
FÖRSTER (705), p. 131. Brief mention of the Paris fragment. See also KENNEDY (8), pp. 123-4, for material on Aelfric's *Grammar*.

k. Heptateuch—*See* (c) Bible.

l. Hexameron of St. Basil (*Exameron Anglice*)—*See* (m) Homilies.

m. Homilies

NOTE: The following free renderings of the Bible and the Apocrypha have often been regarded as homilies: *Esther, Job, Judith* (if Aelfric wrote it), and *Maccabees*. The so-called version of St. Basil's *Hexameron* (*Exameron Anglice*) and *Admonitio ad Filium Spiritualem* are also treated here as homilies.

Bibliography
   WÜLKER (3), pp. 457-81, *passim;* WHITE (679), pp. 211-2.
   BRANDL (5), pp. 1104-5; KÖRTING (6), pp. 71-2; FÖRSTER (829), *passim.*
   GREIN-WÜLKER (672), Vol. 10 (702), (ed. by S. J. Crawford), pp. 30-2.

Text
698. THORPE, B. The homilies of the Anglo-Saxon Church. The first part, containing the Sermones Catholici, or Homilies of Aelfric. ... 2 vols. London, 1844-6. With translation.
699. NORMAN, H. W. The Anglo-Saxon version of the Hexameron of St. Basil. ... London, 1849. With translation. Contains also the *Admonitio ad Filium Spiritualem.*
   MORRIS (830). E. E. T. S. (87), Vol. XXXIV: 101-19, 296-304.
   NAPIER (923). Contains *On the Sevenfold Gifts of the Holy Spirit* and *De Falsis Deis.*
700. SWEET, H. Selected homilies of Aelfric. Oxford, 1885. 2d ed. Oxford, 1896.
   GREIN-WÜLKER (672), Vol. 3, (682) (ed. by B. Assmann): Angelsächsische homilien und heiligenleben. 1889. Contains *Esther, Judith,* and others by Aelfric.
   BROTANEK (452), pp. 3-27. Contains two of Aelfric's homilies for the consecration of a church.
701. WARNER, R. D-N. Early English homilies from ... Vesp. D. XIV. E. E. T. S. (87), Vol. CLII. 1917. Mostly Aelfric's.
702. GREIN-WÜLKER (672), Vol. 10 (ed. by S. J. Crawford): Exameron anglice, or the Old English Hexameron. With an introduction, a collation of all the manuscripts, a modern English translation, parallel passages from the other works of Aelfric and notes on the sources. 1921.

Discussion
   NORMAN (699). Discusses the *Admonitio* and the *Hexameron.*
   DIETRICH (689), Vol. 25: 506-15; Vol. 26: 181, 228-30.
   WÜLKER (3), pp. 457-81, *passim.*
   GREIN-WÜLKER (672), Vol. 3 (682), pp. 246-65, *passim.*
703. FÖRSTER, M. Über die quellen von Aelfrics exegetischen Homiliae Catholicae. I Legenden. Berlin, 1892. II Exegetische Homilien. Anglia (36), Vol. 16: 1-61. 1894. Additional note in E. St. (38), Vol. 28: 421-3. 1900.
   WHITE (679), pp. 101-18; BRANDL (5), pp. 1102-6.
   BROTANEK (452), pp. 49-128. See FÖRSTER (705) and FÖRSTER (829), *passim.*
   GREIN-WÜLKER (672), Vol. 10 (702). See *Text* above.
704. EMERSON, O. F. Aelfrics Hexameron. Archiv (25), Vol. 145: 254-6. 1923.

705. FÖRSTER, M. Die altenglischen texte der Pariser Nationalbibliothek. In Schröer Festschrift (137), pp. 113-31.
    He discusses (pp. 116-21) the two homilies printed and discussed by BROTANEK (452), and also (pp. 130-1) the Paris fragment of *De Falsis Deis.*
705a. SISAM, K. MSS. Bodley 340 and 342: Aelfric's *Catholic Homilies.* R. E. S. (70), Vol. 7: 7-22. 1931. To be concluded.
NOTE: See also (c) Translations of the Bible.

Translation: SKEAT (706).

n. Interrogations of Sigewulf—*See* (q) Lives of the Saints.
o. Job—*See* (c) Bible, p. 97, and (m) Homilies.
p. Judith—*See* (c) Bible, p. 97, and (m) Homilies.

                q. Lives of the Saints

NOTE: The *Abgarus* and the *Interrogations of Sigewulf* are included in the manuscript of the *Lives of the Saints.*

Bibliography
706. SKEAT, W. W. Aelfric's lives of the saints, being a set of sermons on saints' days. E. E. T. S. (87), Vol. LXXVI, LXXXII, XCIV, CXIV. 1881-1900.
    WÜLKER (3), pp. 462-5, 467; WHITE (679), p. 212.
    BRANDL (5), p. 1104; KÖRTING (6), p. 72.

Text
    SKEAT (706). With translation. Does not contain the *Interrogations of Sigewulf.*
707. MACLEAN, G. E. Aelfric's version of Alcuini Interrogationes Sigeuulfi in Genesin. Anglia (36), Vol. 7: 1-59. 1884. Old English and Latin texts.
708. TESSMANN, A. Aelfrics altenglische bearbeitung der Interrogationes Sigewulfi presbyteri in Genesin des Alcuin. Berlin, 1891.

              r. Old and New Testaments, On the
Bibliography
    WÜLKER (3), pp. 473-4; WHITE (679), p. 212; CRAWFORD (681), pp. 12-14.

Text
    GREIN-WÜLKER (672), Vol. I (ed. by Grein): Älfric de vetere et novo testamento, etc. 1872. See also ASSMANN (682), pp. 81-91.
    CRAWFORD (681), pp. 15-75. With translation.

Discussion
    DIETRICH (689), Vol. 25: 516-22; Vol. 26: 231ff.
    SKEAT (706). Mostly concerning the manuscripts.
709. MACLEAN, G. E. Aelfric's version of Alcuini Interrogationes Sigeuulfi in Genesin. Anglia (36), Vol. 6: 425-73. 1883.
710. MITCHELL, F. H. Aelfrics Sigewulfi Interrogationes in Genesin. Zürich, 1888. Critical revision of the text in MACLEAN (709).
    TESSMANN (708). Only *Interrogations.*

711. OTT, J. H. Über die quellen der heiligenleben in Älfrics Lives of the Saints. Halle, 1892.
FÖRSTER (703); WHITE (679), pp. 57, 126-31, 195-6.

Discussion
DIETRICH (689), Vol. 25: 501-5; Vol. 26: 227, 235.
WHITE (679), pp. 152-5; CRAWFORD (681), pp. 1-12, *passim*.

Translation
712. L'ISLE, W. Divers ancient monuments in the Saxon tongue, etc. London, 1638. Reprinted in CRAWFORD (681), pp. 15-75.

s. Pastoral Letters

Bibliography
WÜLKER (3), pp. 471-3, 475-6; WHITE (679), p. 212.

713. GREIN-WÜLKER (672), Vol. 9 (ed. by B. Fehr): Die hirtenbriefe Aelfrics in altenglischer und lateinischer fassung, hrsg, und mit übersetzung und einleitung versehen. 1914. See also Fehr's article in E. St. (38), Vol. 52: 285-8. 1918.

Text
THORPE (803), pp. 441-65. With translation.
GREIN-WÜLKER (672), Vol. 9 (713). See *Bibliography* above. Translated into German. See also ASSMANN (682), pp. 1-12, 243-6.

Discussion
DIETRICH (689), *passim*; WHITE (679), pp. 135-45.
GREIN-WÜLKER (672), Vol. 9 (713). See *Bibliography* above.

Aethelwold

a. De Consuetudine Monachorum—*See* Benedictine Rule, p. 109, and Aelfric: (f) De Consuetudine Monachorum.
b. Edgar's Establishment of Monasteries.

Bibliography: BRANDL (5), p. 1101.
Text: COCKAYNE (674), Vol. III, pp. 432-45.

Discussion
COCKAYNE (674), Vol. III, pp. 406ff.
LIEBERMANN (773); BRANDL (5), pp. 1100-1.

Alcuin's (Pseudo-Alcuinian) De Virtutibus et Vitiis, Translation of

Bibliography: FÖRSTER (829), pp. 55-6.

Text
714. ASSMANN, B. Übersetzung von Alcuin's De Virtutibus et Vitiis Liber. Ad Widonem comitem. Anglia (36), Vol. 11: 371-91. 1889. Text and Latin original, with a few textual notes.
NOTE: A critical text was promised in 1920 by M. Förster (829), p. 56.

Alexander to Aristotle, Letter of

Bibliography
WÜLKER (3), pp. 504-5.

715. RYPINS, S. Three Old English prose texts in MS. Cotton Vitellius A XV. E. E. T. S. (87), Vol. CLXI. 1924. See also his article in M. L. N. (26), Vol. 38: 216-20. 1923.
Contains *Alexander to Aristotle, Wonders of the East, Life of St. Christopher,* Latin versions of all three, introduction, and notes.

Text
COCKAYNE (673), pp. 1-33. Collation by A. HOLDER in Anglia (36), Vol. 1: 507-12.
716. BASKERVILLE, W. M. Epistola Alexandri ad Aristotelem. Anglia (36), Vol. 4: 139-67. 1881.
RYPINS (715), pp. 1-50. Gives also one page of facsimile.

Discussion
COCKAYNE (673), pp. 67-76; RYPINS (715), pp. vii-xlvii, *passim*.
717. PFISTER, F. Auf den spuren Alexanders des Groszen in der älteren englischen literatur. G.—R. Mon. (51), Vol. 16: 81-86. 1928. Gives supplementary bibliography and brief discussion.

Alfred

a) Augustine's Soliloquies (Blooms of Alfred)
b) Bede's Ecclesiastical History
c) Boethius' Consolations of Philosophy
d) Gregory's Pastoral Care
e) Laws
f) Orosius' History of the World
g) Psalms
h) Miscellaneous: Alfred's Jewel, Alfred's Charters, Alfred's Will, Alfred's Hand-Book.

General
PAULI, R. (745), König Alfred und seine stelle in der geschichte Englands. Berlin, 1851. Translated by T. Wright: Life of King Alfred. London, 1852; and by B. Thorpe: Life of Alfred the Great. London, 1853.
The Whole works of King Alfred the Great (727) : with preliminary essays illustrative of the history, arts, and manners of the ninth century. London, 1858.
718. BOWKER, A. (ed.) Alfred the Great. Containing chapters on his life and times. London, 1899.
719. STEVENSON, W. H. (ed.) Asser's Life of King Alfred, together with the annals of St. Neots erroneously ascribed to Asser. Oxford, 1904.
Valuable introduction and notes. Asser's Life of King Alfred has been translated from Stevenson's edition by A. S. Cook (Boston, 1906) and by L. C. Jane (London, 1924).

Bibliography
WÜLKER (3), pp. [387]-398. General bibliography and survey.

720. PLUMMER, C. The life and times of Alfred the Great. Oxford, 1902. Pp. 139-96, *passim*. Valuable discussions of his works, their sources, and his life.
   GROSS (145), pp. 300-304.
721. LEES, B. A. Alfred the Great, the truthteller, maker of England, 848-899. New York, 1915. Good discussions of his works, pp. 321-89. The best biography. Bibliography, pp. 469-71.
   SONNENSCHEIN (147), part III, pp. 1166-67.

   a. Augustine's Soliloquies (Blooms of Alfred)

Bibliography
   WÜLKER (3), pp. 415-20.
722. HARGROVE, H. L. King Alfred's Old English version of St. Augustine's Soliloquies, edited with introduction, notes, and glossary. Y. St. (119), Vol. VIII. 1902.
723. GREIN-WÜLKER (672), Vol. 11 (ed. by W. Endter): König Alfred der grosse: bearbeitung der Soliloquien des Augustinus. 1922. Excellent bibliography, pp. viii-ix.

Text
   COCKAYNE (675), pp. 163-204.
724. HULME, W. H. 'Blooms' von König Alfred. E. St. (38), Vol. 18: 332-56. 1893. Corrections in E. St. (38), Vol. 19: 470. 1894.
   HARGROVE (722), pp. 1-70. Gives also two pages of facsimile.
   GREIN-WÜLKER (672), Vol. 11 (723). See *Bibliography* above.

Discussion
725. WÜLKER, R. P. Über die angelsaechische bearbeitung der Soliloquien Augustins. Beitr. (48), Vol. 4: 101-31. 1877. Considers the sources and authorship.
   WÜLKER (3), pp. 417 ff.
726. HUBBARD, F. G. The relation of the Blooms of King Alfred to the Anglo-Saxon translation of Boethius. M. L. N. (26), Vol. 9: 321-42. 1894. Comparison to show identity of authorship.
   HARGROVE (722), pp. xv-lvii.
   GREIN-WÜLKER (672), Vol. 11 (723). See *Bibliography* above.

Translation
727. GILES, J. A. (ed.). The whole works of King Alfred the Great. Jubilee edition. 3 vols. in 2. London, 1858. E. Thomson's translation of the Soliloquies, Vol. III, pp. 83-118.
728. HARGROVE, H. L. King Alfred's Old English version of St. Augustine's Soliloquies turned into Modern English. Y. St. (119), Vol. XXII. 1904.

   b. Bede's Ecclesiastical History

Bibliography
   WÜLKER (3), pp. 404-6.
729. MILLER, T. The Old English version of Bede's Ecclesiastical History of the English People. E. E. T. S. (87), Vol. XCV, XCVI. 1890-91.

Introduction, text, and translation. A collation by Miller of four MSS. of Bede's History appears in E. E. T. S. (87), Vol. CX, CXI (1898).

730. SCHIPPER, J. Die geschichte und der gegenwärtige stand der forschung über König Alfreds übersetzung von Bedas Kirchengeschichte. Sitzungsberichte der Wiener Akad. der Wiss., Phil. hist. Klasse, Vol. 138. 1898.

731. GREIN-WÜLKER (672), Vol. 4 (ed. by J. Schipper): König Alfreds übersetzung von Bedas Kirchengeschichte. 1899.

Introduction, Latin and Old English texts, and notes. For bibliography, see especially pp. xxxv-xxxviii.

C. H. E. L. (4), pp. 487-8, 490.

BRANDL (5), p. 1070; GROSS (145), pp. 239-40.

Text

MILLER (729). With translation. Gives one page of facsimile.

GREIN-WÜLKER (672), Vol. 4 (731). See *Bibliography* above. Gives two pages of facsimile.

Discussion

MILLER (729), pp. xiii-lix, ix-xxii.

SCHIPPER (730). Largely superseded by the introduction to his edition.

GREIN-WÜLKER (672), Vol. 4 (731), pp. x-xlv. See *Bibliography* above.

732. VANDRAAT, P. F. The authorship of the Old English Bede. Anglia (36), Vol. 39: 319-47. 1916. "A study in rhythm." Supports the hypothesis of non-Alfredian authorship.

Translation

Whole Works of King Alfred (727), Vol. II, pp. 201-413. E. Thomson's translation.

c. Boethius' Consolations of Philosophy

See also Part X: Boethius, p. 62.

Bibliography

WÜLKER (3), pp. 412-15.

733. SEDGEFIELD, W. J. King Alfred's Old English version of Boethius De Consolatione Philosophiae. Oxford, 1899. Gives introduction, critical notes, and glossary. For bibliography, see especially pp. xxi-xxv. Good discussion.

C. H. E. L. (4), pp. 487-8, 490; FEHLAUER (503), pp. 9-10.

Text

734. Fox, S. King Alfred's Anglo-Saxon version of Boethius De Consolatione Philosophiae. Bohn's Antiquarian Library. London, 1864.

Contains also English translation, notes, and glossary. This text, with translation, was reissued in 1890.

SEDGEFIELD (733). The standard text.

Discussion
735. STEWART, H. F. Boethius, an essay. Edinburgh, 1891. Appreciation of Alfred's translation, pp. 170-78.
736. SCHEPSS, G. Zu König Alfreds Boethius. Archiv (25), Vol. 94: 149-60. 1895.
   SEDGEFIELD (733), pp. xxv-xli; SEDGEFIELD (737), pp. xi-lii.
   FEHLAUER (503), pp. 9-31.

Translation
   Whole Works, etc. (727), Vol. II, pp. 421-537.
737. SEDGEFIELD, W. J. King Alfred's version of the Consolations of Boethius. Done into modern English, with an introduction. Oxford, 1900.
   "The prose part is rendered quite literally .... In the version of the alliterating verses ... the metre of the original Old English has been retained as far as is allowed by the limitations of modern English, but literalness has not been thereby sacrificed."—Preface.

d. Gregory's Pastoral Care

Bibliography
   WÜLKER (3), pp. 401-3; C. H. E. L. (4), pp. 487-8, 490.
   KÖRTING (6), p. 67.

Text
738. SWEET, H. King Alfred's West-Saxon version of Gregory's Pastoral Care. E. E. T. S. (87), Vol. XLV, L. 1871-2.
   Contains also English translation, Latin text, notes, and introduction.

Discussion
   SWEET (738), pp. xiii-xlii. Considers chiefly the manuscripts and the language.
739. DEWITZ, A. Untersuchungen über Älfreds des Grossen westsächsische übersetzung der Cura Pastoralis Gregors und ihr verhältnis zum original. Bunzlau, 1889.
740. WACK, G. Über das verhältnis von König Aelfreds übersetzung der Cura Pastoralis zum original. Colberg, 1889.
741. KLAEBER, F. Zu König Alfreds Vorrede zu seiner übersetzung der Cura Pastoralis. Anglia (36), Vol. 47: 53-65. 1923.
   Interesting analysis of the Preface as an expression of Alfred's personality and literary interests.

e. Laws*

Bibliography
   WÜLKER (3), pp. 398-401; LIEBERMANN (217), especially Vol. III.

---

*See also Part V: F. Law and Institutions; see also below: Laws, p. 120.

742. TURK, M. H. The legal code of Alfred the Great. Halle, 1893.
Contains also description of manuscripts, text, and discussion.
Bibliography, pp. 3-9.
C. H. E. L. (4), pp. 487-8, 491; BRANDL (5), p. 1070; KÖRTING (6), p. 70.

Text
THORPE (803); TURK (742), pp. 60-135.
LIEBERMANN (217), Vol. I, pp. 16-88. The standard text for Anglo-Saxon laws. With translation into German.
ATTENBOROUGH (843), pp. 62-93. With translation.

Discussion
TURK (742), pp. 10-55; LIEBERMANN (217).

Translation
Whole Works of King Alfred (727), Vol. III, pp. 119-40. Translated by J. A. Giles. An inferior translation.

f. Orosius' History of the World

Bibliography
WÜLKER (3), pp. 406-12; C. H. E. L. (4), pp. 487, 489, 491.
BRANDL (5), p. 1069; KÖRTING (6), p. 68.

743. HÜBENER, G. König Alfred und Osteuropa. E. St. (38), Vol. 60; 37-57. 1925.

Text
744. SWEET, H. Orosius' history of the world. E. E. T. S. (87), Vol. LXXIX. 1883. With Latin original.

745. THORPE, B. In Pauli, R., The life of Alfred the Great, translated from the German by B. Thorpe, to which is appended Alfred's Anglo-Saxon version of Orosius, with a literal English translation. London, 1853. Reprinted in the Bohn library. London, 1902.

Discussion
746. HAMPSON, R. T. An essay on the geography of King Alfred the Great. In The Whole Works of King Alfred (727), Vol. III, pp. 11-63. See also Vol. II, pp. 10-17 (by J. Bosworth).

747. SCHILLING, H. König Alfreds angelsächsische bearbeitung der weltgeschichte des Orosius. Halle, 1886.

748. MARKHAM, C. Alfred as a geographer. In Alfred the Great (718) (ed. Bowker), pp. 151-67. London, 1899.

749. GEIDEL, H. Alfred der Grosse als geograph. Münchener Geographische Studien, Vol. 15. 1904.

BRANDL (5), pp. 1068-9.

750. NANSEN, F. In northern mists. Arctic exploration in early times. Transl. by A. G. Chater. 2 vols. New York, 1911. See especially Vol. I, pp. 169-81.

HÜBENER (743). König Alfred und Osteuropa.

Translation
751. BOSWORTH, J., in Whole works of King Alfred (727). Vol. II, pp. 17-198. Translation by J. Bosworth, who published a translation also in 1859.
  g. Psalms (attributed to Alfred)—*See* Part X: Psalms, p. 86, and Part XI: Psalms, p. 129.

h. Miscellaneous

1 King Alfred's Jewel. For a facsimile, see The Whole Works of King Alfred the Great (727), Vol. I, frontispiece. For discussion, by J. A. Giles, see (727), Vol. I, pp. 327-35. See especially J. Earle. The Alfred Jewel. Oxford, 1901.
2 King Alfred's Charters. For a translation, by J. A. Giles, from the Latin and O. E. originals in Kemble's Codex Diplomaticus Aevi Saxonici (929), and for excerpts from Kemble's discussion, see Whole Works, etc. (727), Vol. I, pp. 379-97.
3 King Alfred's Will. For a translation, by J. A. Giles, and discussions of the Will, see Whole Works, etc. (727), Vol. I, pp. 399-409.
4 King Alfred's Hand-book. For a discussion, by R. Pauli, of the lost Hand-book (Handbōc), see Whole Works, etc. (727), Vol. III, pp. 5-7.

Andrew, St.*

Bibliography
  KRAPP (544), p. xxi, note 4; BRIGHT (318), p. 218.
Text
752. GOODWIN, C. W. The Anglo-Saxon legends of St. Andrew and St. Veronica. London, 1851. With translation.
  MORRIS (778), pp. 228-49. With translation.
  BRIGHT (318), pp. 113-28. The best text.
Discussion
753. ZUPITZA, J. Zur frage nach der quelle von Cynewulfs Andreas. Z. f. d. A. (79), Vol. 30: 175-85. 1886.
  FÖRSTER (779), pp. 202-6.
754. LIPSIUS, J. Die apokryphen apostelgeschichten und apostellegenden. Braunschweig, 1883-1900.

Apollonius of Tyre

Bibliography
  WÜLKER, p. 504; C. H. E. L. (4), p. 496.
  COOK AND TINKER (676), p. 207; BRANDL (5) pp. 1132-3.
Text
755. THORPE, B. The Anglo-Saxon version of the story of Apollonius of Tyre . . . with a literal translation. London, 1834.
756. ZUPITZA, J. Die altenglische bearbeitung der erzählung von Apollonius von Tyrus. Archiv (25), Vol. 97: 17-34. 1896.

---

*See also Part X: Cynewulfian Poems: (a) Andreas, p. 69.

Discussion
757. ZUPITZA, J. Welcher text liegt der altenglischen bearbeitung von Apollonius von Tyrus zu grunde? Romanische Forschungen (74), Vol. 3: 269-79. 1887.
758. SMYTH, A. H. Shakespeare's Pericles and Apollonius of Tyre. Philadelphia, 1898.
759. KLEBS, E. Die erzählung von Apollonius aus Tyrus. Eine geschichtliche untersuchung über ihre lateinische urform und ihre späteren bearbeitungen. Berlin, 1899.
760. MÄRKISCH, R. Die altenglische bearbeitung der erzählung von Apollonius von Tyrus. Palaestra, (101), Vol. VI. 1899. Discusses the language and gives the Latin text.
761. EMERSON, O. F. The Old English Apollonius of Tyre. Archiv (25), Vol. 145: 256-8. 1923.

Benedictine Rule*

Bibliography
WÜLKER, (3) pp. 498-9.
762. LOGEMAN, H. The Rule of S. Benet. E. E. T. S. (87), Vol. XC. 1888. Latin and Old English interlinear version.
763. LOGEMAN, W. S. De Consuetudine Monachorum. (1) Text. Anglia (36), Vol. 13: 365-48. 1891. (2) Introduction and notes. Anglia (36), Vol. 15: 20-40. 1893.
764. TUPPER, F. History and texts of the Benedictine reform of the tenth century. M. L. N. (26), Vol. 8: 344-67. 1893. Very useful survey.
C. H. E. L. (4), p. 493; BRANDL (5), p. 1099.
FÖRSTER (883), pp. 31-2, 42, 43, 44. Gives brief discussion.
KÖRTING (6), p. 74; GROSS (145), pp. 275-6, 271-3.
765. NAPIER, A. S. The Old English version of the enlarged Rule of Chrodegang together with the Latin original. An Old English version of the Capitula of Theodulf together with the Latin original. An interlinear Old English rendering of the Epitome of Benedict of Aniane. E. E. T. S. (87), Vol. CL. 1916.
KEIM (775). Aethelwold und die mönchreform in England.

Text
THORPE (803), Vol. II, pp. 400-42. Old English translation of the *Capitula of Theodulf.*
766. GREIN-WÜLKER (672), Vol. 2 (ed. by A. Schröer): Die angelsächsischen prosabearbeitungen der Benedictinerregel. 1885-8.
SCHRÖER (692), A. De Consuetudine Monachorum. E. St. (38), Vol. 9: 294-6. 1886. From Cotton Tib. A III.
767. SCHRÖER, A. Die Winteney-version der Regula S. Benedicti.

See also Part X: Benedictine Office; and Aelfric: (*f*) *De Consuetudine Monachorum.*

Lateinisch und Englisch. Mit einleitung, anmerkungen, glossar und einem facsimile zum erstenmale herausgegeben. Halle, 1888.
LOGEMAN (762), H. The Rule of S. Benet.
768. ZUPITZA, J. Ein weiteres bruchstück der Regularis Concordia in altenglischer sprache. Archiv (25), Vol. 84: 1-24. 1890.
LOGEMAN (763), W. S.; NAPIER (765).

Discussion
GREIN-WÜLKER (672), Vol. 2 (766), pp. xiii-xliv. See *Text* above.
SCHRÖER (692), pp. 290-4.
769. SIEVERS, E. Die angelsächsische Benediktinerregel. Tübingen, 1887.
LOGEMAN, H. (762), pp. xv-lxiii.
770. SCHRÖER, A. Die angelsächsischen prosabearbeitungen der Benedictinerregel. E. St. (38), Vol. 14: 241-53. 1890.
ZUPITZA (768); LOGEMAN, W. S. (763); TUPPER (764).
771. BATESON, M. Rules for monks and secular canons after the revival under King Edgar. E. H. R. (149), Vol. 9: 690-708. 1894.
772. TUPPER, F. Anglo-Saxon *Dæg-mæl*. P. M. L. A. (69), 10: 111-241. 1895.
WHITE (679), chapter I and XII.
773. LIEBERMANN, F. Aethelwolds anhang zur Benediktinerregel. Archiv (25), Vol. 108: 375-7. 1902.
774. BLAIR, D. The Rule of St. Benedict. Fort-Augustus, 1906.
NAPIER (765), pp. vii-xi.
775. KEIM, H. W. Aethelwold und die mönchreform in England. Anglia (36), Vol. 41: 405-43. 1917. Bibliography, pp. 405-6.
776. ROBINSON, J. A. The times of Saint Dunstan. Oxford, 1923. See ch. V, St. Ethelwold; ch. VII, The Regularis Concordia; and pp. 159-71.
Translation: THOMSON (459).

Blickling Homilies

Bibliography
WÜLKER (3), pp. 484-5.
777. FÖRSTER, M. Altenglische predigtquellen. I. Pseudo-Augustin und die 7. Blickling Homily. Archiv (25), Vol. 116: 301-07. 1906. Contains bibliography of studies of the sources.
BRANDL (5), p. 1112; KÖRTING (6), pp. 73-4.

Text
778. MORRIS, R. The Blicking Homilies of the tenth century. E. E. T. S. (87), Vol. LVIII, LXIII, LXXIII. 1874-80. With translation. Gives one page of facsimile.

Discussion
MORRIS (778) pp. v-xvi.
779. FÖRSTER, M. Zu den Blickling Homilies. Archiv (25), Vol. 91: 179-206. 1893. On the sources and quality of translation of eight homilies.

780. FIEDLER, H. G. The source of the first Blickling homily. Mod. Lang. Quart., Vol. 6: 122-24. 1903.
    The 18th homily is discussed by A. Napier, "Notes on the Blicking Homilies I. St. Martin," in M. Ph. (56), Vol. 1: 303-8. 1903.
    FÖRSTER (777); BRANDL (5), p. 1110; GRAU (458), pp. 192 ff.
781. FÖRSTER, M. Altenglische predigtquellen. II. Archiv (25), Vol. 122: 246-62. 1909. Sources of the 14th Blickling Homily, pp. 246-56.

Byrhtferth

Bibliography
WÜLKER (3), pp. 506-507.
782. CLASSEN, K. M. Uber das leben und die schriften Byrhtferths, eines angelsächsischen gelehrten und schriftstellers um das jahr 1000. Dresden, 1896.
    KÖRTING (6), p. 77, note 2.
783. SINGER, CHARLES, AND DOROTHEA. An unrecognized Anglo-Saxon medical text. (Reprinted from Annals of Medical History, Vol. 3, No. 2: 136-49). New York, 1921.
    Full bibliography on p. 138.

Text
784. KLUGE, F. Angelsächsische excerpte aus Byrhtferth's Handboc oder Enchiridion. Anglia (36), Vol. 8: 298-337. 1885.
    SINGER (783) pp. 139-140. Facsimile, p. 137.
785. CRAWFORD, S. J. Byrhtferth's Manual (A.D. 1011). Now edited for the first time from MS. Ashmole 328 in the Bodleian Library, ... Vol. I, Text, Translation, Sources and Appendices. E. E. T. S. (87), Vol. CLXXVII. 1929. The second vol. will contain an introduction and a vocabulary of technical terms.

Discussion
CLASSEN (782); SINGER (783). Gives also a translation.
785a. FORSEY, G. F. Byrhtferth's *Preface.* Speculum (75), Vol. 3: 505-22. 1928. Good general discussion of Byrhtferth, with bibliography.

Cato, Distichs (Proverbs) of

Bibliography
WÜLKER (3), pp. 501-3; KÖRTING (6), p. 75; FÖRSTER (829) p. 48.

Text
KEMBLE (639), p. 258. With translation.
786. NEHAB, J. Der altenglische Cato. Berlin, 1879. Contains also a discussion of manuscripts, and notes on the relation of the Old English version to the original.
    WARNER (701), pp. 3-7.
787. SIEVERS, E. Metrische studien IV. Leipzig, 1919. See pp. 601-15.

Discussion
NEHAB (786). Der altenglische Cato.

788. SCHLEICH, G. Review of NEHAB (786). Anglia (36), Vol. 3: 383-96. 1880. Extended criticism and discussion.
WÜLKER (3), pp. 502-3; FÖRSTER (678a), pp. 434 ff.

Chad, Life of St.

Text
789. NAPIER, A. Ein altenglisches leben des heiligen Chad. Anglia (36), Vol. 10: 114-8. 1888.

Discussion
NAPIER (789), pp. 131-40; BRANDL (5), p. 1054.

Christopher, Life of St.

Bibliography
RYPINS (715). Meager bibliography.

Text
790. HERZFELD, G. Bruchstück einer altenglischen legende. E. St. (38), Vol. 13: 142-5. 1889.
791. EINENKEL, E. Das altenglische Cristoforus-fragment. Anglia (36), Vol. 17: 112-22. 1895. Gives also the Latin original. The text is inferior to that of HERZFELD (790).
RYPINS (715), pp. 68-76.

Discussion
HERZFELD (790), p. 142; EINENKEL (791), pp. 110-12.
RYPINS (715), pp. vii-xxix, *passim;* see also pp. xlvii-l.

Chronicle

Bibliography
WÜLKER (3), pp. 440-50.
792. PLUMMER, C. Two of the Saxon chronicles parallel with supplementary extracts from the others, a revised text edited . . . on the basis of an edition by John Earle. 2 vols. Oxford, 1892-9. See especially Vol. 2, pp. cxxvii-cxxxvi (critical bibliography of editions and translations).
BRANDL (5), pp. 1061-2; KÖRTING (6), pp. 75-6.
GROSS (145), pp. 235-7; SONNENSCHEIN (147), Part III, p. 1163.

Text
793. THORPE, B. The Anglo-Saxon Chronicle. 2 vols. Rolls Series. 1861.
Vol. 1, text; Vol. 2, translation. Six parallel texts from different manuscripts.
EARLE -PLUMMER (792), Vol. 1.
794. CLASSEN, E., and F. E. HARMER. An Anglo-Saxon Chronicle from British Museum, Cotton MS., Tiberius B. IV, edited with a glossary. Manchester, 1926.
A very good edition of a single text—the D text, or Worcester *Chronicle.*

Discussion
WÜLKER (3), pp. 442-50.
EARLE-PLUMMER (792), Vol. 2, pp. xvii-cxxxvii; ABEGG (402); KELLER (919); JOST (927a).
BRANDL (5), pp. 1055-61; HOOPS (12), Vol. IV, pp. 63-6.
794a. VIGLIONE, F. Studio critico-filologico su l'Anglo-Saxon Chronicle. Pavia, 1922.
795. POOLE, R. L. Chronicles and annals: a brief outline of their origin and growth. Oxford, 1926.
   Covers the mediaeval chronicles down to the thirteenth century.

Translation
796. GILES, J. A. Bede's Ecclesiastical History, and the Anglo-Saxon Chronicle. London, 1847. (New ed., 1912.)
797. STEVENSON, J. The Church historians of England. London, 1853. Vol. 2, part 1.
798. GOMME, E. E. C. The Anglo-Saxon Chronicle, edited from the translation in Monumenta Historica Britannica, and other versions by the late J. A. Giles. London, 1909.
799. INGRAM, J. The Anglo-Saxon Chronicle. London, 1912. (Everyman's Library).

Dialogues (religious)

Text and Discussion
800. NAPIER, A. Altenglische kleinigkeiten. Anglia (36), Vol. 11: 1-10. 1888.
   On Adam, Sarah, and Noah, pp. 1-3; On the Virgin Mary, p. 3; Be misdæda, pp. 3-4; On Noah's Ark, St. Peter's, Thieves, Solomon's Temple, etc., p. 5. Most of these appear to be catechetical answers, the questions not being given.
801. FÖRSTER, M. Two notes on Old English dialogue literature, in An English Miscellany . . . (121), pp. 86-106. 1901.
   Contains some general remarks on Old English dialogue literature, with specific treatment of Middle English texts.
FÖRSTER (883), pp. 37, 40. Bibliography and brief discussion.

Ecclesiastical Miscellanea: Laws, Canons, Procedures, Computations, etc.

Bibliography
802. BERBNER, W. Untersuchungen zu dem altenglischen Scriftbōc. Bonn, 1907. Pp. 7-16, bibliography for *Ecgberht's Penitential and Confessional*, with some discussion.
BRANDL (5), p. 1100.
FÖRSTER (883), p. 37 (Fast days); "Be Misdaeda," p. 37. Pp. 41-2 (Indicia Monasterialia).
GROSS (145), pp. 270-3: canons, penitentials, etc.; pp. 275-7: Monastic rules.

Text

803. THORPE, B. Ancient laws and institutes of England. London, 1840.

Old English and Latin text of Ecgberht's *Confessional and Penitential*, pp. 343-92; *Canons Enacted under King Edgar*, pp. 395-415; *Law of the Northumbrian Priests*, pp. 416-21; *Institutes of Polity, Civil and Ecclesiastical*, pp. 422-40; *Ecclesiastical Institutes*, pp. 466-88; *Ecclesiastical Compensations* or *Bōts*, pp. 393-4. All but the works of Ecgberht are translated.

COCKAYNE (674), Vol. III. Table of equivalents, mass and fasting, psalms and fasting, pp. 166-7; computation of ecclesiastical festivals, pp. 226-9; propitious days for fasting, pp. 228-9.

Historical fragments: *Of the monastery of St. Mildred in Tanet*, pp. 422-33; *Edgar's Establishment of Monasteries*, pp. 432-45.

HADDAN AND STUBBS (224). Councils and ecclesiastical documents, etc.

804. KLUGE, F. Fragment eines angelsächsischen briefes. E. St. (38), Vol. 8: 62-3. 1885. *Letter to Brother Eadward.*

805. KLUGE, F. Indicia Monasterialia. Internationale Zeitschrift für allgemeine Sprachwissenschaft, Vol. 2: 118-29. 1885. Some improvements by W. S. Logeman in E. St. (38), Vol. 12: 305-07. 1889.

NAPIER (800), pp. 3, 7 ff. *Fast Days* and *Mass Manual.*

806. NAPIER, A. S. Two Old English fragments. II. De Officiis Ecclesiasticis. M. L. N. (26), Vol. 12: pp. 111-14. 1897.

NAPIER (938a), pp. 111-14. Text and brief discussion of Isidor's *De Ecclesiasticis Officiis.*

LIEBERMANN (217), Vol. 1, pp. 380 ff. *Law of the Northumbrian Priests.*

ROEDER (894), p. xii. *Fast Days.*

806a. STEVENSON, W. H. Yorkshire surveys and other eleventh century documents in the York gospels. E. H. R. (149), Vol. 28: 1-25. 1912.

Contains text and translation of several surveys, an inventory, a prayer, and Aelfric's *Festermen.*

BROTANEK (452), pp. 27-8. "*Synodalbeschlüsse*" ("Decisions of a Synod" of the bishops) from MS. Fonds Latin 943 of the Bibliothèque Nationale.

FÖRSTER (705). Text of an Old English translation of a Latin *Absolution* contained in the so-called *Pontificale Egberti* (p. 114). Text (pp. 123-4) of "*Synodalbeschlüsse*", edited also by

BROTANEK (452). Texte und untersuchungen, etc., pp. 27-8.

807. DOUGLAS, D. C. Fragments of an Anglo-Saxon survey from Bury St. Edmunds. E. H. R. (149), Vol. 43: 376-83. 1928.

Text, pp. 381-83. Discussion, pp. 376-81. See also M. Weinbaum, "*Ags. Survey von Bury St. Edmonds*", in Archiv (25), Vol. 157: 77-8. 1930.

Discussion
  NAPIER (924). *Institutes of Polity.*
808. BATESON, M. The supposed Latin Penitential of Egbert and the missing work of Halitgar of Cambrai. E. H. R. (149), Vol. 9: 320-5. 1894. *Ecclesiastical Laws.*
  NAPIER (806). Two Old English fragments.
809. LIEBERMANN, F. Wulfstan und Cnut. Archiv (25), Vol. 103: 47-54. 1899. Evidence against Wulfstan's authorship of the *Institutes of Polity.*
810. BÖHMER, H. Kirche und Staat in England und in der Normandie im XI und XII jahrhundert. Leipzig, 1899.
811. LIEBERMANN, F. Angelsächsischer protest gegen den Cölibat. Archiv (25), Vol. 109: 376. 1902.
  BERBNER (802), pp. 7-16. *Scriftbōc.*
  BRANDL (5), p. 1100. *Canons.*
  FÖRSTER (883), p. 37. *Fast Days.*
  GREIN-WÜLKER (672), Vol. 9 (713), pp. lxxxiii-cxxvi.
  BROTANEK (452), pp. 128-34. *Synodalbeschlüsse.* See *Text* above: BROTANEK (452).
  FÖRSTER (829), pp. 60-3. Discusses the Absolution-form and the *Synodalbeschlüsse.* See *Text* above: FÖRSTER (705).
  DOUGLAS (807). Fragments of an Anglo-Saxon Survey from Bury St. Edmunds. Discussion, pp. 376-81.
811a. HERVEY, F. The history of King Eadmund the Martyr and of the early years of his abbey. New York, 1929. Contains Old English extracts from MS. Corpus 197, with translation, discussion, and bibliography.

Bibliography and Text **Elucidarium**
  FÖRSTER (801), in An English Miscellany (121), pp. 90-2.
  FÖRSTER (829), p. 63. Mostly bibliographical.
  ZUPITZA-SCHIPPER (325). See pp. 84-5 in the 11th edition.

Discussion
  FÖRSTER (801). Two notes on Old English dialogue literature. See also his article in Archiv (25), Vol. 116: 312-14. 1906.
812. SCHMITT, F. Die mittelenglische version des Elucidariums des Honorius Augustodunensis. Würzburg diss., 1909.

Bibliography **Gospels**
  WÜLKER (3), pp. 495-7.
813. COOK, A. S. Biblical quotations in Old English prose writers. Vol. I. London, 1898. Vol. II. New York, 1903. Valuable introduction.
814. BRIGHT, J. W. The Gospels in West-Saxon. Boston, 1904-06.
  Vol. 1, *The Gospel of St. John,* 1904, has an excellent bibliography, pp. 183-8. Bright's *The Gospel of Saint Luke in Anglo-Saxon* (Oxford, 1893) contains useful text and discussion.
  BRANDL (5), pp. 1116-17; KÖRTING (6), p. 74.

Text
815. [KEMBLE, J. M., C. HARDWICK, and] W. W. SKEAT. The Holy Gospels in Anglo-Saxon, Northumbrian, and Old Mercian versions, synoptically arranged with collations exhibiting all the reading of all the MSS.; together with the early Latin version as contained in the Lindisfarne MS., collated with the Latin version in the Rushworth MS. Cambridge [Eng.], 1871-87.

Contains also valuable discussion, especially in the introduction to *St. Mark* (1871). Supersedes the edition of the Lindisfarne and Rushworth Gospels edited by G. Waring and J. Stevenson for the Surtees Society: Vol. XXVIII (1854), XXXIX (1861), XLIII (1863), and XLVIII (1865).

BRIGHT (814). The Gospels in West-Saxon.
816. The Lindisfarne gospels. Printed by order of the trustees of the British museum. London, 1924.

Three plates in color and 36 in monochrome from Cotton MS. Nero D IV in the British Museum. Introduction by E. G. Millar.

Discussion
SKEAT (815). The Holy Gospels in Anglo-Saxon. . . .
817. DRAKE, A. The authorship of the West-Saxon Gospels. New York. 1894.
818. HANDKE, R. Über das verhältnis der westsächsischen evangelienübersetzung zum lateinischen original. Halle, 1896.
819. HARRIS, L. M. Studies in the Anglo-Saxon version of the Gospels. Baltimore, 1901.
COOK (813), Vol. I; BRIGHT (814), Vol. I.
BRANDL (5), pp. 1115-16; MILLAR (816).
820. GLUNZ, H. Die lateinische vorlage der westsächsischen evangelienversion. Leipzig, 1928.
821. GLUNZ, H. Britannien und Bibeltext. Der Vulgatatext der Evangelien in seinem verhältnis zur irisch-angelsächsischen kultur des frühmittelalters. Leipzig, 1930. Kölner anglistische arbeiten (92), Vol. XII. Bibliography, pp. 178-81.

Guthlac, Life of

Bibliography
WÜLKER (3), pp. 491-3; BRANDL (5), p. 1115.
822. GONSER, P. Das angelsächsische prosa-leben des hl. Guthlac. Heidelberg, 1909. Anglist. Forsch. (81), Vol. XXVII.

Contains Latin life of St. Guthlac, and the Old English from the two manuscripts, with introduction and notes.
FÖRSTER (380), pp. 85-6.

Text
823. GOODWIN, C. W. The Anglo-Saxon version of the Life of St. Guthlac. London, 1848. Contains also translation and notes. The text is normalized.
GONSER (822). The preferred text.

Discussion
   GOODWIN (823), pp. iii-v; DIETRICH (689), pp. 522 ff.
   WHITE (679), pp. 134-5; GONSER (822).
Herbarium; Herbarium of Apuleius; Herbarium from Dioskorides, etc.
Bibliography
   WÜLKER (3), pp. 507-8; KÖRTING (6), p. 75.
Text
   COCKAYNE (674). *Herbarium*, Vol. I, pp. 1-69; *Herbarium Apuleii*, Vol. I, pp. 71-249; *Herbarium from Dioskorides*, etc., Vol. I, pp. 251-325. With translation.
Discussion
   COCKAYNE (674), Vol. I, pp. ix-cv, *passim;* HOOPS (236).
824. BERBERICH, H. Das Herbarium Apuleii nach einer frühmittelenglischen fassung. Anglist. Forsch. (81), Vol. 5: 7-64. 1902. Also Heidelberg diss., 1900.
   PAYNE (238), especially pp. 62-82; SINGER (247), pp. 168-98.

*Homilies**
a. Vercelli Homilies†

Bibliography
   WÜLKER (3), pp. 485-93. The Homilies are listed and briefly discussed.
   FÖRSTER, M. (380), in Festschrift . . . Morsbach (125), pp. 20-148. Contains text of the 2d, 6th, 9th, 15th, and 22d Vercelli Homilies, pp. 87-148; description and bibliography of all the Homilies, pp. 20-86. Valuable.
Text
825. WÜLCKER, R. P. Ueber das Vercellibuch. Anglia (36), Vol. 5: 451 ff. 1882.
   "*Die Homilien des Vercellibuches*", pp. 454-65. Text of 13th Homily, and the beginnings and endings of many others.
   NAPIER (923). Text of the 2d and 10th Homilies.
826. BELFOUR, A. O. Twelfth century homilies in MS. Bodley 343. E. E. T. S. (87), Vol. CXXXVII. 1909. Text of the 3d Homily, pp. 40-8.
   FÖRSTER (380), in Festschrift . . . Morsbach (125). See *Bibliography* above.
827. WILLARD, R. Vercelli homily VIII and the *Christ*. P. M. L. A. (69), Vol. 42: 314-30. 1927.
   Also discussion, especially of its relation to the *Christ*. Willard announced in Anglia (36), Vol. 54: 8 (1930) that he has a complete edition of the prose homilies of the *Vercelli Book* in course of preparation.

___

*See also Aelfric: (*m*) Homilies; Blickling Homilies: and Wulfstan: Homilies.
†See also Part XI: Guthlac.

Discussion
WÜLKER (825). Ueber das Vercellibuch.
828. PRIEBSCH, R. The chief sources of some Anglo-Saxon homilies. Otia Merseiana (100), Vol. I: 129-47. Liverpool, 1899.
  Treats the origin of five homilies "which have for their subject a letter purporting to have been sent from heaven in order to inculcate the strict observance of Sunday." Four of these were printed in NAPIER (923). The fifth was edited by Priebsch.
GRAU (458), *passim*. Quellen und verwandtschaften . . .
FÖRSTER (380), in Festschrift . . . Morsbach (125). See *Bibliography* above.
WILLARD (827). Vercelli homily VIII and the *Christ*.

b. Miscellaneous

Bibliography
WÜLKER (3), pp. 493-4; BRANDL (5), p. 1113.
829. FÖRSTER, M. Der inhalt der altenglischen handschrift Vespasianus D. XIV. E. St. (38), Vol. 54: 46-68. 1920. Gives bibliography, *passim*. (Some twenty-seven texts in this manuscript are versions of homilies by Aelfric.)
Text: The texts of some fourteen homilies are listed in BRANDL (5), p. 1113.
  KEMBLE (639). Gives a homily on the capture of the devil by a hermit, pp. 84-6.
830. MORRIS, R. Old English Homilies and homiletic treatises. First series. E. E. T. S. (87), Vol. XXIX, XXXIV. 1867-8. See pp. 296-304.
831. MORRIS, R. Legends of the Holy Rood. E. E.T. S. (87), Vol. XLVI. 1871.
832. KLUGE, F. Zu altenglischen dichtungen. 3. Zum Phönix. E. St. (38), Vol. 8: 474-9. 1885.
  Two homilies (concerning the Phoenix). The second is entitled *De Sancto Johanne*. Both are versions of the same original.
GREIN-WÜLKER (672), Vol. 3 (682), (ed. by B. Assman): Angelsächsische homilien und heiligenleben. 1889. Contains texts of ten miscellaneous homilies and saints' legends.
833. NAPIER, A. S. An English homily on the observance of Sunday. In An English Miscellany (121), pp. 357-62. 1901.
  Discussion, pp. 355-7. The homily is from Corpus Christi Cambr. MS. 162.
FÖRSTER (781), pp. 257-61. Two homilies.
WARNER (701). A rather large collection.
833a. FÖRSTER, M. Kleinere mittelenglische texte. Anglia (36), Vol. 42: 222-3. 1918. Text of an Old English homily on Antichrist.
  See also his article, "Die spätaltenglische übersetzung der pseudo-Anselmschen Marienpredigt," in Anglica (134), Vol. 148: 8-69. 1925. He gives the text of the *Sermo in festis Sancte Marie Virginis*, with Latin original, bibliography, and much discussion.

Discussion
  BRANDL (5), pp. 1112-3. See p. 1113 for a list of discussions of various homilies.
  FÖRSTER (829), *passim*. See also FÖRSTER (833a) and also his article, "Die Legende vom Trinubium der hl. Anna," in Probleme der englischen Sprache und Kultur (132), pp. 105-30. See especially pp. 115-19 for text and discussion of the Old English version.

Horalogium (A Dial)
Bibliography: FÖRSTER (883), p. 45.
Text and Translation
  COCKAYNE (674), Vol. III, pp. 218-23.
      How long the sun's shadow is on certain days, pp. 218-223; duration of moonlight, pp. 222-5. On epacts and the lunar cycle, pp. 282-3.

Jamnes and Mambres
Bibliography
834. FÖRSTER, M. Das lateinisch—altenglische fragment der apokryphe von James und Mambres. Archiv (25), Vol. 108: 15-28. 1902.
Text
  COCKAYNE (673), p. 50. Latin text, p. 67.
835. JAMES, M. R. A fragment of the penitence of James and Mambres. Journal of Theological Studies 2: 572-7. London, 1901. A careful critical edition.
  FÖRSTER (834), pp. 19-21.
Discussion
  JAMES (835); FÖRSTER (834); BRANDL (5), p. 1118.

Jerome's Story of Malchus
Bibliography: BRANDL (5), p. 1118.
Text
  COCKAYNE (675), pp. 35-44.
  GREIN-WÜLKER (672), Vol. 3 (682) (ed. by B. Assmann): Angelsächsische homilien und heiligenleben. 1889. See pp. 195-207.
836. HULME, W. H. Malchus. J. E. G. Ph. (53), Vol. 1: 431-41. 1897. Little discussion.
Discussion
  GREIN-WÜLKER (672), Vol. 3 (682), pp. 266-7; BRANDL (5), pp. 1117-8.
837. HOLTHAUSEN, F. Quellenstudien zu englischen denkmälern. I. 1. Zum altenglischen leben des h. Malchus. E. St. (38), Vol. 46: 177-86. 1913.

Judgment, Fifteen Signs before the
Bibliography: FÖRSTER (829), pp. 54-5.

Text
838. ASSMANN, B. Vorzeichen des jüngsten gerichts. Anglia (36), Vol. 11: 369-71. 1889.
GRAU (458), pp. 261-80; WARNER (701), pp. 89-91.
Discussion
NÖLLE (455); GRAU (458), pp. 261-80; FÖRSTER (829), pp. 54-5.

Lācnunga (Medications, recipes)*

NOTE: A new edition, with notes and translation, by C. Singer and J. H. G. Grattan, is promised.
Bibliography
WÜLKER (3), p. 510.
839. GREIN-WÜLKER (672), Vol. 6 (ed. by G. Leonhardi): Kleinere angelsächsische denkmäler. 1905. Bibliography, p. 157.
Text
COCKAYNE (674), Vol. III, pp. 2-77. With translation.
GREIN-WÜLKER (672), Vol. 6 (839), pp. 121-55. See *Bibliography* above.
Discussion
GREIN-WÜLKER (672), Vol. 6 (839), pp. 157-9. See *Bibliography* above.
SINGER (245); SINGER (247).

Lapidary

Text and Discussion
840. VON FLEISCHHACKER, R. Ein altenglischer Lapidar. Z. f. d. A. (79), Vol. 34: 229-35. 1890.
MANN (571). Anglia Beibl. (37), Vol. 10: 285-6; Vol. 12: 20; Vol. 13: 239 (the latter by A. L. Jellinek). Gives only bibliography.
841. GARRETT, R. M. Precious stones in Old English literature. Münchener Beiträge (98), Vol. XLVII. 1909.
842. EVANS, Joan. Magical jewels of the Middle Ages and Renaissance, particularly in England. Oxford, 1922.

Laws*

Bibliography
WÜLKER (3), pp. 398-401; C. H. E. L. (4), p. 488; KÖRTING (6), p. 70.
GROSS (145), pp. 257-67; LIEBERMANN (217), Vol. III. The best work.
843. ATTENBOROUGH, F. L. The laws of the earliest English kings, edited and translated. Cambridge [Eng.], 1922.

---

*See also Part X: Charms, p. 67.
*See also Part V: (F) Law, p. 28; see also Ecclesiastical Miscellanea, p. 113; and Alfred: (e) Laws, p. 106.

Covers the laws from Ethelbert to Athelstan (c. 939). See
note to ROBERTSON (844), and K. Sisam's review of (843) in M.
L. R. (27), Vol. 18: 98-104. 1923.
844. ROBERTSON, A. J. The laws of the kings of England from Edmund
to Henry I, edited and translated. Cambridge [Eng.], 1925.
A complement to ATTENBOROUGH (843). Together they contain
the text of all the important codes of Old English laws, but they
do not cover the ground so completely as LIEBERMANN (217).
Both Attenborough and Robertson give text and translation parallel, with brief introductions to the codes, notes, and index.

Text and Discussion
SCHMID (212). Die gesetze der angelsachsen.
LIEBERMANN (217). Vol. 1, text and German translation; Vol. 2,
glossaries; Vol. 3, introduction to each section, and notes. Translated extracts are found on pp. 122-4, 169-70, 178-83, 216, 220-2,
251-2, 267-8, 281-3 of CHAMBERS (198).
ATTENBOROUGH (843). With translation. Gives brief introductions to
the various codes.
ROBERTSON (844). With translation.

Leech-book (Læce Bōc)

Bibliography
WÜLKER (3), p. 509.
GREIN-WÜLKER (672), Vol. 6 (839) (ed. by G. Leonhardi): Kleinere
altenglische denkmaler. 1905. Bibliography, p. 110.
BRANDL (5), p. 1072; KÖRTING (6), p. 75.

Text
COCKAYNE (674), "Fly Leaf Leechdoms," Vol. I, pp. 374-83; "Leechbook of Bald," Vol. II, pp. 2-360; Vol. III, pp. 292-3. With translation.
GREIN-WÜLKER (672), Vol. 6 (839), pp. 1-109. See *Bibliography*
above.

Discussion
COCKAYNE (674), Vol. II, pp. xx-xxxiii; WÜLKER (3), 509-10.
PAYNE (238), pp. 39-62, 154-7. With translated excerpts from the
Leech Book and a page in facsimile.
GREIN-WÜLKER (672), Vol. 6 (839), pp. 110-12. See *Bibliography*
above.
BRANDL (5), p. 1072.

Legends, Royal (Kentish)

Bibliography: BRANDL (5), p. 1055.
Text
845. LIEBERMANN, F. Die heiligen Englands. Hannover, 1889.
846. BIRCH, W. DE G. Liber Vitae: register and martyrology of New
Minster and Hyde Abbey. London, 1892. Text, pp. 83-7.

Discussion
LIEBERMANN (845); BRANDL (5), pp. 1054, 1114.

Letters*

Text and Discussion
KEMBLE (929), Vol. III, p. 327. Part of a letter from Bishop Aethelric to Aethelmær.
HADDAN AND STUBBS (224). Gives various texts.
847. KLUGE, F. Fragment eines angelsächsischen briefes. E. St. (38), Vol. 8: 62-3. 1885.
  Only the text and brief literary criticism. *Letter to Brother Eadward.*
BIRCH (846), pp. 96-100. *Letter of Eadwine to Aelfsige.* Translation based on the text in B. Thorpe's *Diplomatarium* (930), pp. 321-4.
BROTANEK (452), pp. 29, 135-49. Text and discussion of *Letter from Aethelric to Aethelmær.*
848. KONRATH, M. Eine altenglische vision von jenseits. Archiv (25), Vol. 139: 30-46. 1919.
  Contains text, Latin original, and a little discussion of a *Letter from Wynfrith* (Boniface) *to Eadburga.*
849. SISAM, K. An Old English translation of a letter from Wynfrith to Eadburga. M. L. R. (27), Vol. 18: 253-72. 1923.
  Text, Latin original, and discussion. For literature on Boniface (Winfrid), see GROSS (145), pp. 280-1. For an English translation of the Latin and for discussion of Boniface, see E. Kylie, *The English Correspondence of Saint Boniface,* London, 1924.
FÖRSTER (705), pp. 125-9. Discussion of *Letter from Aethelric to Aethelmaer.*

Liber Scintillarum, Defensor's

Bibliography: KÖRTING (6), p. 74, note 2.

Text and Discussion
850. RHODES, E. W. Defensor's Liber Scintillarum with an interlinear Anglo-Saxon version.... E. E. T. S. (87), Vol. XCIII. 1889. Contains also other pieces of a similar nature.

Lorica Hymn and Lorica Prayer

Bibliography
KUYPERS (852), p. 232.
GREIN-WÜLKER (672), Vol. 6 (839) (ed. by G. Leonhardi): Kleinere angelsächsische denkmäler. 1905. "Die Lorica des Gildas," pp. 175-242.

See also Alexander, p. 102, and Aelfric: (s) Pastoral Letters, p. 102.

851. SINGER, C. The Lorica of Gildas the Briton (? 547). Reprinted from the Proceedings of the Royal Society of Medicine 12: 124-44. (Section of the History of Medicine) 1919. London, 1920.
SINGER (247), p. 132.

Text
COCKAYNE (674), Vol. I, pp. lxviii-lxxiii. With Latin gloss.
SWEET (388), p. 174. The prayer.
852. KUYPERS, A. B. The Prayer Book of Aedeluald the Bishop. Cambridge [Eng.], 1902.
See pp. 385-8. With facsimile. The MS. of the *Prayer Book* is known as *The Book of Cerne.*
GREIN-WÜLKER (672), Vol. 6 (839), pp. 175-93, 241. See *Bibliography* above.
SINGER (851); SINGER (247), pp. 122-7. Gives the Latin text, with a translation.

Discussion
853. LEONHARDI, G. Die Lorica des Gildas. Hamburg, 1905.
GREIN-WÜLKER (672), Vol. 6 (839), pp. 194-242. See *Bibliography* above.
SINGER (851). Gives a translation of the English and also of the Latin text.
SINGER (247), pp. 111-22; 127-31 (notes). With translation.

Margaret, Life of St.

Bibliography
WÜLKER (3), p. 494; FÖRSTER (883), p. 40.

Text
COCKAYNE (673), pp. 39-49.
GREIN-WÜLKER (672), Vol. 3 (682) (ed. by B. Assmann): Angelsächsische homilien und heiligenleben. 1889. See pp. 170-80.

Discussion
COCKAYNE (673), pp. 80-7.
854. VOGT, F. Über die Margaretenlegenden. Beitr. (48), Vol. 1: 263-87. 1874.
On the spread of the Margaret legend.
GREIN-WÜLKER (672), Vol. 3 (682), pp. 264-5.

Martyrology

Bibliography
WÜLKER (3), pp. 450-1.
855. HERZFELD, G. An Old English Martyrology. E. E. T. S. (87), Vol. CXVI. 1900. Supplies an introduction, text, and notes. Bibliography, pp. xi-xvii, *passim.*

Text
COCKAYNE (675), pp. 29-33, 44-158. With translation.
SWEET (388), pp. 177-8; BIRCH (846).
HERZFELD (855), pp. 2-223. With translation.

Discussion
856. PIPER, F. Die kalendarien und martyrologien der angelsachsen. Berlin, 1862.
   COCKAYNE (675). See *Text* above.
   HERZFELD (855), pp. vii-xliii.
857. LIBERMANN, F. Zum angelsächsischen Martyrologium. Archiv (25), Vol. 105: 86-7. 1900.
   COOK (813), Vol. II.

Mary of Egypt, Life of St.

Bibliography: WÜLKER (3), p. 494.
Text
858. EARLE, J. Gloucester fragments. I. Facsimile of some leaves in Saxon handwriting on St. Swiþun . . . with elucidations and an essay. II. Leaves from an Anglo-Saxon translation of the life of S. Maria Aegyptiaca, with a translation and notes. London, 1861.
   SKEAT (706), Vol. XCIV, pp. 2-53. With translation.
Discussion
   DIETRICH (689); EARLE (858), pp. 99-101; SKEAT (706), Vol. CXIV, pp. 446-7.

Medicina de Quadrupedibus of Sextus Placitus

Bibliography
   WÜLKER (3), pp. 508-9.
859. DELCOURT, J. Medicina de Quadrupedibus. An early Middle English version, with introduction, notes, translation, and glossary, Anglist Forsch. (81), Vol. XL. 1914.
Text
   COCKAYNE (674), Vol. I, pp. 326-73. With translation.
Discussion
   COCKAYNE (674), pp. lxxxix ff; PAYNE (238), pp. 64.5, 68, 134.
   DELCOURT (859). Medicina de Quadrupedibus.

Mildryth, St.

Bibliography: BRANDL (5), p. 1115.
Text: COCKAYNE (674), Vol. III, pp. 423-33. With translation.
Discussion
   COCKAYNE (674). Leechdoms, wortcunning, and starcraft. . . .
   FÖRSTER (872b), pp. 333-4.
860. HERZFELD, G. Zu Leechdoms III, 428 ff. E. St. (38), Vol. 13: 140-2. 1889.

Neot, Life of St.

Bibliography
   WÜLKER (3), p. 494; BRANDL (5), p. 1113; FÖRSTER (829), pp. 57-8.

Text
861. GORHAM, G. C. The history and antiquities of Eynesbury and St. Neot's, in Huntingdonshire; and of St. Neot's in the County of Cornwall. 2 vols. and supplement. London, 1824.
    See Vol. II, pp. 256-61 and pp. xcvii-cii in the supplement. With translation.
    COCKAYNE (675), pp. 12-17. 1864. With translation.
862. WÜLCKER, R. Ein angelsaechsisches leben des Neot. Anglia (36), Vol. 3: 104-14. 1880.
    WARNER (701), pp. 129-34.

Discussion
    DIETRICH (689), pp. 487ff; WÜLKER (862), pp. 102-4.
    WHITE (679), p. 134; STEVENSON (719), pp. 256-61.
    BRANDL (5), p. 1112. See also the article by Mary Bateson in the *Dictionary of National Biography*, Vol. XIV, pp. 221ff.

Nicodemus, Gospel of

Bibliography
    WÜLKER (3), pp. 497-8.
863. FÖRSTER, M. Zum altenglischen Nicodemus-Evangelium. Archiv (25), Vol. 107: 311-21. 1901. Contains a good survey to 1901, with incidental bibliography.
864. HULME, W. H. The Old English Gospel of Nicodemus. M. Ph. (56), Vol. 1: 579-614. 1904.
    FÖRSTER (829), p. 53.

Text
865. HULME, W. H. The Old English version of the Gospel of Nicodemus. P. M. L. A. (69), Vol. 13: 471-515. 1898. Parallel texts of two MSS., and a comparison of the Old English and Latin texts.
    HULME (864), pp. 591-614. Text of a late Old English version of Nicodemus, and text of a homily on the harrowing of hell. This article is supplementary to HULME (865).
    WARNER (701), pp. 77-88.
866. CRAWFORD, S. J. The Gospel of Nicodemus. Edinburgh, 1927.
    NOTE: M. FÖRSTER in 1920 (see FÖRSTER (829), p. 53) promised a critical text based on all manuscripts.

Discussion
867. WÜLKER, R. Das Evangelium Nicodemi in der abendländischen litteratur. Paderborn, 1872.
    HULME (865), pp. 457-70. Notes, pp. 516-41.
    HULME (864), pp. 579-91; FÖRSTER (863).

Peri Didaxeon (Of Schools of Medicine)

Bibliography: LÖWENECK (868), pp. v-vi.
Text
    COCKAYNE (674), Vol. III, pp. 82-145. With translation.

868. LÖWENECK, M. Peri Didaxeon, eine sammlung von rezepten in englischer sprache aus dem 11./12. jahrhundert. Erlanger Beitr. zur englischen Philologie XII. Erlangen, 1896. Gives the Latin text also.

Discussion
LÖWENECK (868), pp. v-vii. See also the notes, pp. 54-7.
PAYNE (238), pp. 143-57; SINGER (247), p. 148.

Phoenix

KLUGE (832). Gives discussion and texts.
WARNER (701). Text of the Phoenix homily, pp. 146-8.
COOK (559), pp. 128-32. Gives bibliography, text, and notes.
FÖRSTER (829), pp. 64-5. Gives bibliography and discussion.

Prayers (including Credo and Pater Noster)
See also Lorica, p. 122.

Bibliography
BRANDL (5), p. 1114; FÖRSTER (883), p. 38. Confessional prayers.

869. COOK, A. S. The Old English glosses of the *Te Deum*. Archiv (25), Vol. 122: 263-8. 1909. Includes also four texts and the Latin original.

Text
NOTE: See in addition to the following texts the list of texts in BRANDL (5), p. 1114.
THORPE (803). A confessional formulary and other confessional instructions, pp. 260-64, 278, 280, 282, 284.
THORPE (698). Vol. II, pp. 594-600. Translation, pp. 595-601.

870. LOGEMAN, H. Anglo-Saxonica minora. Anglia (36), Vol. 11: 97-120. 1889.
Pater Noster, version of the *Creed, Confessions,* and other prayers.

871. LOGEMAN, H. Anglo-Saxonica minora. Anglia (36), Vol. 12: 497-518. 1889.
Five prayers and confessions from MSS. Royal 2 B V and Tiberius A III.

872. ZUPITZA, J. Eine weitere aufzeichnung der oratio pro peccatis. Archiv (25), Vol. 84: 327-9. 1890. Confessional prayers. He gives the text of a *Devotion to the Cross* in Vol. 88: 361-4. 1892.

872a. COOK, A. S. New texts of the Old English Lord's Prayer and Hymns. M. L. N. (26), Vol. 7: 21-3. 1892. See also his "The evolution of the Lord's Prayer in English" in Am. Journ. of Phil. (44), Vol. 12: 59-66. 1891.

FÖRSTER (883), p. 46. Confessional prayers.
COOK (869), pp. 265-8.
STEVENSON (806a), pp. 9-10. Text, translation, and discussion of a *Bidding of Prayer.*

872b. FÖRSTER, M. Die altenglischen beigaben des Lambeth-psalters. Archiv (25), Vol. 132: 328-35. 1914. Gives the text of several prayers, and also of St. Mildryth and St. Seaxburh.
  For a version of the *Nicene Creed*, see S. J. Crawford's article in Anglia (36), Vol. 52: 1-25. 1928.
Discussion: See the preceding texts, and the discussions mentioned in BRANDL (5), p. 1114.

Prognostics

NOTE: There is a considerable number of works in Old English which may be brought under the following general heads: dreams, weather-, sickness-, birth-forecasts, horoscopes, computations, significant days, and general divinations. The most important contributions to the subject are listed below.

873. HAMPSON, R. T. Medii aevi kalendarium; or Dates, charters, and customs of the Middle Ages. 2 vols. in 1. London, 1841.
  Contains, among other material, an Old English phlebotomy. Gives texts and translations of some Old English Prognostics.
COCKAYNE (673), pp. 49 ff. Foetal growth.
COCKAYNE (674), Vol. III. Gives the texts and translation of a large amount of material falling under the general head of Prognostics: Dies Aegyptiaci, pp. 76-7. Determination of sex of unborn child, pp. 144-5. Calendar of foetal growth, pp. 146-7.
  Prognostics by the moon's age: general, pp. 150-1; dream lunar, pp. 154-7; 158-63; birth lunar, pp. 156-9; propitious action, pp. 176-81; sickness, pp. 182-3; general fortune, pp. 184-197.
  Prognostics according to the day of the week: birth, pp. 162-3; mass days, pp. 162-5; thunder, pp. 166-9, 180-3.
  Unpropitious days in the month: for medication and bloodletting, pp. 152-5; for success, pp. 224-5. Rare days in the year: for birth, pp. 154-5.
  Prognostics according to the Christmas twelve nights: wind, pp. 164-5; sunshine, pp. 164-7. Prognostics (Pseudo-Daniel) according to the nature of dreams, pp. 168-77; 198-215.
  Computation of epacts and the age of a past or future moon, pp. 228-9; on epacts and the lunar cycle, pp. 282-3.

874. SIEVERS, E. Bedeutung der buchstaben. Z. f. d. A. (79), Vol. 21: 189-90. 1877. Text and brief discussion.

875. BIRCH, W. DE G. Edition of divination alphabet, in Trans. of the Royal Soc. of Literature, second series, XI, p. 508. 1878.

876. ASSMANN, B. Eine regel über den donner. Anglia (36), Vol. 10: 185. 1888. Prophezeiung aus dem 1. Januar für das jahr. Anglia (36), Vol. 11: 369. 1889. Texts only. See also FÖRSTER (829), p. 52, for bibliography on the *"Prophezeiung"*. See also pp. 55, 68.

877. NAPIER, A. Altenglische kleinigkeiten. Anglia (36), Vol. 11: 1-10. 1889. Text of the *Ages of the World*, pp. 6 ff. Other texts

of the *Ages of the World* are given in KEMBLE (639), Pt. II, p. 184, THORPE (601), p. 112, LOGEMAN (870), pp. 105 ff., BIRCH (846), pp. 81-3, WARNER (701), pp. 139-40; and HOLTHAUSEN, in Anglia (36), Vol. 11: 174. 1889.

878. HELLMANN, G. Denkmäler mittelalterlicher meteorologie. Berlin, 1904. Bauern-Praktik. Berlin, 1896.

879. DIETERICH, A. A B C-Denkmaler. Rheinisches Museum für Philologie. N. F. 56: 77-105. 1901. Discussion of divination alphabets.

880. FÖRSTER, M. Die kleinliteratur des aberglaubens im altenglischen. Archiv (25), Vol. 110: 340-58. 1903.

Gives brief discussion and bibliography for various weather prognostications, propitious days for bloodletting, medication, etc., horoscopes, prognostications according to the day of the week of one's birth, sickness prognoses, influence of the moon, dreams, and *"Himmelsbriefe."*

PAYNE (238), pp. 17-21. Discusses prognostics from the moon's age, and the *Dies Aegyptiaci.*

GREIN-WÜLKER (672), Vol. 6, (839) (ed. by G. Leonhardi) : Kleinere angelsächsische denkmäler. 1905. Text of a phlebotomy, pp. 152 ff.

881. FÖRSTER, M. Beiträge zur mittelalterlichen volkskunde. I. Archiv (25), Vol. 120: 43-52. 1908.

Discusses and gives some five texts and bibliography for several brontologies (according to the month, day of the week, hour of the day or night, canonical hours, quarter of the heaven).

882. FÖRSTER, M. Beiträge zur mittelalterlichen volkskunde. II. Archiv (25), Vol. 120: 296-305. 1908.

Gives discussion, bibliography, and two texts for meteorologies, and one text for a dream-book.

883. FÖRSTER, M. Beiträge zur mittelalterlichen volkskunde. III. Archiv (25), Vol. 121: 30-46. 1908.

Gives chiefly bibliography for the contents of MS Tiberius A. III. Many of the works fall under the head of prognostics, some under ecclesiastical miscellanea, and some under dialogues, prayers, homilies, *Benedictine Rule,* letters, genealogies, and *Horalogium.*

884. FÖRSTER, M. Beiträge zur mittelalterlichen volkskunde. IV. Archiv (25), Vol. 125: 39-71. **1910.**

Gives bibliography, discussion and text of the pseudo-Daniel dream-book.

885. FÖRSTER, M. Beiträge zur mittelalterlichen volkskunde. VI. Archiv (25), Vol. 128: 55-71. 1912.

Gives bibliography, discussion, and texts of books about wind and sunshine.

886. FÖRSTER, M. Beiträge zur mittelalterlichen volkskunde. VII. Archiv (25), Vol. 128: 285-308. 1912.

Gives bibliography, discussion, and texts of prognostications according to birth on the day of the week.

887. FÖRSTER, M. Beiträge zur mittelalterlichen volkskunde. IX. Archiv (25), Vol. 134: 264-93. 1916.
   Gives bibliography, discussion, and text of a dream-book.
   WARNER (701). Weather prophecies, p. 66; brontology (*Emb þunre*), p. 91.
   FÖRSTER (829), *passim*. Bibliography and discussion (pp. 60-3) of the Seven Ages of the World.
888. FÖRSTER, M. Die weltzeitalter bei den angelsachsen. In Luick Festschrift (133), pp. 183-203. 1925.
   Bibliography, texts, and discussion of the Old English and Latin lists of the 5 to 7 divisions of world history.
889. FÖRSTER, M. Die altenglischen traumlunare. E. St. (38), Vol. 60: 58-93. 1925-6. Bibliography, texts, and discussion.
890. FÖRSTER, M. Die altenglischen verzeichnisse von glücks— und unglückstagen. In Studies in Eng. Phil. (139), pp. 258-277. 1929.
   Gives texts, bibliography, and discussion of Lucky Birth-days, Twenty-four Unlucky Days of the Year, Twenty-four Critical Days for Blood-letting, Three Critical Mondays.

Psalms

Bibliography
   WÜLKER (3), pp. 379-84, 435-6; BRIGHT AND RAMSAY (895), pp. 149-56.
   BRANDL (5), pp. 1055, 1114; KENNEDY (8), pp. 137-140, *passim*.
891. GREIN-WÜLKER (672), Vol. 7 (ed. by K. Wildhagen): Der Cambridger psalter (Hs. Ff. 1. 23 Univ. Libr. Cambr.). Zum ersten male herausgegeben mit besonderer berücksichtigung des lateinischen textes. I. Text mit erklärungen. 1910.
   KENNEDY (8), pp. 123, 131.

Text
892. STEVENSON, J. Anglo-Saxon and Early English Psalter. 2 vols. Surtees Soc. Pub. (107), Vol. XVI (1843) and Vol. XIX (1847).
   Vol. I. contains the *Lindisfarne Psalter* and Vol. II the *Saron Psalter*.
   SWEET (338), pp. 183-401. The *Vespasian Psalter*.
893. HARSLEY, F. Eadwine's Canterbury psalter. E. E. T. S. (87), Vol. XCII. 1889.
894. ROEDER, F. Der altenglische Regius-Psalter, eine interlinearversion in Hs. Royal 2. B. 5 des Brit. Mus. Zum ersten male vollständig herausgegeben. St. E. Ph. (106), Vol. XVIII. 1904.
895. BRIGHT, J. W., AND R. L. RAMSAY. Liber psalmorum: The West-Saxon psalms, being the prose portion, or the First Fifty, of the so-called Paris Psalter. Boston, 1907. A very good edition.
896. BRENNER, E. Der altenglische Junius—Psalter... Anglist. Forsch. (81), Vol. XXIII. 1908.

897. LINDELÖF, U. Der Lambeth—Psalter . . . Acta Soc. Scient. Fenniae, tom 35, nr. I: Text und glossar, 1909; tom 43, nr. 3: II. Beschreibung und geschichte der hs., etc. 1914.
898. LINDELÖF, U. Die altenglische glossen im Bosworth Psalter (Brit. Mus, MS. Addit. 37517). Memoires de la Soc. Néo-Philologique de Helsingfors (97), Vol. 5: 138-231. 1909.
899. OESS, G. Der altenglische Arundelpsalter . . . Anglist. Forsch. (81), Vol. XXX. 1910.
GREIN-WÜLKER (672), Vol. 7 (891). See *Bibliography* above.

Discussion
900. WICHMANN, J. König Aelfred's angelsächsische übertragung der psalmen I-LI excl. Anglia (36), Vol. 11: 39-96. 1889. Believes Alfred translated these psalms.
BRUCE (627). The Anglo-Saxon version of the Book of Psalms.
COOK (813). Biblical quotations in Old English prose writers.
901. WILDHAGEN, K. Über die in Eadwine's Canterbury Psalter (Trinity College Cambridge) enthaltene altenglische psalter-interlinearversion. Mit zwei tafeln. Halle, 1903.
ROEDER (894), pp. xi-xxii.
902. LINDELÖF, U. Studien zu altenglischen psalterglossen. Bo. Beitr. (83), Vol. XIII. 1904.
A comparison of the glosses of ten psalms and the *Magnificat*, from the eleven Old English versions.
903. WILDHAGEN, K. Der psalter des Eadwine von Canterbury. St. E. Ph. (106), Vol. XIII. 1905. Bibliography and apparatus.
BRIGHT AND RAMSAY (985). Liber psalmorum . . . .
904. OESS, G. Untersuchungen zum altenglischen Arundel-Psalter. Heidelberg, 1908.
BRENNER (986). Der altenglische Junius—Psalter . . . .
905. WILDHAGEN, K., in Festschrift . . . Morsbach (125), pp. 418-72. Studien zum Psalterium Romanum in England and zu seinen glossierungen. 1913. Also published separately. Halle, 1913.
A useful survey of the Old English psalters, their derivation and linguistic peculiarities. See also his article in E. St. (38), Vol. 54: 35-45. 1920.
906. HEINZEL, O. Kritische entstehungsgeschichte des angelsächsischen interlinear-psalters. Palaestra (101), Vol. CLI. Leipzig, 1926. Covers much the same ground as LINDELÖF (902).
FÖRSTER (705), pp. 129-30.

Quintinus, Passion of

Bibliography and Discussion
Vol. 106: 258-61. 1901.

Text
HERZFELD (860), p. 145; HERZFELD (855), pp. 196-9. With translation.
907. FÖRSTER, M. Zur altenglischen Quintinus—legende. Archiv (25),

Rituals

Bibliography
BRANDL (5).
908. FEHR, B. in Festgabe Liebermann (127). Altenglische ritualtexte für krankenbesuch, heilige ölung und begräbnis. See pp. 20-67. Bibliography in footnotes.
Rituale ecclesiae Dunelmensis (910). Introduction, pp. lxxv-lxxvi.

Text
909. STEVENSON, J. Rituale Ecclesiae Dunelmensis. Surtees Soc. Publ. (107), Vol. X. London, 1840. An extract is given in SWEET (338), p. 176. Stevenson's edition is superseded by (910).
FEHR (908). See *Bibliography* above. Manuscripts with similar texts are mentioned by F. Liebermann in Archiv (25), Vol. 104: 123-4.
910. Rituale Ecclesiae Dunelmensis. The Durham Collectar. A new and revised edition of the Latin text with the interlinear Anglo-Saxon version. Surtess Soc. Publ. (107), Vol. CXL. London and Durham, 1927.
    Introduction, Ch. I, pp. vii-xlii, by A. H. Thompson; Introduction, ch. II, pp. xliii-lxxvi, and text and notes, pp. 1-221, by U. Lindelöf.

Discussion
LINGARD (223), Vol. II, pp. 359ff. A brief but excellent account.
911. LIEBERMANN, F. Das Rituale Dunelmense. Archiv (25), Vol. 104: 122ff. 1900.
FEHR (908), pp. 20-45. See *Bibliography* above.
912. LINDELÖF, U. A new collation of the gloss of the Durham Ritual. M. L. R. (27), Vol. 18: 273-80. 1923. See also his article in Anglia Beibl. (37), Vol. 39: 145-51. 1928.
Rituale Ecclesiae Dunelmensis (910).

Rood-Tree, History of the Holy

Bibliography, Text and Translation
913. MORRIS, R. Legends of the Holy Rood. E. E. T. S. (87), Vol. XLVI. 1871.
914. NAPIER, A. S. The history of the Holy Rood-Tree. E. E. T. S. (87), Vol. CIII. 1894. Text is 12th century. Bibliography, pp. x-xi.
SKEAT (706), Vol. XCIV, pp. 144-59. Text and translation (Morris's, with alterations) of Aelfric's homily. See the notes, p. 450.

Salomon and Saturn, Dialogue of

Bibliography: WÜLKER (3), pp. 500-1.
Text: KEMBLE (639), pp. 178-93; THORPE (601), pp. 110-15.
Discussion: See Part X: Salomon and Saturn, p. 88.

Swithun, Life of St.

Text and Discussion
EARLE (858), pp. 1-13, 15-17. With translation.

SKEAT (706). E. E. T. S. (87), Vol. LXXVI: 440-70. Gives a text and translation of Aelfric's homily.
MORLEY (337), Vol. II, pp. 301-4. Gives a discussion.
WHITE (679), pp. 37-40, 128-9. Discusses the *Life* in relation to Aelfric.

915. GEROULD, G. H. Aelfric's legend of St. Swithin. Anglia (36), Vol. 32: 347-57. 1909.

Veronica, Legend of St. (Vindicta Salvatoris)

NOTE: The *Nathanis Judaei Legatio* is part of this legend.

Bibliography

WÜLKER (3), pp. 494-5; BRANDL (5), p. 1118; FÖRSTER (829), pp. 53-4.

Text

GOODWIN (752), pp. ix-xi, 26-47. With translation.
GREIN-WÜLKER (672), Vol. 3 (682), (ed. by B. Assmann), pp. 181-94.
WARNER (701), pp. 88-9. Text of *Nathanis Judaei Legatio*.

Discussion

GOODWIN (752); GREIN-WÜLKER (672), Vol. 3 (682), pp. 265-6.
FÖRSTER (829), pp. 53-4.

Werferth's Translation of Gregory's Dialogues*

Bibliography

WÜLKER (3), pp. 437-40.

916. GREIN-WÜLKER (672), Vol. 5 (ed. by H. Hecht): Bischof Waerferths von Worcester übersetzung der dialoge Gregors des Grossen. I teil: text. II teil: einleitung. 1900-7.
KÖRTING (6), p. 70.
HOLTHAUSEN (386), p. 402. Gives a text of the alliterative preface, and bibliography.

Text: GREIN-WÜLKER (672), Vol. 5 (916). See *Bibliography* above.

Discussion

917. KREBS, H. Die angelsächsische übersetzung der dialoge Gregors. Anglia (36), Vol. 2: 65-70; 3: 70-3. 1879-80.
     Also gives texts of the preface, introductory chapter, and the conclusion.

918. JOHNSON, H. Gab es zwei von einander unabhängige altenglische übersetzungen der dialoge Gregor's? Berlin, 1884.

919. KELLER, W. Die litterarischen bestrebungen von Worcester in angelsächsischer zeit. Strassburg, 1900. Q. F. (103), Vol. LXXXIV.

GREIN-WÜLKER (672), Vol. 5 (916). See *Bibliography* above.

---

*See also Part X: Werferth, p. 91.

Wonders of the East

Bibliography

WÜLKER (3), p. 505.

920. KNAPPE, F. Das angelsächsische prosastück Die Wunder des Ostens. Überlieferung, quellen, sprache und text nach beiden handschriften. Berlin, 1906.
921. FÖRSTER, M. Zur altenglischen Mirabilien-version. Archiv (25), Vol. 117: 367-70. 1906.

BRANDL (5), p. 1133.

Text

COCKAYNE (673), pp. 33-39; KNAPPE (920), pp. 43-64.
RYPINS (715), pp. 51-67.

Discussion

COCKAYNE (673), pp. 76-80; KNAPPE (920), pp. 5-20.
FÖRSTER (921); RYPINS (715), pp. xliv-xlvii.

Wulfstan
a. Homilies

Bibliography

WÜLKER (3), pp. 481-3; C. H. E. L. (4), pp. 492-4; KÖRTING (6), p. 73.

922. BECHER, R. Wulfstans Homilien. Leipzig, 1910. A very good bibliography. Gives a brief statement of the content of each homily, pp. 40-103.

Text

923. NAPIER, A. S. Wulfstan. Sammlung der ihm zugeschriebenen homilien nebst untersuchungen über ihre echtheit. Berlin, 1883.

Discussion

924. NAPIER, A. S. Über die werke des altenglischen Erzbischofs Wulfstan. Weimar, 1882.
925. EINENKEL, E. Der Sermo Lupi ad anglos ein gedicht. Anglia (36), Vol. 7 (Anz.): 200-3. 1884. A large selection from the sermon, arranged in metrical form, with notes.
926. KINARD, J. P. A study of Wulfstan's homilies: their style and sources. Baltimore, 1897.

PRIEBSCH (828); FEILER (460), pp. 43 ff.; KELLER (919).

927. PRIEBSCH, R. Quelle und abfassungszeit der sonntags epistel in der irischen 'Cáin Domnaig'. Ein beitrag zur entwicklungs- und verbreitungsgeschichte des vom himmel gefallenen briefes Christi. M. L. R. (27), Vol. 2: 138-54. 1906. Contains also portions of a text.

BECHER (922). Wulfstans Homilien.

927a. JOST, K. Wulfstan und die angelsächsische Chronik. Anglia (36), Vol. 47: 105-23. 1923.

b. Ecclesiastical Laws

NOTE: See Ecclesiastical Miscellanea, especially LIEBERMANN (809). See also FEHR (694).

PART XII

MISCELLANEOUS

NOTE: Bibliography of various minor runic remains is given in KENNEDY (8), pp. 78-83, *passim*. Texts are given in SWEET (388), pp. 124-30.

Bewcastle Cross*

Bibliography
C. H. E. L. (4), pp. 476-7; KENNEDY (8), pp. 78-83.

Discussion
NOTE: See Nos. 2334, 2333, 2328, 2326, 2324, 2312, 2277 in KENNEDY (8). An excellent plate showing all four sides of the Cross is found in HOOPS (12), Vol. I, opposite p. 274.
BROWN (240), Vol. V. Much discussion. Brown contributed the article in HOOPS (12), Vol. I, pp. 272-4.

928. COLLINGWOOD, W. G. Northumbrian crosses of the pre-Norman age. London, 1927.
An important contribution to the study of the Northern stone-crosses and similar monuments. Valuable illustrations.

Charters

Bibliography
BRANDL (5), p. 1053; GROSS (145), pp. 45-8, 267-70; KENNEDY (8), p. 127.

Text
929. KEMBLE, J. M. Codex diplomaticus aevi saxonici. 6 vols. London, 1839-48. The most comprehensive collection.

930. THORPE, B. Diplomatarium anglicum aevi saxonici. A collection of English charters. London, 1865. With translation.
SWEET (388), pp. 426-60. From manuscripts antedating 900.

931. BIRCH, W. DE G. Cartularium saxonicum: A collection of charters relating to Anglo-Saxon history. 3 vols. London, 1885-93. In general supersedes KEMBLE (929). Covers A. D. 430-975.

932. EARLE, J. A Hand-book to the land charters, and other Saxonic documents. Oxford, 1888. Occasional pieces are translated.

933. NAPIER, A. S., AND W. H. STEVENSON. The Crawford collection of early charters and documents now in the Bodleian Library. Anecdota Oxoniensia, part 7. Oxford, 1895. Complementary to BIRCH (931). Not all are Old English.

See also Cynewulfian Poems: (c) Dream of the Rood, p. 70.

934. HARMER, F. E. Select English historical documents of the ninth and tenth centuries. Cambridge [Eng.], 1914. Twenty-three documents (grants, deeds, wills, etc.); translation and notes.
NOTE: Translations of various texts from Kemble, Thorpe, Birch, and Harmer are given in CHAMBERS (198), pp. 229-30, 248-51, 252-3, 295-7.

Discussion
NOTE: The most important discussions are listed in BRANDL (5), p. 1053, and GROSS (145), pp. 45-8, 267-70.

935. WALLENBERG, J. K. Studies in Old Kentish charters. In Studia Neophilologica (76), Vol. I. 1928.
936. KEAYS-YOUNG, JULIA. The Eadmund-Aelfric charter, 944 A. D. In R. E. S. (70), Vol. 6: 271-83. 1930. An interesting study of a fairly typical Old English land charter.
936a. FÖRSTER, M. Die freilassungsurkunden des Bodwin-Evangeliars. In A Grammatical Miscellany. . . . (139b), pp. 77-9. 1930.
Discusses and gives texts of some Old English charters, and makes valuable comments on the texts of Old English charters in general.

Codex Aureus Inscription

Text
SWEET (388), p. 175; SWEET (323), p. 195; BENHAM (343), pp. 77-9. With translation.

"Festermen" of Aelfric, The

936b. BJÖRKMAN, E. Die "festermen" des Aelfric. In Festschrift. . . . Morsbach (125), pp. 1-19. Gives bibliography, text, and discussion.
936c. LINDKVIST, H. Some notes on Elfric's Festermen. Anglia Beibl. (37), Vol. 33: 130-44. 1922. STEVENSON (806a), pp. 11-13, also gives text and discussion.

Franks Casket (Clermont or Runic Casket)

Bibliography
WÜLKER (3), pp. 356-9; C. H. E. L. (4), p. 477.
BRANDL (5), p. 951; KENNEDY (8), pp. 78-83.
BROWN (240). The Arts in early England. Vol. VI, Part 1. 1930.

Discussion
NOTE: See Nos. 2332, 2309, 2301, 2298, 2292, 2291, 2290, 2289, and 2285 in KENNEDY (8).
IMELMANN (413). Die Hos-seite des Franks Casket.
937. CLARK, ELEANOR G. The right side of the Franks Casket. P. M. L. A. (69), Vol. 45: 339-53. 1930.
BROWN (240). The arts in early England. Vol. VI. Part 1. 1930. Gives a full critical analysis.

Photographs
938. NAPIER, A. S. The Franks Casket. In An English Miscellany (121), pp. 362-81. Excellent reproductions and important discussion.
   HEUSLER (430), pp. 2-3; CLARK (937); BROWN (240).

Genealogies

Bibliography
   BRANDL (5), p. 1055; FÖRSTER (883), p. 44; KLAEBER (462), pp. 239-40.

Text
   THORPE (793), Vol. I, pp. 86, 126-7, 232-3. Translation, Vol. II, pp. 44, 57-8, 100-1. There are other fragments of genealogies in the *Chronicle*.
   COCKAYNE (674), Vol. III, pp. 444-5. Gives texts and translation.
   GRIMM-STALLYBRASS (351), Vol. IV, *passim*. Gives discussion also.
   SWEET (388), pp. 167-71, 179. Texts of Northumbrian and Saxon Fragments.
   EARLE-PLUMMER (792), Vol. I, pp. 2-5. For harmonized West Saxon genealogical trees, see Vol. II, pp. 1-5. For Mercian, see p. 6.
938a. NAPIER, A. S. Two Old English fragments. M. L. N. (26), Vol. 12: 105-14. 1897. See pp. 106-8.
939. HACKENBERG, E. Die stammtafeln der angelsächsischen königreiche. Berlin, 1918. Gives complete texts of the West Saxon genealogies, with discussion.
   See also A. Brandl, "Die Urstammtafel der Westsachsen und das Beowulf-Epos," in Archiv (25), Vol. 137: 6-24. 1918.
   See also Brandl's "Die Urstammtafel der englischen könige" in Sitzungsb. d. kgl. preusz. Akad. d. Wiss. (93), no. 3, 1918.
   CHAMBERS (198). On p. 58 there is a translation of the Pedigree of the Mercian kings (from MS. C. C. C. C. 183 [English]). On p. 98 is a translation of the Genealogical and Chronological Note prefixed to the Parker MS. of the *Anglo-Saxon Chronicle*.

Discussion
   GRIMM-STALLYBRASS (351), pp. 1709-36.
   EARLE-PLUMMER (792), Vol. II, pp. 1-6; CHADWICK (155), pp. 269 ff.
940. WILLIAMS, O. T. The dialect of the text of the Northumbrian Genealogies. M. L. R. (27), Vol. 4: 323-8. 1909.
   HACKENBERG (939). Die stammtafeln der angelsächsischen königreiche.
941. WHEELER, G. H. The genealogy of the early West Saxon kings. E. H. R. (149), Vol. 36: 161-71. 1921.

Glosses

Bibliography: BRANDL (5), p. 1055; KENNEDY (8), pp. 128-9.
Text: Both BRANDL (5) and KENNEDY (8) mention the important texts.

Liber Vitae
a. Northumbrian
Bibliography: KENNEDY (8), p. 130.

Text and Discussion

942. STEVENSON, J. Liber Vitae. Surtees Soc. Pub. (107), Vol. XIII. 1841.

> A photographic reproduction of the text was issued (Surtees Soc. Pub. (107), Vol. CXXXVI) in 1923. A new text with introduction is being prepared for the society by J. A. Herbert, with contributions also by others.

SWEET (388), pp. 154-66. Text.

943. BJÖRKMAN, E. Zum nordhumbrischen Liber Vitae. Anglia Beibl. (37), Vol. 29: 243-7. 1918. A collation.

> See also titles in KENNEDY (8), and the introduction to the facsimile edition of the text mentioned in the notes to STEVENSON (942).

b. Winchester
Text and Discussion: BIRCH (846).

Mortain Casket

943a. CAHEN, M., AND OLSEN, M. L'inscription runique du Coffret de Mortain. Avec un appendice par C. Osieczkowska. Paris. 1930. Photographic reproduction, description, history, and interpretation of the casket.

Ruthwell Cross*

Bibliography

WÜLKER (3), pp. 134-8; BRANDL (5), pp. 1031-2; KENNEDY (8), pp. 78-83.

Text: ZUPITZA-SCHIPPER (325), pp. 4-7, in the eleventh edition.

Discussion

NOTE: See Nos. 2334, 2328, 2326, 2324, 2312, 2277, in KENNEDY (8).

BROWN (240), Vol. V. Gives extended discussion.

COLLINGWOOD (928). Northumbrian crosses of the pre-Norman age.

Urswick Inscription

943b. COLLINGWOOD, W. G. A rune-inscribed Anglian cross-shaft at Urswick church. Transactions of the Cumberland and Westmoreland Antiquarian and Archaeological Soc., Vol. XI, New Series, pp. 462-8. Kendal, 1911.

943c. OLSEN, M. Notes on the Urswick inscription. Norsk Tidsskrift for Sprogvidenskap (65), Vol. 4: [282]-286. 1930.

---

*See also Cynewulfian Poems: c. Dream of the Rood, p. 70.

INDEX OF MODERN AUTHORS AND PUBLICATIONS

In this index the figures refer to the serial number of the items in the work.

Aarbøger for Nordisk Oldkyndighed og Historie, 41.
Abegg, D., 402.
Aberg, N., 248.
Academy, 42.
Acta Philologica Scandinavica: Tidskrift for Nordisk Sprogforskning, 43.
Adams, G. B., 218.
Adams, H., 213.
A Grammatical Miscellany, 139b.
Agrell, S., 289, 290.
Allison, T., 233a.
Althof, H., 654.
American Bibliography, 23.
American Journal of Philology, 44.
Anderson, L. H., 237.
An English Miscellany, 121.
Anglia, 36.
Anglia Beiblatt, 37.
Anglica, 134.
Anglistische Forschungen, 81.
Anzeiger für deutsches Altertum und deutsche Litteratur, 45.
Archiv für das Studium der neueren Sprachen, 25.
Arkiv för Nordisk Filologi, 46.
Arndt, W., 297.
Arnold Schröer, 137.
Aron, A., 182.
Ashdown, M., 617a.
Ashley, W. J., 202.
Assmann, B., 682, 684, 685, 714, 838, 876.
Athenaeum, 47.
Attenborough, F. L., 843.
Aurner, N. S., 586.
Ayres, H. M., 7, 590.

Baldwin, C. S., 342.

Barnouw, A. J., 406.
Bartels, A., 411a.
Bartlett, H., 628.
Baskervill, W. M., 543, 716.
Bateson, M., 771, 808.
Batiouchkof, T., 646.
Baugh, A. C., 495.
Becher, R., 922.
Beddoe, J., 152.
Behagel (*Festschrift*), 130.
Beiträge zur englischen Philologie, 81a.
Beiträge zur germanischen Sprachwissenschaft, 130.
Beiträge zur Geschichte der deutschen Sprache und Literatur, 48.
Belfour, A. O., 826.
Benham, A. R., 343.
Berberich, H., 824.
Berbner, N., 802.
Berliner Beiträge zur germanischen und romanischen Philologie, 82.
Berthold, L., 525.
Bibliographie der deutschen Zeitschriften-literatur, 33.
Bibliographie der Rezensionen, 35.
Bibliographischer Monatsbericht, 34.
Binz, G., 528, 551.
Birch, W. de G., 846, 875, 931.
Björkman, E., 936b, 943.
Blackburn, F. A., 515, 606.
Blair, D., 774.
Bode, W., 400.
Boer, R. C., 472, 480, 643.
Böhmer, H., 810.
Bond, E. A., 308, 310, 311.
Bonner Beiträge zur Anglistik, 83.
Bonner Studien zur englischen Philologie, 84.

BIBLIOGRAPHY OF OLD ENGLISH

Bosworth, J., 277, 751.
Bourauel, J., 545.
Bowker, A., 718.
Bradley, H., 469, 522.
Brandl (*Festschrift*), 134.
Brandl, A., 5, 456, 558, 939.
Breck, E., 693.
Bremer, O., 153.
Brenner, E., 896.
Brenner, O., 271.
Breslauer Beiträge zur Literaturgeschichte, 85.
Brie, M., 529.
Bright, J. W., 318, 814, 895.
Bright, W., 226.
Britannica, 138.
Brooke, S. A., 333, 334.
Brotanek, R., 452.
Brown, C. F., 533, 535, 538, 539.
Brown, G. B., 239, 240.
Browne, G. F., 181, 227, 231.
Bruce, J. D., 627, 650.
Bruinier, J. W., 360.
Bruning, E., 630.
Buchholz, R., 650a.
Buck, C. D., 286.
Budde, E., 176.
Bugge, E. S., 288.
Bülbring, K., 272.
Burton, R., 421.

Cahen, M., 287a, 943a.
Callaway, M., 275.
Cambridge Book of Prose and Verse, 398.
Cambridge History of English Literature, 4.
Cambridge Medieval History, 143.
Cappelli, A., 298.
Chadwick, H. M., 155, 215, 429.
Chambers, R. W., 198, 335, 376a, 461, 466, 494, 661.
Chase, F. H., 273, 683.
Child, C. H., 488a.
Cheyney, E. P., 206.
Clark, E. G., 937.
Clarke, M. G., 349.
Classen, K. M., 782, 794.

Clubb, M. D., 374, 513.
Collected Papers of Henry Sweet, 124.
Collingwood, W. G., 194, 928, 943b.
Collitz (*Festschrift*), 139a.
Columbia University Studies in English and Comparative Literature, 86.
Cockayne, O., 673, 674.
Cook, A. S., 254b, 391, 483, 484, 498, 542, 549, 553, 559, 574, 609, 629, 660, 676, 719, 813, 869, 872a.
Cosijn, P., 254a.
Courthope, W. J., 422.
Craigie, W. A., 304, 324, 326, 327, 356.
Cramer, J., 582.
Crawford, D. H., 497.
Crawford, S. J., 681, 687, 702, 785, 866, 872b.
Cross, T. P., 1.
Crow, C. L., 504.
Cumulative Book Index, 28.
Cunningham, W., 205.

Davis, H. W. C., 142.
De Baye, J., 235.
Deering, R. W., 457.
Dehmer, H., 473a.
Delcourt, J., 859.
Deutsche Literaturzeitung, 49.
DeWitz, A., 739.
Dickins, B., 281.
Dieter, F., 256.
Dieterich, A., 879.
Dietrich, E., 689.
Dixon, W. M., 428.
Douglas, D. C., 807.
Drake, A., 817.
Dudley, L., 603a, 648.

Earle, J., 316, 332, 449, 635, 792, 858, 932.
Early English Text Society Publications, 87.
Ebert, A., 336.
Ebert, M., 19.

Ehrismann, G., 408, 645.
Einenkel, E., 791, 925.
Ekwall, E., 559.
Elton, C. J., 189.
Emerson, O. F., 249, 570, 704, 761.
Endter, W., 723.
Englische Studien, 38.
English Historical Review, 149.
English Miscellany, An, 121.
English Studies, 39.
Erlanger Beiträge zur englischen Philologie, 87a.
Evans, J., 842.
Essays and Studies by Members of the English Association, 88.

Facsimiles of Ancient Charters, 308.
Faust, C., 397.
Fehlauer, F., 503.
Fehr, B., 694, 713, 908.
Fehrle, E., 163.
Feiler, E., 460.
Feist, S., 291.
Ferrell, C. C., 642.
Festschrift F. Kluge, 136.
Festschrift für Lorenz Morsbach, 125.
Festschrift Wilhelm Viëtor, 123.
Festschrift zu Eugen Mogk, 131.
Fiedler, H. G., 780.
Files, G. T., 172.
Fischer, A., 171.
Fleure, H. J., 159.
Flom, G. T., 263.
Flügel Memorial Volume, 126.
Forsey, G. F., 785a.
Förster (*Festschrift*), 138.
Förster, M., 321, 376a, 379, 380, 382, 678a, 686, 703, 705, 777, 779, 781, 801, 829, 833a, 834, 863, 872b, 880, 881, 882, 883, 884, 885, 886, 887, 888, 889, 890, 907, 921, 936a.
Forstmann, H., 564.
Foster, J. G., 610.
Fox, S., 621, 727, 734.

Frampton, M. G., 507.
Freeman, E. A., 187.
Frings, T., 512.
Furnivall (Anniversary Volume), 121.

Garnett, J. M., 395, 488.
Garrett, R. M., 841.
Gasquet, F. A., 301.
Geidel, H., 749.
Gem, S. H., 680.
Germania, 50.
Germanica, 135.
Germanisch-romanische Monatschrift, 51.
Gerould, G. H., 350, 551, 565, 680a, 915.
Giles, J. A., 584, 727, 796.
Glunz, H., 820, 821.
Goette, R., 13.
Gomme, E. E. C., 798.
Gollancz, I., 373, 376, 550.
Golther, W., 353.
Gonser, P., 822.
Goodwin, C. W., 752, 823.
Gordon, R. K., 396.
Gorham, G. C., 861.
Grammatical Miscellany, A, 139b.
Grau, G., 458.
Green, J. R., 192.
Greene, R. L., 514.
Greg, W. W., 443.
Grein, C. W. M., 280, 385, 672.
Grendon, F., 528, 531a.
Grienberger, T., 636, 666, 580a.
Grimm, J., 351.
Grimm, W., 352.
Gross, C., 145.
Groth, E., 517.
Grundriss der germanischen Philologie, 9.
Guest, E., 634.
Guide to Historical Literature, 148.
Gummere, F. B., 11, 393.

Hackenberg, E., 939.
Haddan, A. W., 224.

BIBLIOGRAPHY OF OLD ENGLISH

Hall, H., 201.
Hall, J. L., 394, 487.
Hall, J. R. C., 278, 490, 491.
Hälsig, F., 530.
Hamilton, G. L., 546.
Hammarström, M., 292.
Hampson, R. T., 746, 873.
Handke, R., 818.
Hanscom, E. D., 404.
Hardwick, C., 815.
Hargrove, H. L., 722, 728.
Harmer, F. E., 794, 934.
Harris, L. M., 819.
Harsley, F., 893.
Hart, W. M., 424.
Harvard Studies and Notes in Philology and Literature, 89.
Hecht, H., 345, 458, 916.
Heinzel, R., 419, 478, 479, 652, 906.
Hellmann, G., 878.
Hempl, G., 270, 283.
Herbert, J. A., 305.
Herrmann, P., 364.
Hervey, F., 811a.
Herzfeld, G., 790, 855, 860.
Hesperia, 90.
Heusler, A., 426, 427, 430, 444.
Hewison, J., 555.
Heyne, M., 467.
Hicketier, F., 607.
Hodgetts, J. F., 234.
Hodgkin, T., 193.
Hofer, O., 451.
Holdsworth, W. S., 219.
Holt, L. H., 561.
Holthausen, F., 386, 448, 468, 521, 541, 571, 623, 631, 632a, 658, 659, 671, 837, 877.
Hoops (*Festschrift*), 132.
Hoops, J., 12, 236, 384.
Howard, E. J., 551a.
Hubbard, F. G., 726.
Hübener, G., 743.
Huchon, R., 251.
Hulme, W. H., 724, 836, 864, 865.
Hunt, W., 228.

Imelmann, R., 407, 413, 620.
Indogermanische Forschungen, 52.
Ingram, J., 799.
International Index to Periodicals, 30.

Jahresberichte der Geschichtswissenschaft, 150.
Jahresbericht über die Erscheinungen auf dem Gebiete der germanischen Philologie, 22.
James, M. R., 300, 835.
Jane, L. C., 719.
Jansen, K., 536.
Jellinek, A. L., 571.
Jespersen (*Festschrift*), 139b.
Jespersen, O., 252.
Jiriczek, O., 361.
Johnson, H., 918.
Johnson, W. S., 519.
Jordan, R., 664.
Jost, K., 680a, 927a.
Journal of English and Germanic Philology, 53.
Jovy, H., 524.

Kaluza, M., 265, 434, 440.
Karsten, T. E., 18.
Kauffmann, F., 14, 355.
Keays,-Young, J., 936.
Keim, H. W., 775.
Keller, G., 184.
Keller, W., 293, 302, 306, 919.
Kellner, L., 599.
Kemble, J. M., 186, 377, 639, 929.
Kennedy, A. G., 8, 331.
Kennedy, C. W., 371, 506, 540.
Kent, C. W., 560.
Ker, W. P., 339, 341, 425, 619.
Kershaw, N., 389.
Kieler Studien zur englischen Philologie, 91.
Kinard, J. P., 926.
Kirkland, J. H., 581.
Kissack, R. A., 431.
Klaeber (*Festschrift*), 139.

Klaeber, F., 462, 485, 505, 520, 523, 531a, 594, 741.
Klebs, E., 759.
Kleinert, G., 649.
Kluge (*Festschrift*), 136.
Kluge, F., 250, 317, 633, 641, 784, 804, 805, 832, 847.
Knappe, F., 920.
Knott, T. A., 262.
Koch, C. F., 264.
Kölner anglistische Arbeiten, 92.
Königliche Preussische Akademie der Wissenschaften, 93.
Königliche sächsische Akademie der Wissenschaften, 94.
Konrath, M., 848.
Körting, G., 6.
Krämer, E., 502.
Krapp, G. P., 331, 374a, 544.
Krebs, H., 917.
Krueger, C., 600.
Kurtz, B. P., 566, 650b.
Kuypers, A. B., 852.
Kylie, E., 849.

Laborde, E. D., 615, 616.
Lappenberg, J. M., 188.
Lawrence, W. W., 331a, 463, 473, 580, 589, 644, 662, 670.
Leach, A. F., 178, 179.
Learned, M. D., 653.
Leeds, E. T., 241.
Lefebvre, G., 190.
Lees, B. A., 721.
Leipziger Beiträge zur englischen Philologie, 95.
Leitzmann, A., 656.
Leonard, W. E., 446, 493.
Leonhardi, G., 839, 853.
Liebermann (*Festschrift*), 127.
Liebermann, F., 217, 482, 614, 773, 809, 811, 845, 857, 911.
Lindelöf, U., 254, 897, 898, 902, 910, 912.
Lindkvist, H., 936c.
Lindisfarne Gospels, 816.
Lingard, J., 223.
Lipsius, J., 754.

Lipson, E., 210.
L'Isle, W., 712.
Literarisches Zentralblatt, 54.
Literaturblatt für germanische und romanische Philologie, 24.
Litteris, 55.
Logeman, H., 762, 870, 871.
Logeman, W. S., 763, 805.
Löhe, H., 454.
Löweneck, M., 868.
Luick (*Festschrift*), 133.
Luick, K., 266, 436.
Lumby, J. R., 453.
Lunds Universitets Årsskrift, 96.

Mackie, W. S., 587, 632.
MacLean, G. E., 707, 709.
Magoun, Jr., F. P., 11.
Maitland, F. W., 165, 214.
Malone, K., 474, 476, 593.
Mann, J. S., 141.
Mann, M. F., 571.
Markham, C., 748.
Märkisch, R., 760.
Marstrander, C. J. S., 290a.
Mason, L., 527.
Mawer, A., 195, 595.
Mayhew, A. L., 269.
Mead, W. E., 403.
Mediaeval England, 142.
Meissner, J. L. G., 233.
Mémoires de la Société Neophilologique à Helsingfors, 97.
Menner, R. J., 638.
Merbot, R., 399.
Meyer, R. M., 359, 420.
Millar, E. G., 305, 816.
Miller, T., 729.
Mitchell, F. H., 710.
Modern Humanities Research Association. Annual Bibliography. 21.
Modern Language Notes, 26.
Modern Language Review, 27.
Modern Philology, 56.
Mogk (*Festschrift*), 131.
Mogk, E., 348, 367.

BIBLIOGRAPHY OF OLD ENGLISH

Möller, H., 478.
Moncrieff, C. K. S., 492.
Moore, M. F., 200, 299.
Moore, S., 262, 516, 551.
Morley, H., 337, 501.
Morris, R., 778, 830, 831, 913.
Morris, W. A., 222.
Morsbach (*Festschrift*), 125.
Moyen Âge, Le, 57.
Much, R., 157, 667.
Müllenhoff, K., 10, 471, 477.
Müller, E., 603.
Müller, H., 598.
Munch, P. A., 366a.
Münchener Beiträge zur romanischen und englischen Philologie, 98.
Munn, J. B., 496.
Murch, H. S., 568.
Mürkens, G., 518.

Nansen, F., 750.
Napier, A. S., 447, 562, 604, 651, 765, 780, 789, 800, 806, 833, 877, 914, 923, 924, 933, 938, 938a.
Nation, 58.
Neckel, G., 15.
Nehab, J., 786.
Neophilologus, 59.
Neue anglistische Arbeiten, 99.
Neuendorff, B., 585.
Neue philologische Rundschau, 60.
Neueren Sprachen, Die, 61.
Neuphilologische Mitteilungen, 62.
Neusprachliche Studien, 133.
New Statesman and Athenaeum, 58.
Nölle, G., 455.
Nordisk Tidskrift för Vetenskap, Konst och Industri, 64.
Nordisk Tidsskrift for Filologi, 63.
Norman, H. W., 699.
Norsk Tidsskrift for Sprogvidenskap, 65.
Northup, C. S., 2.
Notes and Queries, 66.

Olivero, F., 547.
Olrik, A., 357, 362.
Olsen, M., 288, 943a, 943c.
Oman, C. W. C., 197, 244.
Otia Merseiana, 100.
Ott, J. H., 711.

Padelford, F. M., 174.
Paetow, L., 146.
Palaeographical Society, 310.
Palaestra, 101.
Panzer, F., 358.
Parry, A. W., 183.
Patch, H. R., 559.
Paul, H., 9.
Pauli, R., 745.
Payne, J. F., 238.
Peake, H. J., 158.
Pedersen, H., 287.
Peebles, R. J., 572.
Peers, C. R., 246.
Petersen, C., 363.
Petit-Dutaillis, C., 190.
Pfändler, W., 175.
Pfister, F., 717.
Philippson, E. A., 185.
Phillpots, B. S., 369, 617.
Philologica, 67.
Philological Quarterly, 68.
Philologische Studien, 120.
Piper, F., 622, 856.
Pitman, J. H., 574.
Plummer, A., 230.
Plummer, C., 225, 720, 792.
Pogatscher, A., 268.
Pollock, F., 214.
Pons, E., 416.
Poole, R. L., 795.
Pound, L., 511.
Priebsch, R., 828, 927.
Probleme der englischen Sprache und Kultur, 132.
Publications of the Modern Language Association, 69.
Publications of the Victoria University of Manchester, 102.
Purdie, E., 611.

Quellen und Forschungen, 103.
Quennell, M., and C. H. B., 168.

Rademacher, M., 304a.
Ramsay, J. H., 191.
Ramsay, R. L., 629a, 895.
Rankin, J. W., 409, 441.
Readers' Guide to Periodical Literature, 31.
Reum, A., 696.
Review of English Studies, 70.
Revue Critique d'Histoire et de Littérature, 71
Revue Germanique, 72.
Rhodes, E. W., 850.
Ricci, A., 556.
Ricci, H., 414, 417a.
Richter, C., 405a.
Rieger, M., 500.
Ripley, W. Z., 156.
Rituale Ecclesiae Dunelmensis, 909, 910.
Robertson, A. J., 844.
Robinson, J. A., 232, 776.
Robinson, W. C., 387.
Roeder, F., 173, 177, 894.
Romania, 73.
Romanische Forschungen, 74.
Root, R. K., 548.
Rösler, M., 180.
Routh, H. V., 433.
Routh, J., 442.
Rypins, S. I., 383, 715.

Saintsbury, G., 377a.
Salzman, L. F., 208, 211.
Sarrazin, G., 411, 534.
Saussaye, P. D. Chantepie de la, 354.
Savage, E. A., 303.
Schepss, G., 736.
Schilling, H., 747.
Schipper, J., 325, 436, 439, 640, 730, 731.
Schleich, G., 788.
Schlotterose, O., 569.
Schmid, R., 212.

Schmidt, W., 450.
Schmitt, F., 812.
Schmitz, T., 537.
Schneider, H., 366, 370.
Scholz, H. van der M., 432.
Schrader, O., 16.
Schreiner, K., 591.
Schröder, E., 691.
Schröder, F. R., 20.
Schröer (*Festschrift*), 137.
Schröer, A., 602, 692, 766, 767, 770.
Schröer, M. M. A., 346.
Schücking, L. L., 319, 345, 470, 481, 657, 668.
Schütte, G., 162.
Scripture, E. W., 445.
Sedgefield, W. J., 322, 330, 465, 612, 733, 737.
Seebohm, M. E., 209.
Setzler, E., 435.
Shore, T. W., 154.
Siebs, T., 663.
Sieper, E., 412.
Sievers (*Festschrift*), 120, 135.
Sievers, E., 255, 260, 284, 437, 438, 508, 526, 563, 665, 769, 787, 874.
Sims, W. R., 618.
Singer, C., 243, 245, 247, 783, 851.
Singer, D., 783.
Sisam, K., 381, 705a, 843, 849.
Skeat, W. W., 309, 634, 706, 815.
Skemp, A. R., 405, 531.
Small, G. W., 276.
Smith, C. A., 257.
Smith, R. A., 244a.
Smithson, G. A., 410.
Smyth, A. H., 758.
Snell, F. J., 334a.
Sokoll, E., 620.
Sonnenschein, W. S., 147.
Spaeth, J. D., 392.
Speculum, 75.
Stand und aufgaben der Sprachwissenschaft, 129.
Stanford University Publications, 104.
Stefanovič, S., 669.

BIBLIOGRAPHY OF OLD ENGLISH 145

Steinhausen, G., 17.
Stenton, F. M., 194.
Stephens, G., 282.
Stevens, W. O., 557.
Stevenson, J., 608, 797, 892, 909, 942.
Stevenson, W. H., 688a, 719, 806a, 933.
Stewart, H. I., 735.
Stjerna, K., 242.
Streitberg-Festgabe, 128.
Streitberg (*Festschrift*), 129.
Strobl, J., 597.
Strong, A., 494.
Strunk, W., 567.
Strutt, J., 166.
Stubbs, W., 190, 224.
Studia Neophilologica, 76.
Studien zur englischen Philologie, 106.
Studier i modern Sprakvetenskap, 105.
Studies in English Philology, 139.
Studies in Honor of Hermann Collitz, 139a.
Studies in Philology, 77.
Subject Index to Periodicals, 32.
Surtees Society Publications, 107.
Sweet (Memorial), 124.
Sweet, H., 267, 279, 312, 313, 314, 323, 388, 700, 738, 744.
Symons, B., 347.

Taswell-Langmead, T. P., 221.
Taylor, H. O., 144.
Ten Brink, B., 338, 479.
Tessmann, A., 708.
Texte und Forschungen, 127.
Thomas, W., 415.
Thompson, A. H., 910.
Thompson, E. M., 295, 296, 308, 310, 311.
Thompson, S., 397.
Thomson, E., 459.
Thorpe, B., 188, 372, 375, 601, 626, 698, 745, 755, 793, 803, 930.
Threlkeld, F., 390.

Times [London] Literary Supplement, 29.
Tinker, C. B., 391, 486, 489, 676.
Toller, T. N., 277.
Tolman, A. H., 401.
Traill, H. D., 141.
Transactions of the Cambridge Philological Society, 108.
Transactions of the Connecticut Academy of Arts and Sciences, 109.
Trautmann, M., 532, 576, 578, 588, 605, 655.
Treneer, A., 344.
Tupper, F., 540a, 573, 575, 610a, 764, 772.
Tupper, J. W., 579, 677.
Tupper, M. F., 727.
Turk, M. H., 329, 742.
Turner, S., 164.

University of California Publications in Modern Philology, 110.
University of Illinois Studies in Language and Literature, 111.
University of Iowa Studies, 112.
University of Pennsylvania Publications, 113.
University of Toronto Studies, 114.
University of Virginia Monographs, 115.
University of Wisconsin Studies in Language and Literature, 116.
Untersuchungen und Quellen, 122.
Uppsala Universitets Årsskrift, 117.
Usher, A. P., 207.

Van Draat, P. F., 732.
Victoria History of the Counties of England, 140.
Viëtor (*Festschrift*), 123.
Viëtor, W., 554.
Viglione, F., 794a.
Vinogradoff, P., 203, 204.
Vogt, F., 854.
Von Amira, K., 216.

Von der Leyen, F., 365.
Von Fleischhacker, R., 840.
Von Friesen, O., 285, 292a.
Von Inama-Sternegg, K., 167.
Von Kelle (*Festschrift*), 122.
Von Vincenti, A. R., 637.

Wack, G., 740.
Wadstein, E., 160.
Wakeman, H. O., 229.
Wallenberg, K., 935.
Wardale, E. E., 261.
Warner, R. D-N., 701.
Warton, T., 418.
Washington, State University of, 118.
Wattenbach, W., 294.
Weinbaum, M., 807.
Weldon, B. de W., 161.
Wellman, M., 573a.
Wessén, E., 475.
Westwood, J. O., 307.
Wheeler, G. H., 941.
White, A. B., 220.
White, C. L., 679.
Whitman, C. H., 552.
Wichmann, J., 900.
Wildhagen, K., 891, 901, 903, 905.
Willard, R., 827.
Williams, B. C., 596.
Williams, M. W., 196.

Williams, O. T., 940.
Williams, R. A., 592.
Willich, A. F. M., 583.
Wimmer, L. F. A., 283.
Wingfield-Stratford, E. C., 169.
Wolff, L., 368.
Wolters, F., 363.
Wright, E. M., 258, 259.
Wright, J., 258, 259.
Wright, T., 170, 678, 688, 695.
Wülfing, J. E., 274.
Wülker, R., 3, 340, 378, 385, 464, 509, 625, 672, 725, 825, 862, 867.
Wyatt, A. J. 254c, 315, 320, 328, 466, 577.
Wyld, H. C., 253, 417.

Yale Studies in English, 119.
Year's Work in English Studies, 40.

Zachrisson, R. E., 199.
Zeitschrift für deutsche Philologie, 78.
Zeitschrift für deutsches Altertum und deutsche Litteratur, 79.
Zeitschrift für vergleichende Sprachforschung, 80.
Zernial, U., 613.
Zeuss, K., 151.
Zupitza, J., 325, 499, 510, 624, 647, 690, 697, 753, 756, 757, 768, 872.

INDEX OF OLD ENGLISH WRITINGS

An asterisk distinguishes prose writings; ordinary type is used for poetic writings; a dagger is used for miscellaneous items, such as the Bewcastle and Ruthwell crosses, the genealogies, and the Franks Casket.

*ABC. See Prognostics, p. 127.
*Abgarus. See Aelfric: (q) Lives of the Saints, p. 101.
Address of the Soul to the Body. See Soul to the Body, p. 89.
*Admonitio ad Filium Spiritualem, St. Basil's. See Aelfric: (m) Homilies, p. 99.
*Adrian and Ritheus, p. 96.
Aelfric, p. 96.
Aethelwold, p. 102. See also Benedictine Rule, p. 109 and Aelfric: (f) De Consuetudine Monachorum, p. 98.
*Ages of the World. See Prognostics, p. 127.
*Alcuin's De Virtutibus et Vitiis, Translation of, p. 102.
Aldhelm, Praise of, p. 54.
*Alexander to Aristotle, Letter of, p. 102.
Alfred, King, Prose Works of, p. 103.
Alfred, Poems by, p. 54.
Alfred's Capture and Death, p. 54.
*Alfred's Charters, p. 108.
*Alfred's Handbook, p. 108.
*Alfred's Jewel, p. 108.
*Alfred's Laws, p. 106.
*Alfred's Will, p. 108.
Alms, p. 54.
*Alphabet, Divination. See Prognostics, p. 127.
Andreas, p. 69.
*Andrew, St., p. 108. See also X Verse: Cynewulfian Poems: (a) Andreas, p. 69.

*Anglo-Saxon Chronicle, p. 112.
Anglo-Saxon Chronicle, Poems from the. See Alfred's Capture and Death, Brunanburh, Edgar's Coronation, Edgar's Death, Edward the Confessor's Death, Edward the Martyr's Death, Five Cities, William the Conqueror.
*Antichrist. See Homilies: (b) Miscellaneous, p. 118.
*Apollonius of Tyre, p. 108.
*Apuleius, Herbarium of. See Herbarium, p. 117.
Ascension of Christ. See Caedmonian Poems: (b) Christ and Satan, p. 64; see also Cynewulfian Poems: (b) Christ, p. 70.
Athelstan's Victory. See Brunanburh, p. 63.
*Augustine's Soliloquies (Blooms of Alfred), p. 104.
Azarias, p. 55.

*Basil's Admonitio ad Filium Spiritualem. See Aelfric: (m) Homilies, p. 99.
*Basil's Exameron Anglice. See Aelfric: (m) Homilies, p. 99.
Battles of Brunanburh, Finnsburh, Maldon. See Brunanburh, Finnsburh, Maldon.
Bede's Death Song, p. 55.
*Bede's De Temporibus. See Aelfric: (g) Bede's De Temporibus, p. 99.
*Bede's Ecclesiastical History, p. 104.

147

Be Dōmes Dæge, p. 55.
Benedictine Office, p. 56. *See also* XI Prose: Benedictine Rule, p. 109.
*Benedictine Rule, p. 109. *See also* X Verse: Benedictine Office, p. 56; and Aelfric: (*f*) De Consuetudine Monachorum, p. 98.
Benedictional. *See* Halgung-bōc, p. 82.
Beowulf, p. 56.
Bestiary. *See* Cynewulfian Poems: (*i*) Physiologus, p. 74.
†Bewcastle Cross, p. 134. *See also* Cynewulfian Poems: (*c*) Dream of the Rood, p. 70.
*Bible, Translations of the, p. 97. *See also* Gospels, p. 115, and Psalms, p. 129.
Bi Monna Cræftum, p. 61.
Bi Manna Lease, p. 61.
Bi Manna Mode, p. 61.
Bi Manna Wyrdum, p. 62.
*Blickling Homilies, p. 110.
*Blooms of Alfred. *See* Alfred (*a*) Augustine's Soliloquies, p. 104.
Boethius, Metra (Metres) of, p. 62. *See also* XI Prose: Alfred: (*c*) Boethius, p. 105.
*Boethius' Consolations of Philosophy, p. 105. *See also* X Verse: Boethius, Metra of, p. 62.
*Brontology. *See* Prognostics, p. 127.
Brunanburh, Battle of, p. 63.
*Byrhtferth, p. 111.
Byrhtnoth's Death. *See* Maldon, p. 84.

Caedmonian Poems, p. 63.
Caedmon's Hymn, p. 63.
Calendar. *See* Menologium, p. 85.
Calendcwide. *See* Menologium, p. 85.
*Canons. *See* Aelfric: (*s*) Pastoral Letters, p. 102; *see also* Ecclesiastical Miscellanea, p. 113.

*Capitula of Theodulf. *See* Benedictine Rule, p. 109.
*Cato, Distichs (Proverbs) of, p. 111.
*Chad, Life of St., p. 112.
Charms, p. 67. *See also* XI Prose: Lācnunga, p. 120.
†Charters, p. 134.
Christ, p. 70.
Christ and Satan, p. 64.
*Christopher, Life of St., p. 112.
Christ's Descent into Hell. *See* Descent into Hell, p. 76; *see also* Caedmonian Poems: (*b*) Christ and Satan, p. 64.
*Chrodegang. *See* Benedictine Rule, p. 109.
*Chronicle, Anglo-Saxon, p. 112.
Chronicle, Poems of the Anglo-Saxon. *See* Alfred's Capture and Death; Brunanburh; Edgar's Coronation; Edgar's Death; Edward the Confessor's Death; Edward the Martyr's Death; Five Cities; William the Conqueror.
Chronology. *See* Menologium, p. 85.
†Clermont Casket, The, p. 135.
†Codex Aureus Inscription, p. 135.
*Colloquy, p. 98.
*Computations. *See* Ecclesiastical Miscellanea, p. 113.
*Confessions. *See* Prayers, p. 126.
*Consolations of Philosophy, Boethius', p. 105.
*Credo. *See* Prayers, p. 126.
Creed, p. 68.
Cross, Vision of the. *See* Cynewulfian Poems: (*c*) Dream of the Rood, p. 70; *see also* XII Miscellaneous: Ruthwell Cross, p. 137.
*Cura Pastoralis. *See* Alfred: (*d*) Gregory's Pastoral Care, p. 106.
Curse of Urse, The, p. 68.
Cynewulfian Poems, p. 68.

INDEX OF OLD ENGLISH WRITINGS 149

Daniel, p. 65.
Day of Judgment. *See* Be Dōmes Dæge, p. 55, and Last Judgment, p. 83.
*De Consuetudine Monachorum, Excerpts from Aethelwold's, p. 98. *See also* Benedictine Rule, p. 109.
*De Diebus Malis Cujusque Mensis. *See* Prognostics, p. 127.
*Defensor. *See* Liber Scintillarum, p. 122.
Deor's Lament, p. 76.
*De Quadrupedibus. *See* Medicina de Quadrupedibus, p. 124.
*De Rebus in Oriente Mirabilibus. *See* Wonders of the East, p. 133.
*De Sancto Johanne. *See* Homilies: (b) Miscellaneous, p. 118.
Descent into Hell, Christ's, p. 76.
*De Temporibus, Bede's, p. 99.
*De Virtutibus et Vitiis, Alcuin's. *See* Alcuin's De Virtutibus et Vitiis, p. 102.
*Deuteronomy. *See* Aelfric: (c) Bible, p. 97.
*Dial. *See* Horalogium, p. 119.
*Dialogues, Religious, p. 113. *See also* Elucidarium, p. 115.
*Dicta Catonis. *See* Cato, p. 111.
Didactic (Monitory) Poem, p. 77.
*Dioscorides. *See* Herbarium, p. 117.
*Discovery of the Sacred Cross. *See* Rood-tree, p. 131.
*Distichs of Cato. *See* Cato, p. 111.
*Dies Aegyptiaci. *See* Prognostics, p. 127.
*Divinations. *See* Prognostics, p. 127.
Doomsday. *See* Be Dōmes Dæge, p. 55, and Last Judgment, p. 83.
*Dream-book. *See* Prognostics, p. 127.
Dream of the Rood, p. 70.
*Durham, Book of. *See* Gospels, p. 115.

Durham, On the City of, p. 77.
*Durham Ritual. *See* Rituals, p. 131.
*Ecclesiastical History, Bede's, p. 104.
*Ecclesiastical Miscellanea, p. 113.
*Ecgberht's Penitential (*Scriftbōc*). *See* Ecclesiastical Miscellanea, p. 113., and Aethelwold: (b) Edgar's Establishment of Monasteries, p. 102.
Edgar's Coronation, p. 77.
Edgar's Death, p. 77.
*Edgar's Establishment of Monasteries, p. 102.
Edmund's Freeing of Five Cities. *See* Five Cities, p. 80.
Edward the Confessor's Death, p. 77.
Edward the Martyr's Death, p. 78.
Elene, p. 71.
*Elucidarium, p. 115.
*Enchiridion. *See* Byrhtferth, p. 111.
Endowments of Men. *See* Bi Monna Cræftum, p. 61.
*Epistle of Alexander to Aristotle. *See* Alexander, p. 102.
*Epitome of Benedict of Aniane. *See* Benedictine Rule, p. 109.
*Esther. *See* Aelfric: (c) Bible, p. 97.
*Exameron Anglice. *See* Aelfric: (m) Homilies, p. 99.
Exhortation to Christian Living (*Lār*), p. 78.
Exile's Complaint. *See* Wife's Complaint, p. 93.
Exodus, p. 65.
*Exodus. *See* Aelfric: (c) Bible, p. 97.

Fæder Lārcwidas, p. 78.
Falsehood of Men. *See* Bi Manna Lease, p. 61.
Fates of Men. *See* Bi Manna Wyrdum, p. 62.

Fates of the Apostles, p. 72.
Father's Instruction, A. (*Fæder Lārcwidas*), p. 78.
†"Festermen" of Aelfric, The, p. 135.
*Fifteen Signs before the Judgment. *See* Judgment, Fifteen Signs before the, p. 119.
Finnsburh, The Fight at, p. 78.
Five Cities (Boroughs), Edmund's Freeing of, p. 80.
*Forecasts. *See* Prognostics, p. 127.
Fortunes of Men. *See* Bi Manna Wyrdum, p. 62.
†Franks Casket (Clermont or Runic Casket), p. 135.
*Fursaeus, Life of St. *See* Aelfric: (*m*) Homilies, p. 99.

†Genealogies, p. 136.
Genesis, p. 66.
*Genesis. *See* Aelfric: (*c*) Bible, p. 97.
Gifts of Men. *See* Bi Manna Cræftum, p. 61.
Gloria, p. 80.
*Glossary, Aelfric's, p. 99.
†Glosses, p. 136.
Gnomic Verses, p. 80.
*Gospel of Nicodemus. *See* Nicodemus, p. 125.
*Gospels, p. 115.
*Grammar, Aelfric's, p. 99.
Grave, The, p. 81.
*Gregory's Dialogues. *See* Werferth, p. 132.
*Gregory's Pastoral Care, p. 106.
Guthlac, p. 72. *See also* XI Prose: Guthlac, p. 116.
*Guthlac, p. 116.

*Hadrian. *See* Adrian and Ritheus, p. 96.
Halgung-bōc, p. 82.
*Handbōc, Byrhtferth's, p. 111.
Harrowing of Hell. *See* Descent into Hell, p. 76, and Caedmonian Poems: (*b*) Christ and Satan, p. 64.

*Heptateuch. *See* Aelfric: (*c*) Bible, p. 97.
*Herbarium; Herbarium Apuleii; Herbarium from Dioscorides; etc., p. 117.
*Hexameron of St. Basil (*Exameron Anglice*). *See* Aelfric: (*m*) Homilies, p. 99.
*Historical Fragments. *See* Ecclesiastical Miscellanea, p. 113.
*History of the World, Orosius, p. 107.
*Homilies, p. 117. *See also* Aelfric: (*m*) Homilies, p. 99; Blickling Homilies, p. 110; Wulfstan: Homilies, p. 133; *Guthlac, Life of, p. 116.
*Homilies, Aelfric's, p. 99.
*Horalogium, p. 119.
*Horoscopes. *See* Prognostics, p. 127.
Husband's Message, p. 82.
Hymns and Prayers, p. 82. *See also* Creed, p. 68; Gloria, p. 80; Pater Noster, p. 85.

*Indicia Monasterialia. *See* Ecclesiastical Miscellanea, p. 113.
*Institutes of Polity. *See* Ecclesiastical Miscellanea, p. 113.
*Interrogations of Sigewulf. *See* Aelfric: (*q*) Lives of the Saints, p. 101.
*Isidor's De Ecclesiasticis Officiis. *See* Ecclesiastical Miscellanea, p. 113.

*Jamnes and Mambres, p. 119.
*Jerome's Story of Malchus, p. 119.
*Job. *See* Aelfric: (*c*) Bible, p. 97, and (*m*) Homilies, p. 99.
*Joshua. *See* Aelfric: (*c*) Bible, p. 97.
*Judges. *See* Aelfric: (*c*) Bible, p. 97.
*Judgment, Fifteen Signs before the, p. 119.
Judith, p. 83.

INDEX OF OLD ENGLISH WRITINGS 151

*Judith. *See* Aelfric: (*c*) Bible, p. 97, and (*m*) Homilies, p. 99.
Juliana, p. 73.

Kentish Psalm, p. 86.
*Kings. *See* Aelfric: (*c*) Bible, p. 97.

*Lācnunga (Medications, recipes), p. 120. *See also* X Verse: Charms, p. 67.
*Laece-bōc. *See* Leech-book, p. 121.
Lament of the Fallen Angels. *See* Caedmonian Poems: (*b*) Christ and Satan, p. 64.
Lār. *See* Exhortation to Christian Living, p. 78.
*Lapidary, p. 120.
Last Judgment (Doomsday), p. 83.
*Last Judgment, Fifteen Signs Before the, p. 119.
*Law of the Northumbrian Priests. *See* Ecclesiastical Miscellanea, p. 113.
*Laws, p. 120. *See also* V The People and Their Institutions: (F) Law, p. 28; Ecclesiastical Miscellanea, p. 113; and Alfred: (*e*) Laws, p. 106.
*Laws of Alfred, p. 106.
*Leech-book, p. 121.
*Legatio Nathanis. *See* Veronica, p. 132.
*Legends. *See* Saints.
*Legends, Royal (Kentish), p. 121.
*Letter to Brother Eadward. *See* Ecclesiastical Miscellanea, p. 113.
*Letters, p. 122. *See also* Alexander, p. 102; Aelfric: (*s*) Pastoral Letters, p. 102; and Ecclesiastical Miscellanea, p. 113.
*Leviticus. *See* Aelfric: (*c*) Bible, p. 97.
*Liber de Virtutibus et Vitiis. *See* Alcuin, p. 102.
*Liber Scintillarum, Defensor's, p. 122.

†Liber Vitae, p. 137.
*Life of St. Margaret. *See* Margaret, Life of St., p. 123.
*Lindisfarne Gospels. *See* Gospels, p. 115.
*Lives of the Saints, p. 101.
*Lorica Hymn and Lorica Prayer, p. 122.
Lover's Message. *See* Husband's Message, p. 82.

*Maccabees. *See* Aelfric: (c) Bible, p. 97.
*Malchus. *See* Jerome, p. 119.
Maldon, Battle of, p. 84.
Mambres. *See* Jamnes, p. 119.
*Manual, Byrhtferth's, p. 111.
*Margaret, Life of St., p. 123.
*Martin. *See* Blickling Homilies, p. 110.
*Martyrology, p. 123.
*Mary of Egypt, Life of St., p. 124.
Maxims. *See* Proverbs, p. 86, and Gnomic Verses, p. 80.
*Medicina de Quadrupedibus of Sextus Placitus, p. 124.
Menologium (Menology), (Calendcwide), p. 85.
*Meteorology. *See* Prognostics, p. 127.
Metra. *See* Boethius, Metra (Metres) of, p. 62.
*Mildryth, St., p. 124.
Mind of Men. *See* Bi Manna Mode, p. 61.
*Mirabilia. *See* Wonders of the East, p. 133.
Monitory Poem. *See* Didactic Poem, p. 77.
†Mortain Casket, p. 137.

*Neot, Life of St., p. 124.
*Nicene Creed. *See* Prayers, p. 126.
*Nicodemus, Gospel of, p. 125.
*Numbers. *See* Aelfric: (*c*) Bible, p. 97.

*Old and New Testaments, On the, p. 101.
*Orosius' History of the World, p. 107.
Paris Psalter, p. 86.
*Passio S. Margaretae. See Life of St. Margaret, p. 123.
*Pastoral Care. See Alfred: (d) Gregory's Pastoral Care, p. 106.
Pastoral Care. See Alfred, Poems by, p. 54.
*Pastoral Letters, p. 102.
Pater Noster, p. 85.
*Pater Noster. See Prayers, p. 126.
*Penitential. See Ecclesiastical Miscellanea, p. 113.
*Pentateuch. See Aelfric: (c) Bible, p. 97.
*Peri Didaxeon (Of Schools of Medicine), p. 125.
Pharaoh, p. 85.
*Phlebotomies. See Prognostics, p. 127.
Phoenix, p. 73.
*Phoenix, p. 126.
Physiologus, p. 74.
Praise of Aldhelm. See Aldhelm, p. 54.
Praise of Thureth. See Thureth, Praise of, p. 90.
Prayers. See Hymns and Prayers, p. 82.
*Prayers (including *Credo and *Pater Noster), p. 126. See also *Lorica, p. 122.
*Prognostics, p. 127.
*Prophecies. See Prognostics, p. 127.
Proverbs, p. 86. See also Gnomic Verses, p. 80.
*Proverbs. See Cato, Distichs of, p. 111.
*Psalms, p. 129.
*Psalms of Alfred. See X Verse: Psalms, p. 86, and XI Prose: Psalms, p. 129.

Psalms, Metrical (Paris Psalter and Kentish Psalm), p. 86.
*Quintinus, Passion of, p. 130.
*Regularis Concordia. See Benedictine Rule, p. 109.
Resurrection. See Caedmonian Poems: (b) Christ and Satan, p. 64.
Rhyming Poem, p. 87.
Riddles, p. 75.
*Rituals, p. 131.
Rood, Dream of the. See Cynewulfian Poems: (c) Dream of the Rood, p. 70.
*Rood-tree, History of the Holy, p. 131.
*Royal Legends, Kentish, p. 121.
Ruin, The, p. 87.
*Rule of Chrodegang. See Benedictine Rule, p. 109.
*Rule of St. Benedict. See Benedictine Rule, p. 109.
Runic Poem, The (Rune Song), p. 88.
†Ruthwell Cross, p. 137; see also Cynewulfian Poems: (c) Dream of the Rood, p. 70.

*Saints, Lives and Legends of. See Aelfric: (q) Lives of the Saints, p. 101; Andrew, p. 108; Chad, p. 112; Christopher, p. 112; Fursaeus, p. 99; Guthlac, p. 116; Margaret, p. 123; Martin, p. 110; Martyrology, p. 123; Mary, p. 124; Mildryth, p. 124; Neot, p. 124; Quintinus, p. 130; Seaxburh, p. 127; Swithun, p. 131; Veronica, p. 132.
Salomon and Saturn, p. 88.
*Salomon and Saturn, Dialogue of, p. 131.
*Scriftbōc. See Ecclesiastical Miscellanea, p. 113.
Seafarer, The, p. 89.
*Seaxburh, St. See Prayers, p. 126.

INDEX OF OLD ENGLISH WRITINGS 153

*Sigewulf, Interrogations of. See Aelfric: (q) Lives of the Saints, p. 101.
*Sign Language (Indicia Monasterialia). See Ecclesiastical Miscellanea, p. 113.
*Signs Before the Last Judgment, p. 119.
*Soliloquies of St. Augustine. See Alfred: (a) Augustine's Soliloquies, p. 104.
Soul to the Body, Address of the, p. 89.
Spirit of Men. See Bi Manna Mode, p. 61.
*Survey from Bury St. Edmunds (and other surveys). See Ecclesiastical Miscellanea, p. 113.
*Swithun, Life of St., p. 131.

Temptation of Christ. See Caedmonian Poems: (b) Christ and Satan, p. 64.
*Theodulf, Capitula of. See Benedictine Rule, p. 109.
Thureth, Praise of, p. 90.

†Urswick Inscription, p. 137.

*Vercelli Homilies, p. 117.
*Veronica, Legend of St. (*Vindicta Salvatoris*), p. 132.
*Vindicta Salvatoris. See Veronica, p. 132.
*Virtues and Vices. See Alcuin, p. 102.
*Vision. See Letters, p. 122.
Vision of the Cross, p. 70.

Waldhere, p. 90.
Wanderer, The, p. 91.
Werferth's Preface to Gregory's Dialogues, p. 91. See also XI Prose: Werferth, p. 132.
*Werferth's Translation of Gregory's Dialogues, p. 132. See also X Verse: Werferth, 91.
Widsith, p. 92.
Wife's Complaint, The, p. 93.
Wonders of Creation, The, p. 94.
*Wonders of the East, p. 133.
Worcester Fragment, p. 94.
Wulfstan, p. 133.

INDEX OF OLD ENGLISH WRITINGS 155

Ipswich, Intercession of the
Abbot (?) Æthelm (besides
n. 107).
Sine Laudibus (Gloria in Excelsis), see Ecclesiastical
Miscellanea, n. 175.
Signs before the Last Judgement, p. 112.
Soliloquies of St. Augustine, See
Alfred (Ad Augustini's Soliloquies), p. 103.
Soul, to the Body, Address of the, p. 86.
Spirits of Men, Nos. III Magna Moderatio, p. 61.
Survey from Bury St. Edmund (and other surveys), see Ecclesiastical Miscellanea, p. 175.
Swithun, Life of, No. I p. 137.

Temptations of Christ, See Quatuor Poenae, 147 (Christ and Satan), p. 81.
Theodore, Confessio of, see Ecclesiastical Iudic., p. 168.
Thureth, Prayer of, p. 90.

Uterark, lux clarissima, p. 117.
Verselli Homilies, p. 117.
Veronica, Legend of, St. (besides Salvator), ph. 148.
Vindicta salvatoris, See Veronica, p. 135.
Virgines and Vices, See Moralia, p. 102.
Vision, See Letters, p. 122.
Vision of the Cross, pp. 79.

Waldhere, p. 90.
Wanderer, The, no. 31.
Werferth, Prelate to Gregory's Dialogues, p. 31, No. one, 51.
Fresc. Werferth, p. 132.
Werferth's Translation of Gregory's Dialogues, p. 132. See also
S. Verser, Werferth, 91.
Whoydialol, p. 90.
Wife's Complaint, The, p. 95.
Wonders of Creation, The, p. 94.
Wonders of the East, p. 115.
Worcester Fragment, p. 93.
Wulfstan, p. 128.

35 - 1 M
20